STORE
PLANNING/
DESIGN

STORE PLANNING/ DESIGN

History • Theory • Process

LAWRENCE J. ISRAEL, AIA, FISP

JOHN WILEY & SONS, INC.
New York • Chichester • Brisbane • Toronto • Singapore

Library of Congress Cataloging in Publication Data:
Israel, Lawrence J.
    Store planning/design : history, theory, process / Lawrence J.
Israel.
       p.   cm.
    Includes bibliographical references and index.
    ISBN 0-471-59488-1
    1. Stores, Retail—Planning.   2. Stores, Retail—Design and
construction.   I. Title.
HF5429.I77   1994
725'.21—dc20   93-37737

Printed in the United States of America

10 9 8 7 6 5 4 3

TO PETER COPELAND AND ADOLPH NOVAK

Partners and true brothers,
to whom I owe so much

Foreword

The "store" is a building form that is as old as civilization itself and yet, oddly enough, one concerning which there is a relative paucity of information. In writing this book, the author has provided the design community with a long overdue resource of remarkable depth and range. Written by an architect whose distinguished career in store design spans several continents and nearly half a century, this book is unquestionably one of the most informative and comprehensive books published on the subject. In addition to addressing major aspects of the basic theory and elements of store planning and design, and by using the department store as model, the author skillfully chronicles the development of store design over the last five decades. Employing a menu of basic design considerations as a matrix, he provides the reader with a comparative analysis of the design approaches that are representative of each decade.

An added dimension, not often found in reference books of this type, is the historic context that the author furnishes as backdrop for his journey through almost 50 years of store design. He provides this added perspective by prefacing each of the decades explored with a brief, yet scholarly, overview of the major cultural, socioeconomic, and demographic developments influencing the design of that period.

The scope of this book, with its wealth of detailed design, planning, and historic information, its lexicon of current technical terminology, its insights into process and practice, and its abundance of illustrative drawings and photographs, make it a required resource for all who are involved in the planning, design, and construction of retail store environments.

JULIUS PANERO, AIA, ASID
Professor, Interior Design Department
Fashion Institute of Technology

* * *

We all eat, sleep and shop. How often, however, have we thought about what it is that we like or dislike about a store. Is it the merchandise, the prices, the presentation, or the environment? In Larry Israel's definitive book on store planning readers can gain insights into what makes the creation of some retail environments successful and thus can see that store design is indeed a "silent salesman."

Organized in a comprehensive manner, the book gives both the designer and the retailer the fundamentals with which they can plan successful stores. Although there is no one right design solution, there are proven planning, lighting, and presentation techniques that, when coupled with a designer's imagination, shows that a higher level of performance can be achieved.

The step-by-step process of store planning in this book is easy to read and takes into account real-world solutions. Many of the projects illustrated still exist as living case studies.

The lessons from this book can be applied to domestic and international as well as to specialty and department stores.

Written by an architect who was among the handful who gave definition to the discipline of store planning, it is full of insights and observations that only someone who has lived the profession could articulate. It puts store planning in its correct historical perspective and its anecdotal comments bring the work to life.

KENNETH H. WALKER, FAIA
Partner
The Walker Group/CNI

*   *   *

When we think of the legends in architecture and design, it is not unusual to mention Wright, Aalto, and Gropius. There have been major contributors to specialized fields within architecture and design, however, who have been acknowledged by their peers yet have not received the public recognition for their contributions. Lawrence Israel is one such ''legend'' who, with his partners Peter Copeland and Adolph Novak, pioneered and revolutionized the field of store planning and design as we know it today. For five decades, Copeland, Novak and Israel (CNI), which later became Walker Group/CNI, pushed the frontiers of store planning and design to its present level of growth and sophistication. In this book, Lawrence Israel documents this architectural evolution from the 1940s to the 1990s in a unique way, by including a comprehensive historical perspective that links the seven arts and their influence on the store planning model. The analysis is performed by decade and is organized by means of a matrix of categories related to both design and merchandising issues. Such an historical perspective is significant, not only for the student of architecture and interior design, but also for today's practitioner and merchandiser.

Yet this is not just an historical work; it is also a book that provides today's designers with up-to-date practical information on all aspects of store planning and design. Rich in detail and vocabulary, this book provides comprehensive information on the physical elements and vocabulary of store planning and merchandising. Replete with illustrations, the combined narrative and graphics are extremely successful in providing the reader with insights about store planning that, heretofore, were unavailable in other books on this topic. This is manifested in Section III, ''Theory and Elements of Store Planning and Design,'' which sets forth a detailed body of technical information, theory, and practices through the eyes of a professional who has been responsible for the design of tens of millions of square feet of store interiors.

The shortest section of Israel's work is perhaps the most unique and interesting to the student and young practitioner, because it is written almost in diary form, recounting the ''process'' through which every project must evolve: the relationship between designer and client, the interpretation of the client's ''wish list,'' the conflicts, the anecdotes, the personal reminiscences of an architect before, during, and upon completion of an architectural project— all of the insights that are rarely, if ever, included in architectural publications today. Yet, the fact that Israel does include this background information is what makes this book so much more readable, enjoyable, and credible.

MARTIN ZELNIK, AIA, ASID, IDEC
Professor, Interior Design Department
Fashion Institute of Technology

Contents

Credit List

PHOTOGRAPHERS AND ARTISTS

Richard Rykowski
        146
Toshi Yoshimi
        58
John Wadsworth
        119, 145, 216, color insert

Introduction

Recently, as I was preparing a talk to celebrate a major event, I had the opportunity to research the archives of retail projects designed and built by my firm during the past decades. This material was fascinating, and it ignited in my mind the idea for this book.

Not only have the records shown the incredible growth and metamorphosis of the physical nature of stores, their increasing sophistication, complexity, and multidisciplinary development; and have reflected enormous cultural changes during a tumultuous period of our national global life; they also have served to underline the importance of studying the background and reasons for an amazing growth of the retail environment and of projecting definitions, directions, and strategies for the 1990s and indeed the twenty-first century, especially in the context of the "store wars" that have revolutionized the ownership, operation, and character of stores during the past several years.

Although recently there have been several excellent books published describing the characteristics of stores (e.g., found in the Bibliography found at the back of this book), it seemed that another book was necessary to analyze comprehensively the background as well as the theory of store planning and design; to provide practitioners and students with an exciting compendium and reference; and to put together a definitive study that reflects the growing maturity of a relatively young profession, born after World War II, which advanced the state of the art and set the standards in the field.

If these thoughts seemed ambitious and vainglorious, they quickly led to the more sober realization that a serious dedication of effort would be required to compile and record an exciting period of half a century; to seek and obtain documents describing seminal, world-wide examples of outstanding designs; and to secure the necessary clearances and waivers, not only from competing store design firms, but also from their clients (who are always zealously guarding their rights of privacy and proprietary data) and from photographers, of whom many are no longer alive or active—a daunting challenge. However, I felt that I could offer to the bright and dedicated young people just entering the related professions the reasons why this field has been so exciting and fulfilling for me.

After further reflection, it seemed appropriate to plan and organize the book into four major sections. Section I, "Definitions of Store Planning/Design Terms," is a lead-in to the entire book and consists of definitions of store planning terms that have been culled from the disciplines of architecture, design, and retailing. A working familiarity with this vocabulary is truly necessary for anyone in the field. It also will help readers of this book, since many of the terms will appear throughout sections and chapters. Certainly, the accepted use and understanding of them expedite communications between all parties interested in the physical development of stores.

Section II, "History," offers a brief overview of historical, cultural, socioeconomic, and demographic influences. A parallel survey of architecture, cinema, the performing arts, interior design, graphics and fashion design, literature, and so on, is made in order to accentuate the synergistic and interactive dialectics of all creative activities, and to illustrate how store design has contributed to and is influenced by them.

In order to put these influences into a simple, graphic, and easily understood form, I decided to include a "Synoptic Time Line" at the beginning of each chapter, which describes the creative work of each decade. To the reader, this might be a rewarding visualization of the incredibly manifold human activities of our era. Certainly the works cited are personal choices and by no means encyclopedic, but they have been selected to convey a mood and a sense of the ideological and creative spirit of the decades under review.

An analysis of the store designs of each decade are richly illustrated with photographs, renderings, sketches, plans, diagrams, and charts. Projects were sought that showed dominant and seminal trends. A summary of these trends would organize the work into the following categories:

1. Merchandising
2. Visual merchandising
3. Fixturization
4. Planning
5. Design
6. Lighting design
7. Color and materials

Section III, "Theory and Elements of Store Planning and Design," offers a comprehensive analysis of all of the complex components of a multidisciplinary professional practice. These components are subdivided into chapters as follows:

Chapter 6.   Stragegy and Program
Chapter 7.   The Plan
Chapter 8.   Architecture
Chapter 9.   Design
Chapter 10.   Colors and Materials
Chapter 11.   Fixturization
Chapter 12.   Lighting Design
Chapter 13.   Graphics
Chapter 14.   Visual Merchandising

A theoretical discussion is supplemented by photographs, plans, sketches, charts, and schedules, illustrating key projects throughout the world. Fundamentally, this book provides as definitive and as comprehensive a reference as possible, but it does not compile details or architectural and interior standards that are thoroughly covered in other current texts.

Section IV, "Process," concludes with a personal history of projects undertaken and anecdotes that illuminate a different aspect of our professional challenges—the very personal relationship of client and designer. In many respects, it overshadows the objective, theoretical analysis of the elements of store planning and design. It reveals how decisions are made by leaders in the field and how credibility, respect, and belief are established by the designer. Above all, however, it gives evidence to the power, majesty, and humanity of the individual, of that wide-ranging, indefinable warmth, variety, brilliance, and short-sightedness of the decision makers. It shows how the designer must think quickly and be prepared to defend his or her creative work against unimagined reactions. Hopefully, the personal, narrative style will give to this section a controversial human insight into the real, inner nature of our practice.

At this point I believe it is necessary to clarify the objectives of this book with respect to its kick-off point in time. The development of the department store during the 1880s and into the first half of this century has been well documented and is an exciting history in itself, as can be seen from the many books on this topic found in the Bibliography. I have chosen to begin this book during the period following World War II, when our nation and most of the world were striving to make the awesome transition from a wartime to a peacetime culture, and then to discuss the postwar period with which we are familiar. During this period, as the middle class fled from the cities of America, suburban shopping centers swiftly developed and stores themselves reallocated their resources into new building types in the suburbs. Simultaneously, it saw the birth of a new profession: the store planner/designer.

In many respects, the department store will form the model for this book's analysis. Yet, the definition of "department store" has in itself undergone significant changes during this period. From a traditional emporium carrying a full range of merchandise and customer services, the recent definition established by the National Retail Federation (NRF), includes "multidepartment soft goods stores (or specialized department stores) with a fashion orientation, full mark-up policy and operating in stores large enough to be shopping center anchors" (Gill). From the earlier postwar giants that had 300,000–400,000 square feet, more recent installations have a reduced area of 150,000–250,000 square feet, eliminating many of the marginal nonprofit and service-oriented departments. The result is the blurring of the line between department stores and specialty stores. In addition, because of this revolution, the shopping center itself is undergoing radical changes, challenging the very concept of the anchor store and investigating alternate diurnal uses of cultural and leisure activities to enhance and increase the profitability of physical constructions now perceived as the centers of the new edge cities. Result: utter confusion within the retail world, the unprecedented challenge to survive and to find a new niche, health, and a profitable market share.

In this context, *The New York Times* article of October 15, 1989 anticipated and described the problem:

> Retailing suffers from overcapacity and is in the process of being restructured. It is moving from big store dominance to an era characterized by stores that provide merchandise for specific groups. Mass marketing and centralization have given way to specialty providers and alternate channels of distribution like direct mail, telemarketing and home shopping.

Yet the department store, with its economic leverage, critical mass, pluralism, flexibility, and outstanding human leadership, remains and will continue as the paradigm of store design. It will form the center of our analysis. In the last analysis, it encompasses all of the elements, all of the challenges of store design. It is necessary, however, to define and to include in this book all of the varieties and categories of store design. Accordingly, I will review and illustrate the following subtypes:

Mass merchandiser
Discounter

Warehouse and catalogue operator
Specialty shop
Boutique
Franchiser
Food supermarket

The list of items sold by these types of stores is virtually limitless—from fashion to food to hardware, to bicycles and boats, to sporting goods and antiques, to arts and crafts, to electronics, books, cassettes to reflecting every form of human activity. In this sense, the metamorphosis of store design is an encyclopedia of our civilization.

The problems of retailing and their resolution have occupied many of us during the 1980s and 1990s. What is the future of the department store? Is it, in its last stages of decline, a dinosaur? We have seen and witnessed an unprecedented, violent, frustrating, distressing, and volatile series of events involving liquidations, acquisitions, and Chapter 11 restructurings that have transformed the department store universe. (Many of the stores illustrated will have gone through innumerable changes of ownership and names. In the interest of simple reference, I will use the names of the stores as they were at the time of planning and construction.) Having created physical and competitive advantages by all of our arts and sciences, by complexity and sophistication, style, dramatic spatial excitement, a memorable place to shop, see and be seen, have we also spawned a paradox? Has the price of the advantages and the increasing high cost of planing, construction, and operation in an inflationary economy blown the department store out of the water? One can only speculate on its future in the twenty-first century. Certainly, these retailers must reformulate their fundamental strategy, form, and content. They must take new risks and find new ways of selling, of offering services, and of being responsive to a changing customer. Merchandise will have to be presented in a new, compelling, and cost-effective environment. It is in this context that this book was written. In my opinion, the problems and challenges must be faced by a new generation of store planners/designers. Talent, imagination, and creativity are uniquely positioned to contribute to the birth of a new and successful store structure. Hopefully, this book will assist and inspire those who are participating in this process. Control of the past controls the future.

While the stores in America were fiercely fighting for position and market share, the department store was competing with mass merchandisers, discounters, and specialty stores. As telemarketing and the upsurge of catalogue operations jumped into the vacuum caused by the decline of the department store, the lessons of retail planning and design were being exported throughout the rest of the world. The concept of the "global village," with the predominance of America in every conceivable entrepreneurial, industrial, economic, military, and cultural sphere, spread like a fire storm during the 1980s and into this decade. The experience of the American stores was to be appropriated and then converted to fit into the pluralistic cultures of other nations. The disintegration of the Iron Curtain between Western Europe and Eastern Europe, concurrent with the ratification and acceptance of the European Common Market, established a vast new and hungry market for the expansion of new ideas in retailing. The enlightened store planner/designer had to adjust his or her experience and reshape it to reflect the myriad regions, economics, and cultures, each with a different time line of development. The international style thus moves forward toward the pluralistic regional styles. This is no different from the American development during the 1970s and 1980s in which an ubiquitous, corporate, centralized style ultimately transformed itself into regional searches for identity and special imagery. In addition, if American department stores have followed the flight to the suburbs, with the weakening and loss of the downtown "flagship" stores, in Europe, the Pacific Rim, and other parts of the world, the viability and growth of the large metropolis have encouraged the renewed development and formulation of the central, urban, major multistoried store. This is now heir to all of the theories and experiences of the American models.

One example of this can be seen in a world-famous Paris department store that is now expanding into other capital cities, such as New York, Berlin, and Singapore. Each installation is varied, dependent upon different building codes, architectural traditions, market, and the condition of their pluralistic cultures. This simultaneous, multiple variety is mind-boggling and challenging. It is, in this context, an introduction and symbol to the complexities of our shrunken globe with one dynamic market—a challenge that we must surmount or perish.

I have enjoyed a lifetime of practice in the store design field and have, I believe, accumulated experience and skills that I now wish to share with a new generation. I should be extremely egotistical and provincial, however, if I did not mention here the many colleagues, friends, and even competitors who have helped make this book possible. Let me, therefore, give full but brief credit to those contributors. First and foremost, I would like to thank my dear wife Beul. Without her quiet, determined, but totally reliable dedication (using old-fashioned equipment), this book could not have happened: She typed tirelessly, making sense of my indecipherable, crabbed handwriting, numerable drafts, and endless correspondence to clients, publishers, photographers, and professionals. She was always there to help.

At Walker Group/CNI, my thanks go to Bob Carullo, who compiled technical and systemic data, who in a fiercely busy schedule was always interested and cooperative; to Marty Jerry, who was always available to discuss esthetic and design issues and who helped select recent, advanced projects; to Odine Kleiner, who had a sorcerer's touch in locating and retrieving obscure names and marketing data; to Steve Kitezh, one of my first supporters, who had an amazing, encyclopedic grasp of questions and answers in every conceivable direction; to Mark Pucci, who graciously gave me complete access to every facility in the office; to his secretary, Nancy Luces, who was always comforting and cheerful; to Diana Mesh, who laid out much of the information related to store lighting technics; and finally to George Dewey, whose eager cooperation in a thousand details made onerous tasks pleasant and easy.

At the Fashion Institute of Technology, my thanks go to Professor Julius Panero, AIA, who planted the seed and urged me to undertake writing this book, and who constantly helped me through the unchartered waters (to me) of organizing and publishing; to his partner, Professor Martin Zelnik, son of Simon—my first professional mentor—who was always gracious, scholarly, and supportive; to Professor Frank Menoli, whose brief and precise analysis of New York's building codes adds scope and depth to the challenges of store architecture; and to Professor Joan Melnick, Department Chair, whose interest and delightful smile were a constant, subliminal sign of encouragement.

My gratitude also extends to my partners, Peter Copeland and Adolph Novak, who inspired in me my love for store planning and design and who illuminated in their daily acts and concepts the range, vitality, and rewards of a new, developing professional field; to my dear old friend, Herman Litwack, FAIA, whose devotion both to me and to the architectural profession set the ideals and standards; to Josephine Russo, my administrative assistant at CNI for ten years, whose efficiency and unflagging, warm interest made my professional activities easy, who encouraged me to share my experiences and point-of-view by writing; and to Ed Hambrecht, FISP, an associate, colleague, and competitor, who was generous and gracious in his help.

At John Wiley, I wish to thank editor Everett Smethurst, my first contact in the publishing universe, who was warm, sympathetic, and a true cicerone; his assistant editor, Linda Bathgate, whose good cheer and support were always marvelous, and who taught me daily the mysteries, intrigues, and responsibilities of publishing; and to Diana Cisek, who steadfastly guided me through the maze of book production.

And also and always, my gratitude goes to the unnamed legions, the men and women with whom I worked, each one of whom reflected a special talent and devotion in a multifaceted field. From each of them, I learned and reflected in turn an understanding and perhaps a mastery of this always exciting profession. And to all of you workers, associates, designers, artists, renderers, decorators, draftspersons, technicians, administrators, coordinators, secretaries, consultants, clients, clients' staff, contractors, and artisans in the field—to all, thanks!

I

DEFINITIONS OF STORE PLANNING/ DESIGN TERMS

At the outset it seems wise to define the terms that will be used in this book. This is, however, as complex a task as the subject itself. Why, for example, is the book's title *Store Planning/Design?* For one thing, the parent professional society is called the Institute of Store Planners (ISP). This omits the more comprehensive word *designer*, which embraces professionals in a multitude of other fields, such as fashion design, industrial design, interior design, and so on. Yet, to exclude this word is to ignore one of the most vital disciplines necessary to produce successful stores. In addition, the word *planning* limits the creative-imaginative reference. The word *planner* includes connotations of urban planning, regional planning, economic planning, space planning, and so on.

Without prolonging this debate, I offer the following general definitions of "store design." Each has a merit.

1. Store design is the formulation of all aspects of the retail, physical environment to achieve image, operational performance, and successful sales results.
2. Store design is helping the client add value to the physical product through the provision and management of imagination.
3. Store design is the creation of a compelling environment for competitive retail selling at profit.

Because of the very special language developed in store design practice and its importance for the store planner/designer, it is vital that the historical and theoretical analysis of stores be introduced by the following definitions of store planning terms (Israel). Many of the terms and expressions will be used throughout this book.

PHYSICAL ELEMENTS

ADJACENT STOCKROOM: Also called forward stock. The area immediately behind selling space that is devoted to stock reserves and is an adjunct to selling capacity.

BEHIND THE SCENES: All spaces behind perimeter partitions, inclusive of selling and nonselling functions.

BOUTIQUE: A shop designed to present specially selected associated merchandise with specialty shop appeal and ambience.

BUILDING FUNCTION AREA: An area not available for selling functions, including walls, columns, entrances, stairs, escalators, elevators, mechanical equipment rooms, machinery rooms, electrical equipment rooms, toilets, pipe spaces, ducts, permanent passageways, and fixed building elements.

CURTAIN WALL: A wall system that hangs from a ceiling structure and is normally installed at the front face of a wall fixture to give it recessed treatment.

DOUBLE-DECK STOCK: Utilization of stockroom facilities by mezzanine construction to develop maximum cubic contents.

DWARF PARTITION: A wall system lower than the ceiling and unattached to the ceiling structure, its height being variable.

FOOTPRINT: The configuration of a building at the ground level.

GROSS BUILDING AREA: The total amount of area occupied by a building calculated to outside building walls.

HID: High-intensity discharge lighting, including mercury vapor, metal halide, and high-pressure sodium light sources.

HVAC: Heating, ventilating, and air conditioning.

LAMP: A light source, commonly called a "bulb" or "tube."

NET SELLING AREA: The space available for direct selling to customers, including forward areas, immediately adjacent stockrooms, fitting and alteration rooms, cash wraps, and service desks.

NONSELLING AREA: The space available for store functions, including show windows, remote reserve areas, receiving and marking, truck docks, storage rooms, locker rooms, maintenance rooms, general offices, employees' facilities, cashiers, etc.

OPEN PLANNING: A planning and design concept that avoids the use of subdividing wall systems (or shop treatment) to achieve a totality of flexible, open, visual, sales space.

PERIMETER PARTITION: Also called peripheral partition. A wall system that divides selling spaces from fitting rooms, adjacent stock, and other behind-the-scenes spaces; the enclosing wall system that defines forward customer spaces.

PLENUM: The space between a suspended ceiling and the overhead structure containing mechanical equipment and building systems.

REMOTE STOCKROOM: An area assigned for storage of merchandise that is remote from the selling floor and is used as warehousing space.

SHELL: The structural framework of a building, including columns, girders, beams, floor construction, exterior walls, and roof.

SHOP: The physical subdivision of selling space into a specific room normally developed to present one department of merchandise.

SHOP TREATMENT: A planning and design concept utilizing the principle of various physical shops for the housing of departmental merchandise categories.

SOFFIT: A dropped ceiling treatment at variable designated heights.

SPACE DIVIDER: Also called a room divider. A physical element used to subdivide selling spaces, usually of flexible construction not attached to the building structure.

TURNKEY-JOB: A total retail facility, including structural shell, mechanical and electrical equipment, and all interior improvements, fixtures, and decor.

VALANCE: Also called a cornice. A physical horizontal member at the top of a selling fixture, normally used to conceal a continuous light source.

FIXTURIZATION

AISLE: The space devoted to customer and/or materials circulation within the selling area.

ALLOCATION: The technique of placement and calculation of sizes of sales departments and service areas within a store plan.

BACK FIXTURE: A fixture within an island behind the counter line and sales clerk aisle, normally with a combination of merchandise display and reserve stock.

BARGAIN SQUARE: An arrangement of fixtures within a store that is meant to encourage the sale of highly promotional or clearance merchandise, usually attended by a clerk-cashier.

CASH WRAP: A fixture designed for the placement of a cash register and facilities for the wrapping of merchandise; generally located in the consumer sales area.

CASHIER WRAP: A cash wrap specifically designed as a station for an assigned cashier-clerk.

CENTRAL WRAP: Also called regional wrap. A major cash wrap that is conveniently located to service complete departments within the sales area, designed for the self-selection principle, with important decor and signing for quick identification.

CHECKOUT:: A cash wrap designed and located to further the self-selling technique, generally located at the exit of sales areas so as to enclose those areas in a controlled customer traffic pattern; generally designed for a permanently assigned cashier and wrap clerk, and prominently decorated and signed.

CONVERTIBILITY: A technique of fixturing that includes flexibility as well as the facility to change merchandise presentation—for example, hanging to shelfing.

COUNTER: An enclosed selling fixture used for forward merchandise storage and some display; normally used for over-the-counter selling by sales personnel.

CUBAGE: A description of the three dimensions of space, normally associated with vertical utilization for achieving maximum merchandise capacity.

DENSITY: The ratio of the area occupied by selling fixtures to the total area of selling space.

DOUBLE HANG: Two hang rods, one over the other.

ÉTAGÈRE: A special modular display fixture consisting of levels or steps of shelving, generally associated with the stainless steel and glass style.

FACE OUT: A sloping hang rod that permits a waterfall effect for frontal presentation of merchandise.

FIXTURE: Selling equipment designed to display, present, and store merchandise.

FIXTURE TYPE: The designation and design of selling equipment to achieve appropriate presentation according to the special requirements of merchandise classifications.

FLEXIBILITY: A technique of fixturization in which the component parts are movable and not attached to the structure.

GARMENT RACK: A store fixture designed for the hanging of coats, suits, and dresses.

GONDOLA: A fixture located on the selling floor and arranged for self-selection presentation of merchandise, frequently designed to be convertible.

HARDWARE: Metal-fixture components.

ISLAND: An arrangement of showcases, counters, and back fixtures that creates a departmental merchandise sales unit, normally associated with over-the-counter selling by sales personnel.

LAYERAGE: The technique of placing the sales departments and the service areas vertically, according to the number of floors available.

LIGHTING FIXTURE: The instrument designed to contain sources of illumination and to emit such illumination according to a design program.

MAINTENANCE: Also called housekeeping. The provision of cleanliness, repairs, and utilization of all components within the store.

MATERIALS HANDLING SYSTEM: The technique of receiving, storing, and moving goods within the store facility from truck dock to point of sales, including manual, mechanical, and automatic equipment.

MERCHANDISING PRESENTATION: The technique of displaying, storing, and promoting merchandise categories.

MODULE: A dimensional standard to unify size or merchandise presentation of fixture construction.

OVER-THE-COUNTER SELLING: A service technique in which a sales clerk presents merchandise to the consumer across a selling fixture and generally completes the sales transaction.

POINT OF PURCHASE: The placing within the selling space of a highly concentrated merchandise presentation, at which place a sale is to be consummated.

ROUNDERS: Circular hang racks.

SELF-SELECTION: A selling technique in which customers choose merchandise from exposed specially designed fixtures. This technique normally involves a sales clerk in the final sales transaction.

SELF-SELLING: A selling technique that is similar to self-selection but is normally associated with a checkout or discount operation

SERVICE: All supporting activities within a store operation other than selling.

SERVICE CORE: The concentration of physical, building function, materials handling, and nonselling facilities within a selected store area.

SHOWCASE: A selling fixture with a glass enclosed section for merchandise display and possibly a bottom section for stock reserve, used for over-the-counter selling in association with sales personnel.

SLOTTED STANDARD: A vertical hardware element designed for the adjustable support of hanging or shelving units.

STANDARDS AND BRACKETS: Adjustable metal hardware that supports shelving and hang rods.

SUPERSTRUCTURE: Also called build-up. A movable modular fixture element that organizes the presentation of merchandise, normally placed on top of a table.

TABLE: An enclosed selling fixture generally designed to contain stock reserves, of which the horizontal upper surface is used for merchandise presentation.

TRAFFIC: The movement of people or goods horizontally and/or vertically.

WALL FIXTURE: A fixture attached to a perimeter partition for the display, presentation, and storage or merchandise. It may be an integral part of the partition construction or a prefabricated case, open or glass enclosed.

DESIGN

AMBIENCE: Also called atmosphere. The general quality of an interior design expresssing the store image.

ASSOCIATED MERCHANDISING: The merchandising technique in which selling is encouraged by placing related merchandise together within a space, without reference to buying or departmental administration.

ASSORTMENT DISPLAY: The technique of presenting one unit of every available item of merchandise within a department.

BLOCK PLAN: A schematic plan showing the placing, area calculations, and relationship of selling, nonselling and building function elements.

CONTEMPORARY: The architectural or interior design approach that seeks to express a modern life-style and uses a wide range of technological systems and materials.

DECORATING: The art of composing and selecting colors, materials, furniture, furnishings, and accessories to enrich the design of a store interior in order to create an attractive selling environment and to enhance the presentation of merchandise.

DESIGN: The art of store conceptualization, including all elements of architecture, planning, interior styling, decorating, and merchandising.

DISPLAY: The art of dramatically presenting merchandise in order to excite and to encourage consumer interest.

ECLECTIC: An architectural or interior style that indiscriminately borrows from various historic and/or contemporary styles.

ELEVATION: A drafting technique that presents an architectural or interior vertical composition in a direct, linear, two-dimensional point of view.

FIXTURE LAYOUT: A plan that shows the arrangement of selling fixtures, customer aisles, peripheral partitions, behind-the-scenes services, and all major elements of the store interior.

GRAPHICS: The art of typography and lettering extended in store design to include all components of identification and departmental background effects, including mural painting and signing; the study of written department identifications, including techniques of merchandise presentation with price, size, and promotional information.

ILLUMINATION: The art of lighting a store interior, including the process of selecting light sources and output according to a design program.

IMAGE: The character of a store resulting in an institutional personality immediately recognized by the consumer public.

ITEM DISPLAY: The technique of presenting a coordinated group of specifically selected merchandise to promote its sale.

PERSPECTIVE: A drafting technique presenting an architectural or interior composition in a three-dimensional point of view approximating that of the human eye.

PLAN: A drafting technique presenting an architectural or interior composition in a two-dimensional point of view as seen directly above a floor plane.

SAMPLE DISPLAY: The technique of presenting one of a specific item of merchandise attractively, with the back-up housed in a forward stockroom.

STYLE: A quality or mode of design and decoration frequently associated with historic architectural and decorative forms.

VISUALIZATION DRAWING: A drafting technique that is used to explain a design concept.

MERCHANDISING

AS-IS MERCHANDISE: Inventory normally put up for clearance after a season, regardless of the condition of the merchandise.

BASEMENT OPERATION: A budget merchandising subdivision of a department store similar to a discount operation that attempts to widen the store's image by appealing to the low end of a market.

BIG-TICKET ITEM: A large sales transaction normally associated with the purchase of furniture, media equipment, and major appliances.

CLASSIFICATION: Also called category. A subdivision of department merchandise.

CLEARANCE: The selling of inventory at a loss at the end of a season in order to deplete inventory.

CONVENIENCE GOODS: Merchandise consumed daily and purchased frequently, such as food and drugs.

DEMAND SELLING: The technique of presenting merchandise for preselected and planned purchases in which location is not a factor.

DEPARTMENT: An administrative subdivision of store selling.

EXPOSURE: The ability of potential customers to see and to recognize a store or merchandise.

FASHION: A prevailing style currently in vogue, generally associated with women's apparel and accessories and referring to highly volatile seasonal consumer tastes.

HOME FASHIONS: A broad designation of departments within a store relating to furnishing and accessories for the home, including hard and soft goods.

IMPULSE SELLING: The technique of presenting merchandise at high traffic locations in order to stimulate unplanned purchases.

INITIAL MARKON: The spread between invoice cost and initial retail selling price.

LINEAGE The length of fixtures measured on the floor plan, normally associated with calculations of merchandising capacity.

MARGIN: The excess of sales over the cost of sales.

MARKDOWN: Total reductions from the originally set retail price of merchandise.

MARKET: A portion of the consumer public whose taste, life-style, purchasing power, and economic standards can be defined.

MARKET PENETRATION: The amount of sales that a retail operation captures in a specific market area.

MERCHANDISING: The art of buying, distributing, handling, administering, presenting, and selling consumer goods at retail to the public, generally for a profit.

MERCHANDISING MIX: The arrangement of classifications or departments of merchandise so as to produce a balanced sales presentation or, alternatively, a special store character.

OPEN-TO-BUY: The value of merchandise at retail added to inventory at a given time without exceeding planned figures.

OPERATIONS: A generic term expressing all of the service processes of retail selling.

OUTPOST: A small presentation of a merchandise classification that is remote from its parent department and often duplicates that merchandise.

PROFIT: The excess of sales over the cost of sales, including all administration and overhead costs; extended to pretax or after-tax profits.

PROMOTION: The technique of stimulating sales usually by advertising, displaying, selecting, and presenting merchandise.

READY-TO-WEAR: Prestyled and prefabricated apparel presented according to size and type of consumer, including misses, women's, men's, and children's.

RETAIL: The process of selling merchandise directly to the consumer.

RETURNS: Merchandise brought back by customers.

SALES PRODUCTION: The annual volume of earnings divided by gross sales area.

SALES VOLUME: The annual gross earnings at retail.

SHRINKAGE: The loss of inventory at retail caused by stealing, inefficiency, and administrative errors.

SIMPLIFIED SELLING: The technique of merchandise presentation that depends on self-selection.

SKU: Stock-keeping unit, a designation used to enumerate every different merchandise size, color, and style.

TRADING DOWN: The technique of lowering the image of a store by cheapening merchandise selections and presentations and appealing to the lower sector of a market.

TRADING UP: The technique of raising the image of a store by improving merchandise selections and presentations and appealing to the upper sector of a market.

TRANSACTION: The completion of a retail sale.

TURNOVER: The ratio of net sales per year divided by average inventory at retail.

VOLUME: *See* Sales volume.

WHOLESALE: The process of buying or jobbing merchandise from point of manufacture and selling to a retail operation.

II

HISTORY: FIVE DECADES OF STORE DESIGN

... that unreal part ... the external, actual part, liable to everyone's control is but the prolongation, was the part become purely imaginary, of a colour which no longer existed ... that part which has detached itself from the outer world, to take refuge in our soul, to which it gives a surplus value, in which it is assimilated to its normal substance, transforming itself— houses that have been pulled down, people long dead, bowls of fruit at the suppers which we recall—into that translucent alabaster of our memories, the colour of which we are incapable of displaying, since we alone see it, which enables us to say truthfully to other people speaking of things past, that they cannot form any idea of them, that they do not resemble anything that they have seen, while we are unable to think of them ourselves without a certain emotion, remembering that it is upon the existence of our thoughts that there depends, for a little time still, their survival, the brilliance of the lamps that have been extinguished and the fragrance of the arbours that will never bloom again.

—MARCEL PROUST, *Remembrance of Things Past*, Volume II.

This section will describe store work completed during the five decades since World War II. Starting with a time line spread sheet to illustrate the seminal creative events of each decade, a brief summary of the cultural, social, and economic background and influences will lead into an analysis of selected projects according to the following rather arbitrary categories:

1. Merchandising
2. Visual merchandising
3. Planning
4. Design
5. Fixturization
6. Decoration
7. Lighting design

It should be kept in mind that this type of overview can only outline the main currents and trends that will engender the forms developed in the following decade and lead to the current state of the art. This is the historic method. However, in each decade, there are enormous variations and countercurrents. The field is infinite. While the examples express a prevailing élan vital, eclectic and contrary influences should also be noted, based on the history, traditions, strong personalities, regions, locations, and the constant, fierce, competitive effort to dominate a share of the market, of the multitudes and varieties of stores.

If our historical analysis begins after World War II, a seminal watershed of our century, it seems pertinent briefly to describe the condition of store design just prior to December 7, 1941, the date of the bombing of Pearl Harbor and the entry of the United States into World War II.

The heyday of urban department store construction in America spread across the fin de siècle into the early decades of the twentieth century, disrupted by Word War I and then sputtering to a halt during the Great Depression. The great palaces of the merchant princes were architectural monuments celebrating America's imperial and entrepreneurial expansion. Their interior plans and designs were generally executed by building architects, assisted by some of the prominent store fixture contractors, but occasionally by European designers who had achieved fame and recognition in the field. The designs were dominated by classical architectural elements— columns decorated in plaster according to the Roman orders, open atria surmounted by Tiffany glass skylights or mosaic vaults—providing light and ventilation into the vast multistoried, mercantile spaces.

During the late 1930s, two developments brought a new viewpoint to store design. The first was the awareness of the importance of the automobile and its influence on the expansion of the suburbs. Enlightened merchants understood the potential of this trend and began the building of the first suburban branch stores. Wanamaker's, Lord & Taylor, Bullock's, The Broadway, Famous Barr, Best & Company were leaders in this trend, ultimately stopped in their tracks by the economic mobilization consequent to America's entering the war. The second was the emergence of a group of architects and designers who understood the complex requirements of the department store as a challenging type of building and who imported from Europe the exciting design concepts of the International Style: Victor Gruen and Morris Ketchum, Jr., Raymond Loewy, Eleanor Le Maire, Kenneth C. Welsch and Morris Lapidus. Although few department stores were planned or built during this period, this talented group applied their new notions to the designs of specialty stores and displayed many of the exciting possibilities of a new style, underpinned by new technological developments in lighting, architectural materials, and systems, and merchandise presentation. Stopped by the war, these bold new concepts were prepared and ready to erupt into that incredible burst of energy that generated the postwar boom of suburban store construction which forms the subject of this book.

1

The 1950s

The new profession of store planning and design was born with simple and naive beginnings in a new age of hope after World War II. The exodus of people from the cities, their flight to the suburbs, followed by the proliferation of regional, enclosed mall shopping centers that were anchored by two or more department stores, led to the realization that a new architectural building type was forming. It was the time of the baby boom, of economic expansion, and of a new affluence.

In architecture, the International Style was ascendant. Buzz words were "functionalism" and "less is more." Work by Le Corbusier, Van der Rohe, Johnson, Skidmore Owens, and Merril were models. Pop and op art opened new visions, and were introduced quickly and boldly into commercial communications media and interior and fashion design. Television overshadowed all aspects of mass culture.

Under Eisenhower's administration, there was a drift toward conformity attributed to the mass media, technology, and a prevailing political conservatism. "The silent generation" and "togetherness" were advertising slogans. Books like *The Lonely Crowd* and *The Organization Man* reflected the subordination of ideological concerns to the quest for a steady job and a house in the suburbs.

In television, there was a proliferation of dramatic shows: one weekly program was able to devour all of the works of Shakespeare in just one season. Yet the variety was mind-boggling: Edward R. Murrow, Sid Caesar, Jack Benny, Milton Berle, Bob Hope, Liberace, Harry Belafonte, Elvis Presley. The U.S. film industry was in a slump, overtaken by such foreign films as *Rashomon, Hiroshima, Mon Amour, The 400 Blows,* and *Room at the Top.* In literature revolt and alienation were expressed by writers J. D. Salinger, James Baldwin, Saul Bellow, Allen Ginsberg. The first counterculture involving drugs and sexual freedom began to appear. Dr. Jonas Salk developed the vaccine against polio. Nuclear technology, the hydrogen bomb, and ballistics missiles revolutionized military strategy. J. Robert Oppenheimer was fired as a security risk. Space flight was a glamour industry, but, in seeking to catch up with the Russians, symbolized the cold war—containment of the expansion of the Soviet Union.

By 1956, more than half of all U.S. wage earners were in the service sector. A consumer economy emerged, together with increasing automation of industrial processes. Advertising and the expansion of credit payments played a major role in the flourishing prosperity.

MERCHANDISING

Merchandising controls and the development of packaging led to ideas of self-selection selling techniques. All were under the influence of economic forces to replace high-cost sales personnel with efficient, cost-effective

1950'S SYNOPTIC TIME LINE

CULTURE

Akira Kurosawa
"Rashomon"
1951
•

Francis Bacon
Study–Pope Innocent X
(1953)
•

Jackson Pollack
•

Robert Rauschenberg
•

Mark Rothko
•

Jasper Johns
•

David Riesman
"The Lonely Crowd"
(1951)
•

Elvis Presley
•

Allen Ginsberg
"Howl"
(1955)
•

Charles Eames
Lounge Chair
(1956)
•

Stanley Kramer
"On the Beach"
(1959)
•

Rachel L. Carson
"The Sea Around Us"
(1951)
•

Frank Lloyd Wright
Solomon R. Guggenheim
Museum
(1959)
•

Le Corbusier
Notre Dame du Haut
(1950–1955)
•

Mies van der Rohe
& Phillip Johnson
Seagram Building
(1956–1958)
•

Nervi
Palazzetto dello Sport
(1958)
•

Marilyn Monroe
•

HISTORY

Korean Conflict
(1950–1953)
•

Cold War
Truman-Acheson
Policy: Containment of
Soviet Union
•

Senate Perm.
Investigations Committee
Joseph McCarthy
•

"Togetherness"
•

Pres. Gen. Eisenhower
(1952–1956)
•

Dr. Jonas Salk
Anti-polio Vaccine
(1955)
•

Sputnik I
(Launched 1957)
•

Joseph Stalin
•

Chas. De Gaulle
1st Pres. French
5th Republic
(1958)
•

Apartheid: Policy of Racial
Separation in South Africa
•

Supreme Court
Desegregation Decision
(1954)
•

Peaceful Uses
of Nuclear Power
•

Silent Salesman: The Gondola
Raleigh's, Tyson's Corner, VA
Store Design: Copeland, Novak & Israel

equipment. The self-selection fixture, the gondola, was called ''silent sales-man.'' It was designed to make the shopping experience and final sales transaction more comfortable, faster, and more efficient. The entire nation gradually became accustomed to shopping and purchasing as an individual action without the pampering and pressured cajoling of salespeople. The concept of automation was introduced to the store. The supermarket with total self-selling and checkout, became an accepted and habitual experience. Advertising and catalogues encouraged shoppers to plan and organize their shopping in the comfort of their home. This liberated the shoppers' time, allowing them to spend more time on leisure activities, travel, or a second job.

VISUAL MERCHANDISING

The term ''visual merchandising'' was not yet known. There was the display director, the window trimmer, and the merchandising engineer. Each functioned independently and usually reported to a different officer. Display consisted largely of mannequins on platforms strategically placed with uniform architectural background motifs. Point-of-purchase and signing, pricing techniques proliferated to stimulate and to encourage the self-selection transaction process.

Mannequin Platform with Background Motif
John Wanamaker, Cross County Center, Yonkers, NY
Store Design: Copeland, Novak & Israel

Mannequin Platform with Background Motif
Gimbel Brothers, Upper Darby, PA
Store Design: Copeland, Novak & Israel
Photograph: Alexandre Georges

PLANNING

Open, regular, and rectilinear plans embodied principles of flexibility and interchangeability. They allowed continuity of flooring materials, ceilings, and lighting. Modular fixture components conformed to these principles. Perimeter partitions subdivided selling from behind—the scene spaces conformed geometrically to the basic coordinate structural grid. Elements designed to define and subdivide departmental spaces were screenlike; somewhat higher fixtures were kept well below the ceiling line and were self-supporting. These techniques solved the problems of visibility, security surveillance, and control. Conversely, however, they imposed a disciplined, uniform interior ambience, reducing opportunities for expressing varied designs relating to the departmental merchandise or for contributing to moods enhancing varied life-styles.

Screenlike Elements Subdividing Departments
Gimbel Brothers, Upper Darby, PA
Store Design: Copeland, Novak & Israel
Photograph: Alexandre Georges

DESIGN

The design influence of Raymond Loewy, the quintessential industrial designer, who designed everything from elite railroad trains to Coca-Cola vending machines and the famous postwar Studebaker automobile, dominated. Decorative murals with birds, ribbons, and flowers, and romantic and poetic images with feminine allusions and associations; nostalgic and eclectic mouldings and paneling; highly decorative, iconographic chandeliers in strategic locations: These elements all contributed to the ambience of the period. Peripheral partitions consisted generally of the decorated Sheetrock wall, an illuminated valance above eye level of variable dimensions and form, and hardware below the valance that allowed a certain flexibility and interchangeability of hang rods and/or shelving. The valance provided for direct, local lighting of the inventory of merchandise below, as well as an indirect wash of light above, contributing to a fairly bright general level of illumination. Occasionally, the incorporation of a curtain wall treatment provided a design contrast, recessing and highlighting selected merchandise. Occasionally, a shop feeling was developed for higher priced units, encouraging more exclusive, specialty-shop character and service by hand-picked, customer-loyal salespeople.

Nostalgic Decorative Style
Bonwit Teller, Jenkintown, PA
Store Design: Copeland, Novak & Israel

Specialty Shop Character
Davison-Paxon, Lenox Square, Atlanta, GA
Store Design: Copeland, Novak & Israel

FIXTURIZATION

The store-selling fixture retained most of the traditional elements seen in the store before World War II: glass-enclosed showcases with provision for stocking merchandise in drawers below; arrangements of showcases and back fixtures in "islands" of varying plan formation, in which the back fixture providing height for display and storage and the clerk aisle between them allowed direct sales assistance; tables and racks for self-selection; the newly developed "gondola," which was designed to present merchandise flexibly on shelving or hang rod arrangements, or both. Under the influence of the International Style and the doctrine that "less is more," heavy wooden cabinetry was refined gradually to simple, contemporary, elegant enclosures to permit the dominance of the merchandise itself. Hardware components were invented to provide limitless opportunities for the flexible conversion of shelves to hang rods and for their easy adjustability. Under the control of the plan, with its principle of flexibility, the concept of modular, dimensional control was developing. Accordingly, various fixtures could be grouped as required by seasons or by changing merchandise requirements. To permit the movement and unplanned combinations of fixtures, they were generally surfaced and finished in a storewide uniformity. As generated by the plan, this reinforced the discipline of the uniform, total continuum of the interior spaces.

Showcases and Island Back Fixtures: The Ubiquitous 4 × 4 Fluorescent Fixture
John Wanamaker, Cross County Center, Yonkers, NY
Store Design: Copeland, Novak & Israel

DECORATION

Colors and materials were generally muted pastel tones. Although some efforts were made to reflect the different departmental merchandise, the open plan forced colors to be chromatically and harmoniously related. If, for example, a pink color tone was considered appropriate for reflecting the soft, feminine qualities of a lingerie department, the adjacent ladies shoe department might be decorated in beige or soft blues or grays. The entire interior space was symphonically and harmonically controlled. Occasional wallpapers with nostalgic patterns set a decorative scheme, prudently contrasting with the Loewesque murals. Flooring solutions were simple. Because of the flexible space utilization requirements, carpeting had to be largely continuous and uniform. Some variations of selling to circulation surfaces, soft to hard flooring, were developed—all under the strict discipline of continuity.

LIGHTING DESIGN

The commercial development of the fluorescent lamp became, after World War II, almost universally acceptable. In a long, linear light source, it was

Recessed Incandescent Lighting
John Wanamaker, Cross County Center, Yonkers, NY
Store Design: Copeland, Novak & Israel

efficient and economical, generating opportunities for uniform brightness. Advances in the chemistry of the fluorescents gave reasonable choices of color—the ideal being the color and tone of outdoors, provided, however, that it did not distort the color of the merchandise or the decor. The 4′–0 × 4′–0 recessed fluorescent fixture, with either open egg crate or acrylic plastic lens, spaced in a uniform, nondirectional pattern, became ubiquitous. Occasionally, in the more prestigious, up-scale stores, recessed, incandescent light fixtures were used. These gave a point-source sparkle to the space and merchandise, a tactile highlighting of merchandise, and a flattering quality to people's complexions. The concept of dramatic contrasts of light level was in its infancy. The overriding demand for lighting in the stores was efficiency, brightness, and uniformity. Because of the planned openness and need for flexibility, the ceiling plane containing the light source was kept simple, with very little change of height or interest. Generally, in the department store, the ceiling was high, creating a monumental sense of space and providing a large surface area for wall decorations above the fixture and merchandise line at the periphery.

2

The 1960s

The 1960s was the age of the counterculture. The new humanism; the new ecology; the rebirth of individualism and of human responsiveness; the new interest in clothing, fashions, and handicrafts; the growth of leisure and hobbies; the demand for color in everything; the birth of the consumer protest movement—all led to improved standards of public taste. With the incredible growth of television, the effects of mass media, product design, and forms of marketing were instantaneous, universal, and omnipresent. Pressures to innovate for the sake of novelty and of commercial exploitation were contrasted every day with the search for logical development of a contemporary style. The proliferation of life-styles, of fashions, and of new forms became an overbearing reality. The result was an immeasurable mobility of public demand and acceptance.

The tumult and tragedies surrounding the assassination of President Kennedy and public heroes, the explosion of the Vietnam War, the astronauts landing on the moon, the race riots during LBJ's efforts to develop equality in "The Great Society"—all of these contrasting events were unprecedented and soul piercing. The generation gap led to "Woodstock," youth's revolt against a complaisant, materialistic society, and mind-blowing rituals of drugs and driving rock music.

Andy Warhol undercut the notion of beauty in art with his paintings of cans of soup. With pop and op art, historic preservation, and community activism, Venturi's gentle manifesto precipitated a process of disintegration in design away from the homogeneous purity and logic of the International Style. Postmodernism as expressed in architecture was a rebellion that paralleled the restless counterculture movements transforming all of Western society. Context as a criterion in design emerged into regionalism, diversity, and richness.

It was the end of the bipolar world of the postwar era in which the United States and the former Soviet Union dominated. A global and pluralistic system emerged in which each nation asserted itself politically. Marshall McLuhan proclaimed a modern world without boundaries: "Time has ceased, space has vanished. We now live in a global village . . . a simultaneous happening."

Segregation in the South and racial job discrimination declined. Martin Luther King, Jr., delivered his unforgettable "Freedom Now" speech at the Lincoln Memorial. The decolonization of Africa began. The Arab-Israeli conflict erupted into open war in 1967.

Major works in literature included *One Hundred Years of Solitude,* by Gabriel Garcia Marquez; *One Day in the Life of Ivan Denisovich,* by Alexander Solzhenitsyn; *The Feminine Mystique,* by Betty Friedan; and *Unsafe at Any Speed,* by Ralph Nader. Cinema was dominated by such films as *La Dolce Vita,* *Persona, I Am Curious (Yellow), Dr. Zhivago,* and *2001: A Space Odyssey.* Bob Dylan was the rock poet of the "Now Generation." The Broadway hits *Hair* and *West Side Story* reflected the kaleidoscopic energy that swept America.

1960'S SYNOPTIC TIME LINE

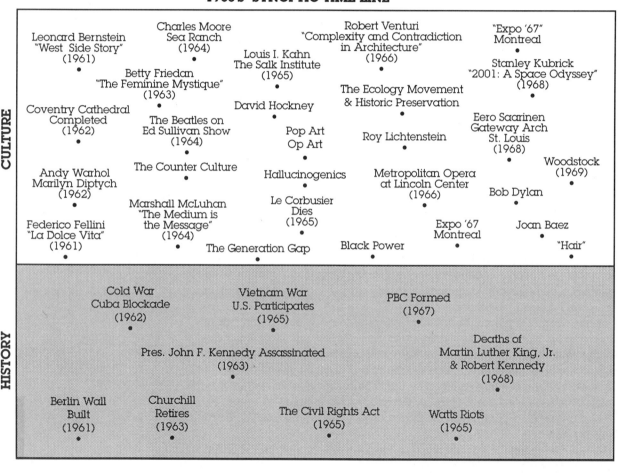

CULTURE

Leonard Bernstein "West Side Story" (1961)

Charles Moore Sea Ranch (1964)

Louis I. Kahn The Salk Institute (1965)

Robert Venturi "Complexity and Contradiction in Architecture" (1966)

"Expo '67" Montreal

Stanley Kubrick "2001: A Space Odyssey" (1968)

Betty Friedan "The Feminine Mystique" (1963)

David Hockney

The Ecology Movement & Historic Preservation

Coventry Cathedral Completed (1962)

The Beatles on Ed Sullivan Show (1964)

Pop Art Op Art

Roy Lichtenstein

Eero Saarinen Gateway Arch St. Louis (1968)

Andy Warhol Marilyn Diptych (1962)

The Counter Culture

Hallucinogenics

Metropolitan Opera at Lincoln Center (1966)

Bob Dylan

Woodstock (1969)

Marshall McLuhan "The Medium is the Message" (1964)

Le Corbusier Dies (1965)

Expo '67 Montreal

Joan Baez

Federico Fellini "La Dolce Vita" (1961)

The Generation Gap

Black Power

"Hair"

HISTORY

Cold War Cuba Blockade (1962)

Vietnam War U.S. Participates (1965)

PBC Formed (1967)

Pres. John F. Kennedy Assassinated (1963)

Deaths of Martin Luther King, Jr. & Robert Kennedy (1968)

Berlin Wall Built (1961)

Churchill Retires (1963)

The Civil Rights Act (1965)

Watts Riots (1965)

MERCHANDISING

Merchandising was dominated by the engineering, variations, and refinements of the self-selection fixture. Glass binning was discovered, together with the dictum in merchandise fixture design that "less is more." Woodwork and decorative traditional enclosing materials were suppressed to display the merchandise itself.

VISUAL MERCHANDISING

Display concepts continued the trend of the 1950s and were fixated at the level of mannequin platforms and point-of-purchase signing techniques.

PLANNING

Sophisticated planning concepts began to reflect a new experimentation and maturity. The use of angles, polygons, and curves was a departure from the rigid coordinate grid. The goal was to create opportunity for excitement and variety. The first developments of the center core or atrium plan created

"Less is More" in Fixture Design

Mannequin Display Platforms
Macy's, Rego Park, NY
Store Design: Copeland, Novak & Israel
Photograph: Henry S. Fullerton, 3rd

Center Core or Atrium Plan
Bonwit Teller, Eastchester, NY
Store Design: Copeland, Novak & Israel

effective, defined selling spaces at the center of the large building rectangle. It multiplied the use of full-height partitions, with all of their background treatment of merchandise, decorations, and graphics. Simultaneously, it allowed for ramifications of the aisle circulation system, irrigating major aisles throughout the surface of the plan and permitting an appropriate relationship between maximum frontage and optimum depth for sales departments. This was a revolution of planning. It converted the large, open, continuous department store spaces into a complex pattern of separate, articulated shop—like spaces, each of which could express the varieties of life-styles then blooming in society. It permitted infinite variations of form and design ideas, reinforcing the awareness among store executives that a strong design image was necessary.

DESIGN

Generated by the flexible, complex, and variable possibilities of the central core plan, there was a growing awareness that strong design achieved a strong image and personality. Design gradually was understood to be a vital tool to express store character in the context of ever-fiercer competition. The eclectic and traditional design of the 1950s shifted radically toward the reflection of contemporary culture. The International Style was brought indoors and, in turn, was modified by psychedelic and op art influences. A glass and chrome style was retrieved from the modernistic style of the 1920s. Industrial forms, for example the airplane and the automobile, suggested streamlined and highly finished elements that led to futurism, with sophisticated variations. Graphics, with bold typography and photographic blow-ups was brought into the store design vocabulary. The House of Cards picture—card game designed by Charles Eames, first produced in the 1950s, became a universal pastime. It introduced new images that exposed an esthetics based on imaginative combinations of machine culture and natural forms (*see color insert*).

Design Reflecting Contemporary Culture
Bonwit Teller, Chicago, IL
Store Design: Copeland, Novak & Israel

Bold Typography, Futurism
Joseph Magnin, Fashion Square, La Habra, CA
Store Design: Skidmore, Owings, & Merrill
Photograph: Retail Reporting Corp.

Glass and Chrome Style
Woodward & Lothrop, Landover Mall,
Landover, MD
Store Design: Robert Young Associates
Photograph: Retail Reporting Corp.

FIXTURIZATION

The trends of the 1950s continued. Designers and fixture manufacturers, in various collaborative combinations, sought to exploit the booming market with refinements of self-selection techniques, materials, and color. The compartmentalization of space permitted by the complexities of the plan challenged the idea of universally applicable, flexible, and convertible fixtures. Specialized fixtures to highlight and contribute to an ambiance, under the influence of pluralistic life-style expressions of the various sales departments, contributed to the development of a host of new ideas. It was recognized that a fixture properly presenting crystal or giftware must be entirely different from that displaying shirts or sweaters. Thus, the germ of differentiation and plurality enriched the store interior by means of varied fixture designs.

Refinements of Self-Selection Techniques
Galeries Lafayette, Paris, France
Store Design: Copeland, Novak & Israel

Specialized Self-Selection Fixture Design
Burdines, Dadeland, Miami, FL
Store Design: Walker/Grad

DECORATION

Uninhibited, bold colors and patterns dominated. Dramatic and psyche-delic shock effects reflected the frenzy and violence of the period. Patterns suggested by the contemporary geometrics of pop art were everywhere, on flooring, walls, and ceilings. Since the spaces were no longer a unified continuum, each department or association of related departments could be designed and colored to fit the mood of its merchandise. The store interior became a compelling kaleidoscope. Drama and variety were the requirements. The store simulated the nightclub—concepts of drama were underlined by purples and oranges and other shocking colors. Pattern upon pattern produced a richness of effect, multiplied by highly reflective surfaces, within a very contemporary viewpoint.

Uninhibited Psychedelic Patterns
Garfinkel's, Landover Mall, Landover, MD
Store Design: Copeland, Novak & Israel
Photograph: Norman McGrath

LIGHTING DESIGN

Two commercial developments of lamps and lighting fixtures—the high-intensity discharge lamp and the incandescent light track broke into the stereotyped usage of regimented fluorescent light fixtures in a simple ceiling plane.

The high-intensity discharge (HID) lamp provided an efficient single-point light source with high lumen output. It was a new alternative to the ubiquitous 4' x 4' fluorescent fixture. It provided nearly the same efficiency and output as the fluorescent lamp with a small-diameter fixture that reflected the current esthetics of minimizing the light source itself. If the color emission of the lamp tended toward the cool end of the spectrum, corrections were developed daily and the fixture itself was modified by "scientific"

HID Light Fixtures; Incandescent Track Lighting
Thalheimer's, Crab Tree Mall, Raleigh, NC
Store Design: Copeland, Novak & Israel
Photograph: Louis Reens

applications of color. The advantage of the single-point light source was fundamental; it gave sparkle, punch, and excitement to the space, and it enhanced the merchandise by accenting its textural and tactile values.

The incandescent light track provided a new, flexible system that utilized the PAR 38 or R 40 to project incandescent spot lamps plugged into an electrified ceiling component. This component was a simple, open, linear metal channel, wired and energized to allow the fixture to be placed anywhere along its length. The Globus Store in Zurich, Switzerland, had the first major installation. It generated world-wide influence and led instantaneously to experimentation to create dramatic and flexible lighting systems integrated into the ceiling design. It introduced a new concept—developing an esthetic appreciation of the importance of the ceiling plane to create design elements. The matrix of the linear elements formed interesting modules. Suspending the matrix below the ceiling plane offered new forms that were

Light Track and Ceiling Design Elements
Proffitt's, Alcoa, TN
Store Design: Copeland, Novak & Israel

themselves infinitely variable, recalling high-tech patterns of the industrial landscape. At one blow, it provided reasonable possibilities for rendering interior store spaces in a theatrical way and for converting uniform, flat lighting to dramatic contrasts based on principles of modulating light and shadow.

Both developments changed forever the department store look. An entirely new vocabulary of forms drew attention to the ceiling as a major design element.

The 1970s

America was perceived as a world superpower—economically, industrially, militarily, as well as culturally. Merchandising know-how and store design concepts were exported worldwide. With the demise of the International Style in architecture, there was an eruption of postmodernism and then a more sustained renewed search for a contemporary, pluralistic, and enriched expression. Crises of the inner cities engendered a consequent movement toward replanning and revitalizing urban centers. The downtown department store, now losing business to its own constellation of suburban branch units, began to reduce selling space in its traditional "palace" and to convert it to a multiuse facility, generating new economic returns on its real estate equity. Concurrently, in its analysis to reduce space and to increase efficiency and profit, the complete department store began to liquidate nonprofit service-oriented departments and to convert itself into a strong, dominant, fashion specialty store. Specialty stores, in turn, picked up many of the businesses "given away." The war between department stores and specialty stores emerged.

During the 1970s, Michael Graves questioned modernism and turned to a classical language of architecture with strong anthropocentric associations. Postmodernism led architecture away from the Miesian authority, just as society was breaking down a monolithically WASP conception of itself. Blacks were demanding equal rights; women were entering the work force; gays were coming out of the closet; the disabled were claiming access; the elderly were recognizing their political power base and their needs. America was giving voice to its constituent minorities. Architecture was emerging as a pluralistic expression of richness and diversity instead of functionalism and uniformity. Everything from urban design to furniture was affected.

The corruption spread by Watergate and the preoccupation with the Vietnam War, watched by Americans every day on their televisions, were the dominant events and infected every aspect of life. Conflict and confrontation were the chief characteristics of the decade. Antiwar demonstrations rocked college campuses. Third World nationalism continued to challenge the primacy of the industrialized nations. A foreign policy of détente was to produce a geopolitical balance of power by containing the former Soviet Union and China and by curbing radical revolutions in the Third World. President Jimmy Carter sought to convert that policy into a global defense and extension of human rights. In 1973, during the Yom Kippur war, America suffered fuel shortages and realized the vulnerability of economic and living standards. Western Europe's postwar economic miracle was jolted to a halt.

Spectacular achievements were made in space by both the United States and the former Soviet Union. Humanity's knowledge of the universe expanded. "Operation Sail" in New York City celebrated the 200th birthday of the United States and gave a renewed impetus to man's hope for good. America's taste in film was for disasters: *Earthquake, Jaws, Star Wars. The Deer Hunter* dealt with the tragedy suffered by veterans of the Vietnam War. *Patton* won seven Oscars.

1970'S SYNOPTIC TIME LINE

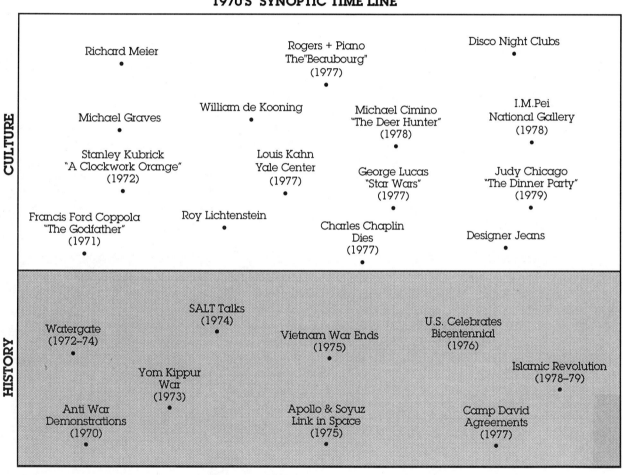

CULTURE

Richard Meier

Rogers + Piano
The "Beaubourg"
(1977)

Disco Night Clubs

Michael Graves

William de Kooning

Michael Cimino
"The Deer Hunter"
(1978)

I.M. Pei
National Gallery
(1978)

Stanley Kubrick
"A Clockwork Orange"
(1972)

Louis Kahn
Yale Center
(1977)

George Lucas
"Star Wars"
(1977)

Judy Chicago
"The Dinner Party"
(1979)

Francis Ford Coppola
"The Godfather"
(1971)

Roy Lichtenstein

Charles Chaplin
Dies
(1977)

Designer Jeans

HISTORY

SALT Talks
(1974)

Watergate
(1972-74)

Vietnam War Ends
(1975)

U.S. Celebrates
Bicentennial
(1976)

Yom Kippur
War
(1973)

Islamic Revolution
(1978-79)

Anti War
Demonstrations
(1970)

Apollo & Soyuz
Link in Space
(1975)

Camp David
Agreements
(1977)

MERCHANDISING

Principles of drama and variety stressed the trend toward defined life-style presentations in the various zones of the department store. Under this need for character and differentiation, the universal, standard self-selection fixture was suppressed. Instead, there was an explosion of different fixture designs, each expressing a zonal and departmental style. Notions of flexibility and interchangeability disappeared under the pressure of excitement, drama, interest, and a new special dynamics highlighting an incredible proliferation of high-style fashion merchandise.

VISUAL MERCHANDISING

Props, Grids, Structures, Blow-ups
Burdines, Town Center,
Boca Raton, FL
Store Design: Walker Group
Photograph: Mark Ross

Seizing the manifold opportunities created by complex interior plans, visual merchandising changed overnight. Instead of sculptured mannequins posing on strategically placed platforms, the merchandise itself became the display. Utilizing the partition systems multiplied by the complexities of the center core plans, visual merchandising elements incorporated the full height of the partition. In this "use of the cube," vertical zones were developed that provided inventory stock at the base, color coordinated or style groupings at the center, and compelling life-style presentations at the top

(*see color insert*). This presentation system revolutionized the historic fixturization of the wall. No longer would there be hang rods or shelving below a light valance or curtain wall, with decorative treatments above. Now the design of the wall would totally reflect ideas of merchandise presentation and would permit infinite variations based on merchandise and fashion trends. The mannequin was replaced by multiple props, grids, structures, sculptural systems, neon lighting displays, all of which applied the possibilities of modern art and stage design. The display director became the visual merchandiser.

PLANNING

Complex store planning ideas dominated, leading to mature, sophisticated, and diverse architectural and spatial elements. Under the influence of the new techniques of visual presentation at the partitions, the modeling of the ceiling planes was seen as a device to draw attention to the merchandise elements; it simultaneously introduced a whole new series of possibilities by integrating with wall systems, with a broader use of illumination elements. It changed the look of the store forever, creating drama, variations of emphasis, and an understanding of human scale. Escalators, generally located at the center of the store to foster quick, efficient, and direct access to all of its departments, now became the symbolic center or icon (*see color insert*). They were opened up, emphasized by monumental spaces, skylights, and imaginative architectural systems. The monumental design of these spaces permitted the shopper to see activities on multiple floor levels and by visual excitement be drawn in to browse and shop everywhere. Additional interest on each floor level was provided by elevating special departments by means of several steps. The concept of the center core plan survived but was

Adding Interest by Elevating
a Department
Bamberger's, Livingston Mall,
Livingston, NJ
Store Design: Copeland, Novak & Israel
Photograph: Gil Amiaga, NYC

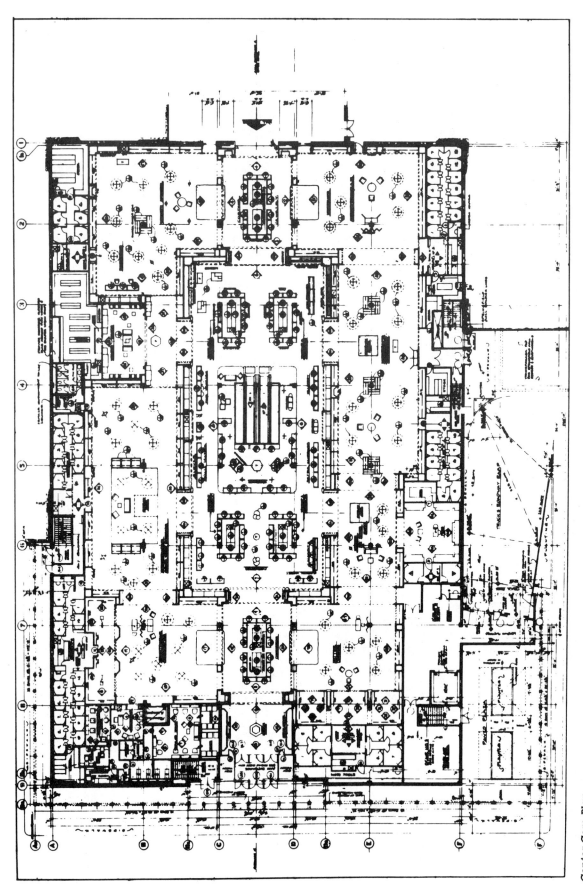

Center Core Plan
Garfinkels, Springfield Mall, Springfield, VA
Store Design: Copeland, Novak & Israel
From Israel, "Basics of Store Design," *Visual Merchandising,* National Retail Merchants Association: New York, 1976.

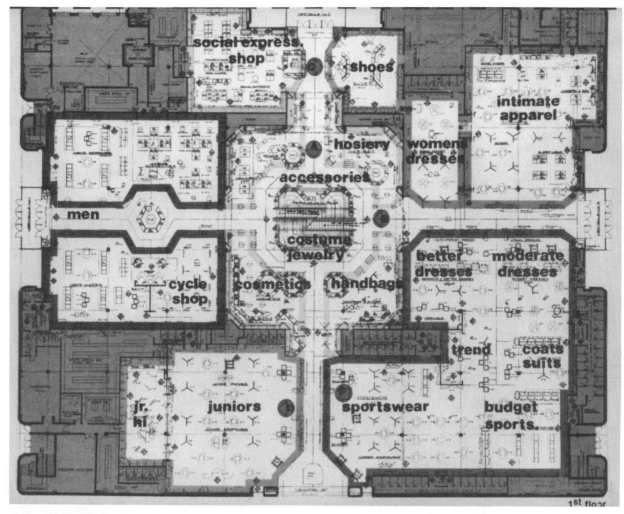

A "Zone-and-Cluster" Plan
Steinbach's Shore Mall, Pleasantville, NJ
Store Design: Copeland, Novak & Israel

developed into countless variations. A "zone-and-cluster" plan expressed larger groupings of associated merchandise. Each of the spaces was defined by enclosing full-height partition systems; the subdivisions of departments within these spaces was accomplished by clustering special modular floor fixtures, flexible and movable, above the eye line. Each such space, then, was specially designed to incorporate and enhance the quality and mood of the merchandise being presented. The total, combined experience was pluralistic, exciting, and dramatic.

DESIGN

The store was conceived as theater. Design direction was contemporary, pluralistic, and rich. This was the classic period of postwar contemporary retail style (*see color insert*). If there were hosts of different approaches and variations generated by the personality both of client and designer and by regional influences, nevertheless, a kind of international, ubiquitous, corporate department store style emerged. The speed of communication and the knowledge of what was happening in a booming expansion of stores throughout America, in an age of shopping malls, tended to make most stores look alike. If the illustrations show an amazing variety of ideas and forms, nevertheless, the shopper had difficulty identifying the store in which he or she was shopping, especially after having explored two or three similar stores in a major, regional shopping center anchored by three or more department stores. The search for identity, personality, and image had begun.

In July 1992, Donald Woutat of the *Los Angeles Times*, had this to say of the shopping mall:

> As ubiquitous as the automobiles and suburbs that created it, the shopping mall— there are now 38,000 in this country, 5,000 in California alone—has been described as the signature structure of our age, the cathedral of post-World War II culture. . . . The mall is praised as a stage for communal rituals and a place for seniors to exercise in winter, it is condemned for blandness and its role as climate-controlled fortress against the real world. Futurists have called it a prototype for habitats in space. It affords pleasure to millions but gives some the heebie-jeebies—a mix of claustrophobia and sensory overload that William Kowinski, author of the book *The Malling of America*, calls "mallaise" or "mal de mall."

Classic Period of Contemporary Style
Bonwit Teller, Chicago, IL
Store Design: Copeland, Novak & Israel

Classic Period of Contemporary Style
Sak's 5th Avenue, South Coast Plaza,
Costa Mesa, CA
Store Design: Copeland, Novak & Israel

FIXTURIZATION

Innumerable variants of special fixture design continued the trend of the 1970s. An entire industry was born. Manufacturers in Europe, Japan, and America developed systems of metal fixtures and hardware components that were modern in style, universal in application, quick to install in the field, and adaptable to infinite variations of merchandise presentation techniques. "Pegboard" was replaced by "slatwall." Countertrends, however, showed a search for special fixture designs and an attempt to avoid the universal, prefabricated look of the systems.

Slatwall Diagrams & Details
From Spacewall®, Spacewall International, Stone Mountain, GA

DECORATION

Bold, psychedelic color and patterns gave way to warm, subtle, flattering palettes. Earth tones, peaches, dusty pinks, and warm whites dominated. Patterns were suppressed. There was a striking use of tactile materials and textures to create depth and richness. Natural wood, veneers, stones, and metals of rich tonality added substance and quality. Color was carefully selected to complement and enhance the merchandise and its package. Simultaneously, dramatic and different moods related to associate merchandise zones were projected. The expanding and sophisticated decorative resources, with incredible richness and variety of contemporary materials, techniques and systems, were fully used (*see color insert*).

Tactile Materials & Textures
I. Magnin, White Flint Center, Bethesda, MD
Store Design: Copeland, Novak & Israel

Tactile Materials & Textures
Bamberger's, Christiana Mall, Wilmington, DE
Store Design: Copeland, Novak & Israel

LIGHTING DESIGN

Lighting design participated in the new, revolutionary opening up of space and developed as an inherent part of a complex interior architectonics, affecting an entirely new vocabulary of overhead elements. As part of the new fixturization of the wall, it became understood that a lowered ceiling plane intersecting the peripheral partition would bring the eye down and would accentuate the merchandise presentation. At the same time, it helped transform the traditional, high-ceiling, monumental, hangarlike space into a more humanistic one, related to personal scale, and created a sequence of intimate scenes to which controlled use of different spotlights rendered the merchandise and presentations in a theatrical contrast. As a result, ceiling designs explored light coves, vaults, domes, stepped planes, suspended structures, fins, and beams. All of these created an ambience of complex richness and variety, integrating with these rediscovered forms the new-found devices and equipment of theatrical lighting.

Simultaneously, crisis in the United States' energy supply forced the enactment of state-controlled regulations, limiting wattage use per square foot according to building type, function, and task. This discipline forbid the design of high-lumen output lighting. If department store lighting had previously approached the 100-foot candle level, quite similar to that employed in the mass merchandising or supermarket stores, with uniform lighting an objective, now it had to be reduced to a 35-foot candle level. Similarly, the high cost of energy began to force store owners to establish their own energy savings criteria. Both of these new limitations led to the realization that modulations of light and shadow, the principle of chiaroscuro, was a seminal solution to the lighting design of department stores. Minimal levels of illumination at aisles and nonselling areas, dramatic contrasts of high-intensity light at merchandise and presentations, and the use of the most efficient fluorescent lamp in coves and ceiling planes, integrating these into architectural spaces all helped to produce an entirely new look, saved energy and its maintenance cost, and contrasted at one blow with the flat illumination of the supermarket, discounter, and mass merchant.

HID lighting was rejected. It could not conform to required wattage per square foot reductions. Its color rendition and control were never truly satisfactory.

Lighting: Ceiling Design Theatrics
Sak's 5th Avenue, South Coast Plaza, Costa Mesa, CA
Store Design: Copeland, Novak & Israel

Principles of Chiaroscuro in Lighting
Carson, Pirie, Scott, Randhurst Mall, Mt. Prospect, IL
Store Design: Copeland, Novak & Israel

4 The 1980s

America was the global center. Europe and the Pacific Rim were increasingly interested in the U. S. retail planning and design concepts and methodology. Europe was on the threshold of organizing its 1992 community. There were important population changes: a declining birthrate at home and a growing mature population with a greater number of retirees. The baby boomers of the 1950s were now the wage earners in the two-income nuclear family. Travel and leisure activities accelerated, leaving less and less time for the shopping adventure. Changes in the domestic market resulted in a dizzying series of liquidations, acquisitions, and restructurings of the department store, which was struggling fiercely to win back its eroding share of the market. In the midst of unparalleled competition, the need for service, added value and distinctive offerings ballooned and made desperate the search for signature elements, store image, and special character. The specialty store took advantage of the chaos and emerged stronger. Simultaneously, alternate channels of distribution flourished: direct mail, catalogue operations, discount clubs, telemarketing. The computer and in-store video were marshalled to bring a new excitement in the department store and to help promote store sales.

In architecture, postmodernism and classicized buildings came to epitomize a movement that expressed establishment values, affluence, and elitism. Under the administration of Ronald Reagan, Americas' taste turned conservative. This conservatism found its way into shopping malls and store interiors. However, in a complex reaction to postmodernism, other architects formulated another response. They rejected the boring, tired expression of modernism in glass box buildings. Instead of referring to eclectic and historic styles, they renewed the revolutionary experiments of the Russians during the 1910s and 1920s, when designers responded to the heady excitement of their brave new world and invented new forms.

New, spectacular designs emerged that changed architectural character and direction. Led by Gehry, Tschumi, and Hadid, the term "deconstructivism" was coined to describe a fragmented, asymmetrical work that eliminated any element that dominated the parts. Parts became independent and scattered, colliding and interactive with other discrete pieces. They intersected and exploded into unpredictable organisms. They behaved as though they were moving through a field of forces, shards and planes and rods liberated from the laws of gravity. Discontinuity evolved into a strategy. "There can be no symmetries when the center no longer holds," said William Butler Yeats. In one of the most intellectually and artistically ambitious movements since World War II, it was an architecture of doubt that embodied the fragmented and precarious times.

"Even if, as Hegel says, history is inevitable, then only God anticipated the events that concluded the eighties."* Popular democratic movements over-

*Lois Gordon and Alan Gordon, *American Chronicle 1920–1989* (New York: Crown Publishers, Inc., 1990).

1980'S SYNOPTIC TIME LINE

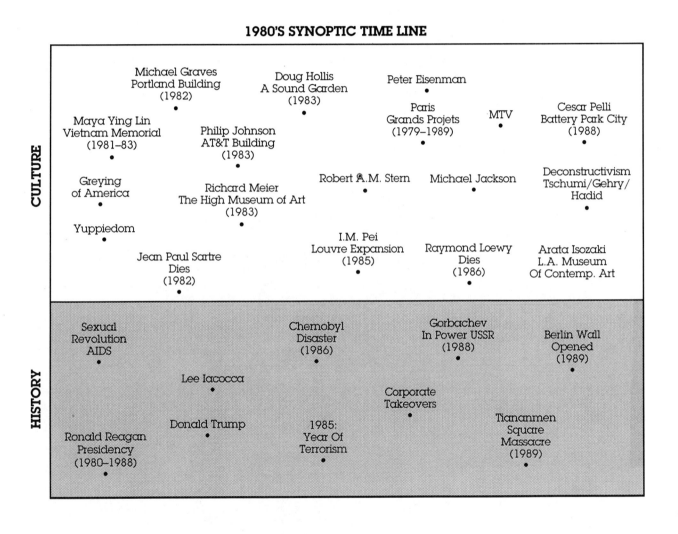

Michael Graves
Portland Building
(1982)

Doug Hollis
A Sound Garden
(1983)

Peter Eisenman

Maya Ying Lin
Vietnam Memorial
(1981–83)

Philip Johnson
AT&T Building
(1983)

Paris
Grands Projets
(1979–1989)

MTV

Cesar Pelli
Battery Park City
(1988)

Greying
of America

Richard Meier
The High Museum of Art
(1983)

Robert A.M. Stern

Michael Jackson

Deconstructivism
Tschumi/Gehry/
Hadid

Yuppiedom

I.M. Pei
Louvre Expansion
(1985)

Raymond Loewy
Dies
(1986)

Arata Isozaki
L.A. Museum
Of Contemp. Art

Jean Paul Sartre
Dies
(1982)

CULTURE

Sexual
Revolution
AIDS

Chernobyl
Disaster
(1986)

Gorbachev
In Power USSR
(1988)

Berlin Wall
Opened
(1989)

Lee Iacocca

Corporate
Takeovers

Ronald Reagan
Presidency
(1980–1988)

Donald Trump

1985:
Year Of
Terrorism

Tiananmen
Square
Massacre
(1989)

HISTORY

turned totalitarian Communist governments in Eastern Europe. Gorbachev initiated "perestroika" and "glasnost" in the former Soviet Union. The nuclear plant at Chernobyl melted down. The United States exalted heroes like Lee Iacocca and Donald Trump. Yuppiedom witnessed incessant multibillion dollar corporate takeovers. The Yuppie work and play ethic was everywhere. The two-income family became necessary and common. The sexual revolution encountered a powerful adversary within the formidable spread of a fatal and sexually transmitted disease—AIDS.

Saul Bellow and John Updike were the dominant writers. The musicals *Cats, Phantom of the Opera*, and *Les Miserables* were popular. *Amadeus* and *Sunday in the Park with George* revealed vitality in the American theater. Michael Jackson and Bruce Springsteen were the rock superstars. Movies reflected the diversity and energy of America: *Atlantic City, Reds, E.T. the Extraterrestrial, Out of Africa*, and *Platoon*. The range of television embraced shows like "Dallas," "M.A.S.H.," "Archie Bunker's Place," "The Cosby Show," "L.A. Law," "Miami Vice," and "Brideshead Revisited."

MERCHANDISING

Merchandising moved from mass presentation to preselected, coordinated themes and expressions of life-styles. The changes developed by visual merchandisers during the 1970s gave merchants the techniques of stocking and

Merchandise Coordination by Color, Function, Lifestyle
Bullock's, Thousand Oaks Mall, Thousand Oaks, CA
Store Design: Copeland, Novak & Israel
Photograph: Marvin Rand/Retail Reporting Corp.

Special Images Provided by Franchisers
Bloomingdale's: Polo Shop by Ralph Lauren, New York, NY
Store Design: HTI/Space Planning International

presenting groups of merchandise dramatically coordinated by color, function, and style. These banished forever from stores the phalanxes of straight or round garment racks crammed with a full inventory of goods of all colors, styles, and sizes. Primarily, it permitted stores to reduce their volume of merchandise and its high cost of investment.

Boutique franchisers moved into the department store. They brought their name brands, fashions, and sales techniques into the emerging fashion supermarket and, by the variety provided by their special images, multiplied the pluralistic drama of the store.

VISUAL MERCHANDISING

The role of the visual merchandisers assumed a revolutionary importance. They became "Renaissance people," incorporating in one executive authority, leadership and a skillful understanding of merchandising, planning, design and decorating, lighting design, and visual presentation. They became the artistic soul of the store. In the upper levels of store management,

Electronic Display and Marketing Technology
Burdines, Town Center, Boca Raton, FL
Store Design: Walker Group
Photograph: Mark Ross

they sat with the president, influenced store planning design decisions, and brought together the many disparate voices in the large store organization. They were the voice of the client. They synergized the complex disciplines and elements of store design and contributed vastly in creating the compelling excitement and rich texture and physical quality of the contemporary store.

The development of video, programmed and coordinated with advertising promotions, brought movement, sound, special presentations, and all of the advances of stunning electronic display and marketing technology from Madison Avenue into the store, challenging the visual merchandiser and store designer to integrate these devices imaginatively into the interiors (Van DeBogart, 1989).

PLANNING

Creativity and originality continued to infuse variations into the center core and zonal plans. Imaginative application of these principles was as varied as the stores themselves, together with the growing number of professional planners and designers who emerged in America and Europe. Sophisticated, theatrical excitement was the goal. The proliferation of boutique and shop franchises added a heterogeneous mix to plan, space, and merchandise. Concepts of complexity, pluralism, and continuity prevailed.

Plan Concepts: Pluralism and the Center Core
Davison-Paxon, Lenox Square, Atlanta, GA
Store Design: Walker Group/CNI

DESIGN

Design became obsessed with searching for a signature—a style that would reflect a unique store image and a selling environment that would be different from the competition. A customer would subconsciously perceive the inherent difference between a Macy's and a Bloomingdales, for example. If the one appeared classically traditional, using wood paneling, marble, and glass, subdued colors, and a decorative palette that was subservient to the merchandise, the other flaunted bold colors, strong contrasts of materials and reflective finishes, chrome, brass, and glass, and the glitz of New Yorker chic.

A new consciousness of regional culture and style reinforced this search for identity. A Burdine's group of department stores advertised itself as "Florida's department store" and unashamedly exploited motives taken from the palm tree as its own icon (*see color insert*).

The escalator's structure and configuration, as the geometric center of the store, became more and more lavish. Open spaces surrounding imaginative, sculptural arrangements of the escalator trusses, connecting bridges, skylights, architectural emphasis to columns and ceilings, vaults, domes, light coves—an entire vocabulary of space forms became the celebratory centerpieces for the design statement. These spaces were deemed essential, even if they subtracted from profitable selling areas for impulse merchandise at 100 percent traffic locations on the several floors.

Signature Elements of Style
Bloomingdale's, New York, NY
Store Design: Barbara D'Arcy
Photograph: Retail Reporting Corp.

Signature Elements of Style
Macy's, Galleria, Dallas, TX
Store Design: Copeland, Novak & Israel

FIXTURIZATION

The trends of the 1970s continued. Variations of style and presentation techniques multiplied under the discipline of a special, total store image. The revolution of visual presentation affected the design of fixtures, with each major store seeking to invent its own look. Additional, contrasting, subconsciously identifiable design elements furnished by the growing number of boutique franchiser installations contributed to the pluralistic impact.

Escalators—Celebratory Elements at the Geometric Center
The Broadway, Beverly Center, Los Angeles, CA
Store Design: Cole Martinez Curtis & Associates, Marina del Rey, CA
Photograph: Toshi Yoshimi/Retail Reporting Corp.

*The Fixture as an Expression
of Store Image*
Gimbel Brothers, Philadelphia, PA
Store Design: Copeland, Novak & Israel
Photograph: Retail Reporting Corp.

Marble and Differentiating Materials
Rich's, Lenox Square, Atlanta, GA
Store Design: Walker Group

DECORATION

Always the partner to design, decoration impacted the search for store image. The return to regional cultural and artistic influences widened the vocabulary. The infinite resources of modern technologies in the decorative arts were brought into play. In differentiating the materials of aisle circulation systems from the selling areas, the use of marble became literally standard and mandatory. The marble from quarries in Italy, Greece, Turkey, and other parts of the world brought richness and monumental character into the department store (*see color insert*). The technical development of man-made and computerized patterns in the textile industries gave the decorator limitless choices of selections for carpeting and wall coverings. Wood flooring, man-made veneer patterns, limitless colors, finishes, and designs in the plastic laminates—everything was possible, limited only by considerations of budget and ease of maintenance.

LIGHTING DESIGN

The concepts explored during the 1970s still governed. The importance of using light to create the store as theater was helped by the commercial development of the low-voltage incandescent lamp and theatrical spotlight fixtures. These provided new qualities of flexibility, great intensity, sparkle, and contrast (*see color insert*). The small lamp and diminutive fixture offered a complete new scale and character to the interior space. The concurrent modifications of design and manufacture of the compact fluorescent lamp and light fixture brought efficiency and relatively low-current consumption into a point source configuration. These gave the lighting designer still another tool to generate diffuse general illumination, high-lumen output with relatively low wattage per square foot, and a ceiling pattern based upon small units minimizing glare and light source.

5 | The 1990s

Since we are still at the threshold of the last decade of the twentieth century, it is fruitless to try to describe new trends. In the dialectics of history, it is understood that the germ of the future lies within current organisms. In the Hegelian tradition, thesis begets antithesis and ultimately synthesis. So it is in store design. However, store design is also enormously influenced by the demise of hosts of department stores, the interwarfare between department stores and specialty stores, and the fierce competition of all of the varieties of retailing operations seeking to dominate their "niche" markets in a stagnant economy in which cost inflation still persists.

In addition, there is a new awareness of what is now called "environmentally conscious design." The condition of our technology and the recognition of the potentially tragic depletion of the earth's natural resources have led designers and clients toward a new objective—to look at environmental quality in a holistic sense throughout the entire design process. There is a new professional ethics and a new esthetics—a social and moral responsibility in design to enhance the quality of life and protect the health, safety, and welfare of the public. There are now moral, healthy, and "green" buildings. There are environmentally friendly "green" products to respond to questions of ecosystems and to provide sustainability. Governmental regulations, such as the National Environmental Policy Act (1969) and the Clean Air Act (amended 1990), underpin these responsibilities. Private industries and manufacturers of products for buildings and interior furnishings have established their own certification initiatives that recognize a growing public awareness as well as a marketing necessity. Principles of recycling and of resource-efficient building elements are finding favor simultaneously with renewed notions of the quality of the urban environment as a cultural testimony to the historic growth of cities and of architecture harmonious to that context (*see color insert*).

Retailers are realizing that store planning and design is environmental marketing that must reflect customer behavior, microdiversity, generational versus cultural attitudes, and the influence of communications and media on behavior. Technology will support new business practices to increase profitability and affect merchandise assortment, presentation, and replenishment. It will improve customer services through the application of sophisticated serving up of data, interlinks, and interactions. Telemarketing will grow and compete but will force the retailer to find new devices and techniques to make the store more exciting, dramatic, and efficient—a place to be, to see, and to be seen. The principles of virtual reality will be applied within the store environment to take advantage of emotions and the senses of taste, sound, and smell.

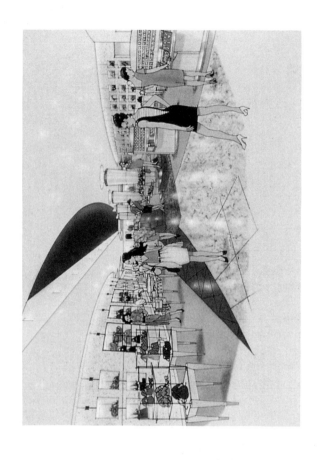

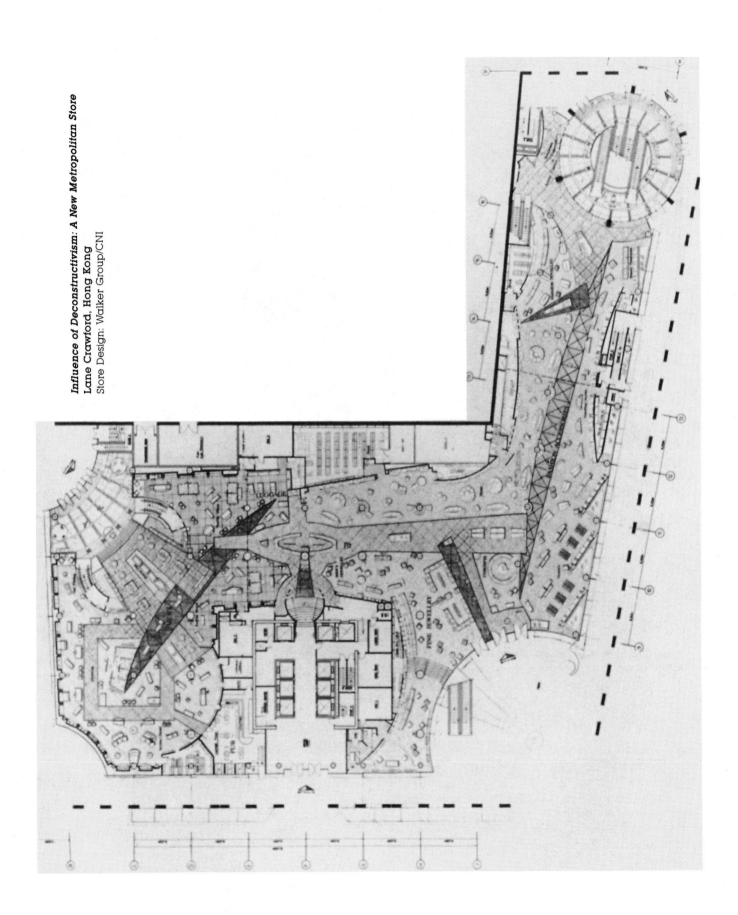

Influence of Deconstructivism: A New Metropolitan Store
Lane Crawford, Hong Kong
Store Design: Walker Group/CNI

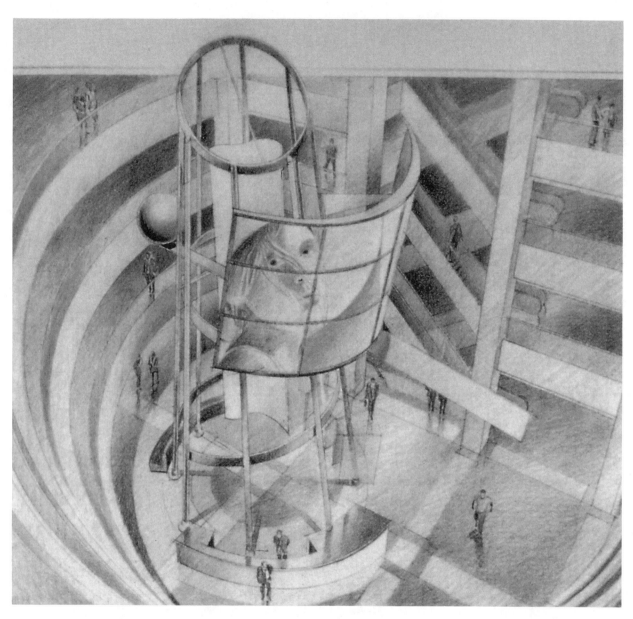

Video Display Tower: Concept Sketch
Store Design: Walker Group/CNI

Historic References with Up-scale Presentation
Bergdorf-Goodman Men, New York, NY
Store Design: J.T. Nakaoka Associates Architects
Photograph: Jaime Ardiles-Arce

As Arthur M. Schlesinger, Jr., has said in the book, *Chronicle of the Twentieth Century,*

> The twentieth century is glorious and damned—a century of triumph and tragedy, of grandeur and misery, of vision and disaster ... filled with anguish and blood and atrocity, filled too with heroism and hope and dream ... it has seen science and technology sweep humanity into the electronic epoch. The onward rush is now carrying humanity even further—beyond the planet Earth itself ... It is the end of the Eurocentric world ... The Third World threw off the shackles of Western empire. The age of the Atlantic wanes. The age of the Pacific is upon us.

So it is that store design reflects the culture that sustains it and from which it springs. That is the essence of the enfolding process: the metamorphosis of store design.

Store of the Future: Shop Front in a Ghetto

III

THEORY AND ELEMENTS OF STORE PLANNING AND DESIGN

6 Strategy and Program

In a theoretical discussion of the elements of store design, it should be emphasized that any analysis is only a convenient way of describing the numerous components that constitute the essence of the total design. Any itemizing or compartmentalizing of the elements runs the risk of destroying the character, mood, style, and image that are the true objectives. The categories that follow are arbitrary. There is an inherent danger of repetition or omission. Such an overview suggests the complexities and interdisciplinary responsibilities that the store planner/designer must master. In this sense, he or she is the director of a large team that involves merchants; visual merchandisers; architects; structural, mechanical, and illumination engineers; operations specialists; quantity and cost surveyors; and construction managers and building contractors in interactive, multitudinous related fields. It is the store planner/designer who with imagination, creativity, experience, and managerial skill can organize and produce a successful store project.

To initiate and set the scene for this kind of project, a valid and comprehensive program must be established. Not only will it clarify procedures, objectives,

PHASE I

DESIGN STRATEGIES
- ROI SUCESS CRITERIA
- MARKET RESEARCH
- COMPETITIVE ENVIRONMENT
- PRODUCT MIX
- MERCHANDISE/PRESENTA-TION CRITERIA DATA
- PLANNING/DESIGN CRITERIA
- OPERATIONSCRITERIA
- PROJECT SCHEDULE
- PROJECT BUDGET PARAMETERS

GOAL
STRATEGIC DESIGN OBJECTIVE

- ANALYZE PRODUCT MIX BY CATEGORY
- ESTABLISH QUANTITIES PER CATEGORY BY S.K.U.
- VALIDATE QUANTITIES AGAINST FINANCIAL MODELS
- MERCHANDISE DATA & AREA PROGRAM CRITERIA
  ESTABLISH BLOCK PLAN

GOAL
BLOCK PLAN / MERCHAN-DISE ANALYSIS REPORT

PHASE II

CONCEPT DESIGN
- MERCHANDISE / DESIGN PLAN
- CONCEPT CEILING / FLOORING
- MERCHANDISE CRITERIA REVIEW (SENIOR MERCHANTS)
- VSUAL MERCHANDISE CRITERIA
- CONCEPT SIGN OFF
- STATEMENT OF PROBABLE CONSTRUCTION COSTS

GOAL
CONCEPT PRESENTATION

PHASE III

DESIGN DEVELOPMENT
- FLOOR PLANS /ADJACENCY LAYOUTS / CIRCULATION PAT-TERNS
- VISUAL MERCHANDISE PLANS
- CEILING DESIGN
- LIGHTING SPECIFICATIONS
- FLOORING DESIGN
- COLORS AND MATERIALS SPECIFICATIONS
- FURNISHINGS AND FIXTURES SPECIFICATIONS
- INTERIOR ELEVATIONS
- STATEMENT OF PROBABLE CONSTRUCTION COSTS

GOAL
FINAL PRESENTATION

PHASE IV

CONTRACT DOCUMENTATION
- FLOOR PLANS / ADJACENCY LAYOUTS / CIRCULATION PATTERNS
- FIXTURE PLANS
- PARTITION PLANS AND DETAILS
- POWER AND SIGNAL PLANS AND DETAILS
- REFLECTED CEILING PLAN AND DETAILS
- FLOOR COVERINGS PLAN AND DETAILS
- INTERIOR ELEVATIONS AND DETAILS
- COLORS AND MATERIALS SPECIFICATIONS
- STATEMENT OF PROBABLE CONSTRUCTION COSTS
- QUALITY/CONTENT REVIEW

GOAL
BID SUMBISSION

PHASE V

CONSTRUCTION ADMINISTRATION
- REVIEW OF BID PROPOSALS
- INTERPRETATION OF CONTRACT DOCUMENTS
- SHOP DRAWINGS AND SAMPLES
- OBSERVATION VISITS BY PHASED COMPLETION
- MERCHANDISE AND DISPLAY OVERVIEW
- EVALUATION

GOAL
STORE OPENING

Chart of Project Process for Walker Group/CNI

Code	Item	FORM X BUDGET 6/6/92		WG/CNI BUDGET 1 8/14/91			WG/CNI BUDGET 2 9/6/91		
		Second Floor	$/SF	Form-X	Cost	Variant	Form-X	Cost	Variant
20000	Site Improvements, Building	$0	$0.00	$0			$0		
30000	Excavcation and Foundation								
32000	Structural	$91,975	$1.39	$91,975	$105,000		$91,975	$105,000	9
33000	General Shell Architectural								
33000	Architectural Interior Finishes	$92,625	$1.40	$92,625	$92,625	5	$92,625	$92,625	9
34000	Demolition - Building Shell	$137,000	$2.07	$137,000	$152,492		$137,000	$152,492	9
34002	Asbestos								
	Sub Total Building	$321,600	$4.86	$321,600	$350,117	($28,517)	$321,600	$350,117	($28,517)
41000	Vertical Transportation	$0	$0.00	$0			$0		
42000	Electrical - Building Shell	$1,800,000	$27.21	$1,800,000	$1,671,589		$1,800,000	$1,400,000	6
43000	Plumbing	$18,525	$0.28	$18,525	$10,000		$18,525	$12,000	6
44000	HVAC	$251,335	$3.80	$251,335	$468,936		$251,335	$400,000	6
46000	Fire Protection	$280,210	$4.24	$280,210	$213,375		$280,210	$215,000	6
47000	Misc. Building Equipment	$0	$0.00	$0	$0		$0		
	Sub Total Building Equipment	$2,350,070	$35.53	$2,350,070	$2,363,900	($13,830)	$2,350,070	$2,027,000	$323,070
96000	General Conditions	$0	$0.00	$0	$0		$0	$0	
0	A&E Fees / Reimburs. / Related	$0	$0.00	$0	$0		$0	$0	
92000	Owners Direct / Related								
93001	Space(s) Project Admin & Related								
93001	Space(s) Proj Dvl Pmt/Eng/Plng/Relt								
93001	Space(s) Capital Purchasing								
93009	Space(s) Travel/Reimbursables								
	C.O. Reserve / Contingency								
	Sub Total Direct and Indirect	$0	$0.00	$0	$0	$0	$0	$0	$0
	TOTAL BLD EQUIP/DIRECT/IND.	$2,671,670	$40.39	$2,671,670	$2,714,017	($42,347)	$2,671,670	$2,377,117	$294,553
60000	Partitions / Walls	$583,200	$8.81	$583,200	$495,799		$583,200	$444,400	7
61000	Dec. Superstructure & Per Fixtures	$1,640,252	$24.79	$1,640,252	$1,510,816	1	$1,640,252	$1,510,816	9
61030	Fitting / Dressing Rooms	$67,200	$1.02	$67,200	$207,500		$67,200	$237,000	7
61040	Stock Shelving / Storage Eqpt.	$111,000	$1.68	$111,000	$200,000	2	$111,000	$159,200	7
71020	Loose Wood Fixtures	$264,630	$4.00	$264,630	$374,600		$264,630	$256,000	7
71021	Loose Metal Fixtures	$62,370	$0.94	$62,370	$70,990	3	$62,370	$70,990	9
71022	Showcases / Back Islands	$37,000	$0.56	$37,000	$26,600		$37,000	$26,600	9
71031	Glass & Mirror and Hardware	$0	$0.00	$0	$0		$0	$0	
81020	Floorcovering	$900,000	$13.60	$900,000	$752,000	4	$900,000	$802,000	8
81060	Decorative Materials	$326,000	$4.93	$326,000	$383,873	5	$326,000	$383,873	9
81066	Display & Store Design	$220,000	$3.33	$220,000	$220,000	5	$220,000	$220,000	5
	Decorative Furniture and Lights	$82,000	$1.24	$82,000	$82,000	5	$82,000	$82,000	5
88001	Food Service Equipment & Decor	$0	$0.00	$0	$0		$0	$0	
67001	Beauty Shop - X sched.								
	Fixture Electical								
52000	Telephone System & Lines	$39,000	$0.59	$39,000	$39,000	5	$39,000	$39,000	
52020	Registers / POS / Rtdl Eqpt. and Lines	$38,000	$0.57	$38,000	$38,000	5	$38,000	$38,000	
47000	Misc. / All other Operating	$34,000	$0.51	$34,000	$34,000	5	$34,000	$34,000	
79140	Exterior Signs								
34005	Demolition / Rubbish - Interior								
	Sub Total Decor & Equipment	$4,404,652	$66.57	$4,404,652	$4,435,178	($30,526)	$4,404,652	$4,303,879	$100,773
9900x	Interior Design Fees / Reim/ Related	$0	$0.00	$0	$0		$0	$0	
	Int. Gnl Conditions, Div/Corp Desgn	$0	$0.00	$0	$0		$0	$0	
	Reserve and Contingency	$0	$0.00	$0	$0		$0	$0	
	TOTAL INTERIORS	$4,404,652	$66.57	$4,404,652	$4,435,178	($30,526)	$4,404,652	$4,303,879	$100,773
	Interest	$0	$0.00	$0	$0		$0	0.00	
	Non-Operating	$0	$0.00	$0	$0		$0	0.00	
	TOTAL CAPITAL	$7,076,322	$106.96	$7,076,322	$7,149,195	($72,873)	$7,076,322	$6,680,996	$395,326

Itemized Budget Control
Form X Budget
Walker Group/CNI Spread Sheet

and strategies, but also it will confirm the time, the man-hours of work necessary, to accomplish it. Not so incidentally, it will also confirm the scope of work and the resultant store planner/designer fee for professional services. A candid and serious meeting with the client should define the interrelationships and clearly establish the functions and responsibilities of the contractual parties. Honesty and mutual respect should be clearly recognized. The client's philosophy and goals, the limits of the budget, and the planned, scheduled comple-

WALKERGROUP/CNI

Name	Hrs. Budgt	Staff	Start	Finish	June	July	August	September	October	November
FINAL MERCHANDISE PLANS	187.5h		6/3/93	7/7/93	6/3 ███████ FINAL MERCHANDISE PLANS					
DESIGN DEVELOPMENT	75h		6/21/93	8/2/93	6/21 █████████ DESIGN DEVELOPMENT					
SCHEMATIC DESIGN PRESENTATION	0h		7/28/93	7/30/93		7/28 ◆ SCHEMATIC DESIGN PRESENTATION				
PRELIMINARY P&S / CLG LIGHTING	187.5h		7/6/93	8/6/93		7/6 ████ PRELIMINARY P&S / CLG LIGHTING				
ELEVATIONS	750h		7/6/93	9/13/93		7/6 ████████ ELEVATIONS				
FIXTURE BIBLE	75h		8/9/93	8/13/93			8/9 ■ FIXTURE BIBLE			
PARTITION / CLG CONSTRUCTION PLANS	300h		7/6/93	8/5/93		7/6 █████ PARTITION / CLG CONSTRUCTION PLANS				
OTHER PLANS	337.5h		8/16/93	9/13/93			8/16 ████ OTHER PLANS			
OUT TO BID PARTITION & CEILING PLANS	0h		8/4/93	8/6/93			8/4 ◆ OUT TO BID PARTITION & CEILING PLANS			
FINAL DESIGN PRESENTATION	75h		8/18/93	8/20/93			8/18 ◆ FINAL DESIGN PRESENTATION			
FINAL P&S / CLG LIGHTING SUBMISSION	0h		8/15/93	8/27/93			8/15 ███ FINAL P&S / CLG LIGHTING SUBMISSION			
BID RETURNS FOR PARTITION & CEILING	0h		8/31/93	9/3/93				8/31 ■ BID RETURNS FOR PARTITION & CEILING		
START PARTITION & CEILING	0h		8/24/93	8/26/93			8/24 ■ START PARTITION & CEILING			
PRE-BID DOCUMENTS SUBMISSION	0h		9/10/93	9/14/93				9/10 ◆ PRE-BID DOCUMENTS SUBMISSION		
FINAL DESIGN IMPACT BUDGET	0h		9/10/93	9/14/93				9/10 ◆ FINAL DESIGN IMPACT BUDGET		
CLIENT REVIEW	0h		9/15/93	9/23/93				9/15 ██ CLIENT REVIEW		
CLIENT COMMENTS & REVISIONS	300h		9/24/93	10/6/93				9/24 ███ CLIENT COMMENTS & REVISIONS		
OUT TO BID	0h		10/5/93	10/7/93					10/5 ◆ OUT TO BID	

Planning and Construction Schedules
Walker Group/CNI Bar Chart

tion date must be put on the table, understood, and agreed upon by both parties. If other consultants, such as architects, engineers, and construction managers, are involved, the questions of responsibility, coordination, and authoritative direction must be defined. If the client's organization is large and diverse, then the client must select an executive, or an executive committee that will be delegated with the authority to act and make binding decisions during all stages of the planning and construction. Without this apparently simple procedure, frustrating and costly delays will inevitably result, leading to basic misunderstandings and ultimately to possible claims and lawsuits.

In establishing cost objectives, architectural, structural, mechanical engineering systems, interiors and store selling fixtures, visual presentation elements and all operational equipment should be defined as separate categories. Each of these should have its budget clearly itemized. Absolute candor is necessary to achieve realistic control and to clarify the responsibility of each professional consultant. Costs should be estimated ahead to the project completion date in order to account for the possible inflationary cost cycle during planning and construction time. Contingencies—that host of unknown probabilities ranging from changes of executive personnel to labor shutdowns, to "acts of God"—should be built into both the budget and the schedule. It is important as well to set planning and construction schedules, providing a critical path in which store management and designer will know when responsibility for decision-making events must be taken.

SITE SELECTION

Very often a prospective client will have chosen its building site before selecting a store planner/designer. While this is sometimes understood as inevitable, given the pressures of shopping center developers, financial planning schedules, and the quick decision necessary in the face of competitor's acts, it can be unfortunate. The site may be ideal with reference to a market and demographic analysis, but it may be fraught with problems and hidden costs with reference to topography, shape, access, subsoil conditions, and numerous other physical limitations. Ideally, the store planner/designer should be consulted before the site is chosen. He or she can be extremely helpful in appraising the site's physical characteristics. Further, the store planner/designer's experience and imagination can be invaluable and might easily save the client the cost of its fee by timely, professional, and astute advice. If the site is a part of the planned shopping center, the store planner/designer's knowledge and experience of negotiations with the landlord, including analysis of the technical exhibits to the lease documents and of the stipulated contributions of landlord or lessee to different parts of the construction costs, can avoid costly future misunderstandings.

ANALYSIS OF GOAL DOLLAR VOLUME

Part of the site selection process includes a demographic and financial market analysis. This study might be done by a marketing division within the client's organization or by consultant specialists. The objective of such a study is to understand market demographics, conditions, and forecasts; to determine customer driving time and access; and to chart the purchasing power of the target market area and the percentage of share of the market that the store can anticipate based on the competition and its own history and character. From this data, the client can calculate its annual dollar volume, generally established at a projected opening date and then over a cycle of ensuing years. This dollar volume projection is the strategic heart of the store planning program.

ESTABLISHING THE PROJECT AREA

Given the dollar volume projection, a simple mathematical formula allows for the conversion of this quantity to store building area. The formula is

$$\text{Area} = \frac{\text{Dollar volume}}{\text{Productivity}}$$

Productivity is the average, historic volume of annual earnings divided by gross sales area. The client will assess this calculation and modify it according to its planned sales strategies, merchandise composition, and mix and expectation of potential business, based on marketing evaluations.

ESTABLISHING AN IMAGE

Together with the determination of store building area, it is necessary that the client express its strategic objectives with reference to the image it wishes to create. Like so many terms in the field, the term "image" is not easily defined. Image is store character resulting in an institutional personality immediately recognized by the consumer public. It is generally established over a long period of time. It is in constant flux, reflecting current and proposed requirements of service. It is updated and refined in relationship to competitor's acts and their struggle for share of its market. In practice, one finds that most clients have real difficulty in articulating this most fundamental attribute. In this author's experience, many executives, leaders in their field, sharp buyers, and astute retailers with insights into community, business, and artistic matters will say, "Well, it should be like————————," mentioning in this roundabout way their admiration for a successful competitor's look. This formulation inherently is no better than their directive to produce a store design that is creative, imaginative, different, and advanced, and then to follow with the admonition, "But where can I see it?"

Image as a concept should also include a definition of the target customer. Obviously, store design will have a different orientation depending upon whether the projected customer is young or old, affluent or middle class, conservative or liberal, or male or female. Many stores think of themselves as "clubs," appealing to a distinct breed of customers sharing the same background, life-style, and goals. One of the most difficult and crucial parts of the store planner/designer's services is to identify these customers and then to develop an appropriate and imaginative design that has a compelling appeal for them. This appropriate design must also conform to the budget, which in itself establishes the degree of complexity and the quality of materials and finishes. It is thus apparent that many of the directions and possibilities of the successful design are formulated during the initial interviews with the client, before a line is even drawn.

Another challenge in achieving an appropriate image refers to cultural differences. A successful design in New York would be disastrous in Florida or California. The merchandise composition, style, and color (e.g., wools, cottons, and polyesters) cry out for a different space and setting that will project and enhance their values. The historic traditions of a region, its established architecture, building codes, and use of indigenous building materials, and other related special qualities should be understood and incorporated into the design program, but in a creative context.

In today's world, in which both ideas and competition travel at the speed of light and in which the leadership of designers in America remains ascendant, this understanding is vital. The store planner/designer must enrich his or her own special creative skills and literally become a student of the culture in which he or she proposes to work. The fragmentation of nations in this decade, the suppressed yearning of people for freedom and self-expression, and the limitless expressions of a pluralistic society—these forces require specific and diverse store designs that contrast with the monolithic and uniform dissemination of information and technics everywhere.

PRINCIPLES OF LAYERAGE

Having established a program that defines the gross building area and image, it is now necessary to relate these elements to the site. The building footprint, the form and size of the store on the land, must be tested with respect to the amount of ground around it and the parking ratios encoded by the community and, often, by the client's own criteria. Frequently, in order to satisfy the number of customer cars in ratio to gross building area, a multiple-level parking structure is needed. The size, height, and area of this structure have a contextual relationship to the mass of the store building. A major store should be dominant and should be seen from any direction. The two factors of land utilization and visual dominance lead to layerage decisions: the number of floors and the placement of both sales and service areas vertically, according to the number of floors available.

WalkerGroup/CNI	**AREA ANALYSIS BY FLOOR**									**PAGE**		1
320 W. 13TH ST NEW YORK NY 10014 (212)206 0444 FAX(212)645 0461	**CLIENT**					**JOB NO.**				**ISSUE DATE**		
	LOCATION					**FLOOR**						

SELLING, FITTING RMS., STOCK AREA REQUIREMENTS					[x] SQ.FT.	[] SQ.M.		QUAN. OF FIT.RMS.		QUAN. OF SHOW CASES		
DEPT. NO.	DEPARTMENTS		EXIST AREA	REQUESTED AREA	PLANNED AREA			EXIST	PLANNED	EXIST'G	REQ.	PLANNED
			0.0	0.0								

NONSELLING		EXISTING	REQUESTED	PLANNED	BUILDING FUNCTIONS		AREA	SUMMARY	
								TOTAL SELLING	0.0
								TOTAL NONSELLING	0.0
		0.0						TOTAL BUILDING FUNCTIONS	0.0
TOTAL NONSELLING				0	TOTAL BUILDG FUNC.		0.0	TOTAL GROSS AREA	0.0

Analytic Area Matrix
Area Analysis by Floor

Additional internal physical and merchandising conditions come into play. Ideally, a client prefers that all sales departments be on one level, preferably the ground floor. This makes them easily accessible to customer traffic. In addition, this one-level building structure is the most economical and the quickest to erect. It eliminates the need for escalators, elevators, and stairs. Its foundation and structural system are designed with relatively light occupancy and deadweight load factors. It produces the greatest percentage of usable to gross area. However, physical limits of size, that is, internal visibility and convenient walking distances, as well as unavailability of ground area, generally prohibit this configuration. Accordingly, the question of how many floors to build must be answered.

In reality two problems are posed. The first problem stems from a merchandising viewpoint. The size of a floor should be related to the number of associated sales departments ideally positioned together, resulting in a total required sales area per floor. A statistical, analytical matrix of these areas can be plotted, ranging from a relatively small floor area containing only one homogeneous department to a relatively large floor area with more

WalkerGroup/CNI	AREA ANALYSIS SUMMARY			PAGE	
320 W. 13TH ST NEW YORK NY 10014					
(212)206 0444 FAX(212)645 0461	CLIENT		JOB NO.	ISSUE DATE	
801 S. FLOWER ST LOS ANGELES CA 90017	LOCATION				
(213)629 0993 FAX(213)629 2118					

GROSS FLOOR AREAS	∏SQ.FT.	∏SQ.M.	ADDITIONAL DATA & NOTES
GROSS BUILDING AREA			

BREAKDOWN OF FLOOR AREAS									
FLOOR									
SELLING & FITTING RMS.									
NON-SELLING & REMOTE STOCK									
BUILDING FUNCTIONS									
LEASE DEPARTMENTS									
ADJACENT STOCK									
TOTAL GROSS AREA									

Analytic Area Matrix
Area Analysis Summary

heterogeneous groups of related departments. The choice is influenced by the character or the image of the store. Should it present itself as a series of specialty shops? Should it provide a variety of merchandise together, to induce most customer traffic? Answers to these questions can also be modified by the notion that not all selling floor areas need be equal. Traffic originates at the ground floor or mall level and decreases in geometric ratio to the number of levels above or below it. Architectural interest could indeed be generated by a program of unequally sized floors, leading to sculptural or ziggarat-like exterior forms. But it should also be kept in mind that nonselling and sales-supporting spaces can be assigned to each of the floors in order to balance out and equalize the total floor areas. In addition, a building with unequal floor areas, while exciting from an esthetic viewpoint, does increase the cost of construction substantially. These factors have to be related to the cost objectives established by the budget.

The second problem stems from an architectural viewpoint. The exterior dominance of the building depends upon both floor area and height. Two floors may not contribute sufficient height or mass to compete with adjacent structures. This contextual analysis governs, whether or not the store is in an urban or suburban location, or even whether or not it is an inherent part of a shopping center. If it is the latter, competitive dominance should also clearly harmonize with the total architectural quality of the center (see also Chapter 8).

Building exterior mass versus building an ideal sized series of selling floors—these are the two principles of layerage, not always in accord and certainly not always in opposition, that must be reconciled in the final decision regarding space. Sometimes, to complicate the program, it is desirable to locate a selling floor below the main level. It is then relatively close—only one floor away—from the vertical center of the traffic flow. It may indeed be connected to a lower mall level, and it may have direct access to customer parking, dependent upon the topography of the site and an intelligent, imaginative use of exterior, contours, terraces, and levels to generate traffic to more than one floor.

MERCHANDISING

Once the gross building area has been established, it is necessary to allocate this total area into the following categories:

1. Building function area
2. Nonselling area
3. Net selling area

The definitions of these three categories are almost universally accepted, although some of the larger corporate clients may have variations tailored to their own logistical usage. In Section I, "Definitions of Store Planning/Design Terms," these definitions have been generalized.

In recent practice, the goal for net selling area is no less than 85 percent of gross area. Building function area is dependent upon the layerage. It should be kept in mind that the greater the number of floors, the greater the building function area, since the space dedicated to vertical circulation (stairs, elevators, and escalators) is precisely multiplied by that number. All of the nonselling functions are programmed according to the client's needs and experience: they also are dependent upon the client's facilities, equipment, and logistics. For example, if it has a large central distribution facility and warehouse, with a fleet of trucks to service a multistore chain, the space requirements for branch store receiving, marking, and remote reserve stockrooms can be minimal. As another example, suppose that a client has a computer center and large central administrative and accounting offices. The branch office facilities can be reduced to a relatively small space for manager and staff. This reduction can obviously be extended into maintenance, paint and sign shops, display storage and work rooms, and so forth. Recent store programs have shoe-horned the building function and nonselling areas, into 15 percent or less of gross building area. The purpose of a store is to sell merchandise. It is vital, then, that selling space be at a maximum in order to achieve high productivity.

If the gross area and the net selling area have been established now the net selling area must be subdivided into selling departments. Each department has its own history of productivity (i.e., dollar volume divided by sales area) and capacity requirements by merchandise classifications. The department's history must also be reviewed with regard to the new store objectives, image, market, and competition. Fashion trends and forecasts also have an effect upon these calculations. The ultimate result of this review and audit is the completion of an authorized program of selling department areas.

The same procedure applies to the breakdown of functions within the nonselling area categories. The projected number of employees to service the store leads to space requirements for locker rooms, toilet facilities, rest rooms, employees' dining rooms, and so on. The logistics of materials handling and merchandise distribution facilities lead to space required for receiving, marking, and remote storage.

It is only then, with the completion of these statistical analyses and programs, that the store planner/designer can truly proceed with planning.

7

The Plan

The plan is the generator. . . . The whole structure rises from its base and is developed in accordance with a rule which is written on the ground in the plan: noble forms, variety of forms, unity of the geometric principle. A profound projection of harmony: this is Architecture.

The plan is at its basis. Without the plan there can be neither grandeur of aim and expression, nor rhythms, nor mass, nor coherence. Without plan we have the sensation, so insupportable to man, of shapelessness, of poverty, of disorder, of wilfulness.

A plan calls for the most active imagination. It calls for the most severe discipline also. The plan is what determines everything; it is the decisive moment.

The plan bears within itself a primary and predetermined rhythm: the work is developed in extent and in height following the prescriptions of the plan, with results which can range from the simplest to the most complex, all coming within the same law. Unity of law is the law of a good plan: a simple law capable of infinite modulation.*

God is in the plan. This dictum, with apologies to Mies Van Der Rohe, incorporates within it the concept of total, Godlike creation and conception. The plan is the logos, the germ of all that follows in the structure. It anticipates all of the functional relationships, the spatial forms, and the inherent design character and style. The plan must encompass, in the first sketch of these relationships, every aspect of the program. It must embrace every given condition and resolve it in a holistic solution pointing toward excitement and imaginative forms that reflect in themselves the requirements of the program. That solution becomes in itself a work of art. Compare the plans of classic, medieval, Renaissance, and contemporary architecture. Each is a beautiful diagram, which, at a glance, reveals the space, heights, structural system, rhythm, and form of the resultant building. In store planning, these conditions also apply. The store plan must resolve the following functional principles:

Circulation
Adjacencies
Department space allocation
Commitment and flexibility
Plurality and continuity

CIRCULATION

Paths of circulation, the aisles, are the arterial system of the store plan. In the large interior areas of the department store, the mass merchandiser, the discounter, the hypermarket, or the supermarket, the aisles are the equivalent of an urban street pattern. They must have clarity; that is, they must lead the customer clearly to every part of the interior space, to each department.

*Le Corbusier, *Towards a New Architecture* (London: John Rodker, 1931).

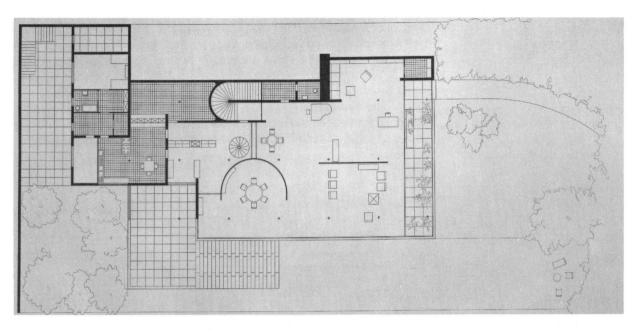

The Plan: Diagram Expressing Total Solution
Lower floor plan, Tugendhat House, Brno, Czechoslovakia, 1930
Architect: Ludwig Mies van der Rohe

The Plan: Diagram Expressing Total Solution
Sak's 5th Avenue, New York, NY
Store Design: Copeland, Novak & Israel

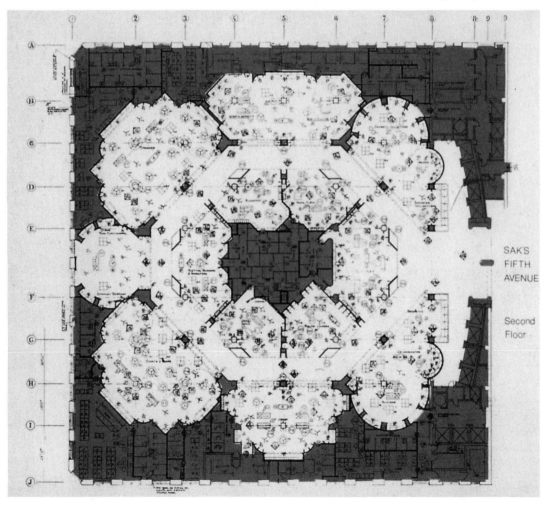

SAK'S
FIFTH
AVENUE

Second
Floor

They must irrigate the traffic flow to every part and also ensure that every part is of an appropriate, functional geometric shape. They must do all of this and also generate a visual excitement as the customer is led through the spaces, creating vistas of surprise and opportunities for compelling merchandise displays. In this sense, if the store is to function as theater, the organizing aisle system must provide a continuous, flexible, interchangeable, dramatic series of enfolding vistas—a kaleidoscope of colorful and moving activities, of people, presentation, and merchandise. In this sense, the store is

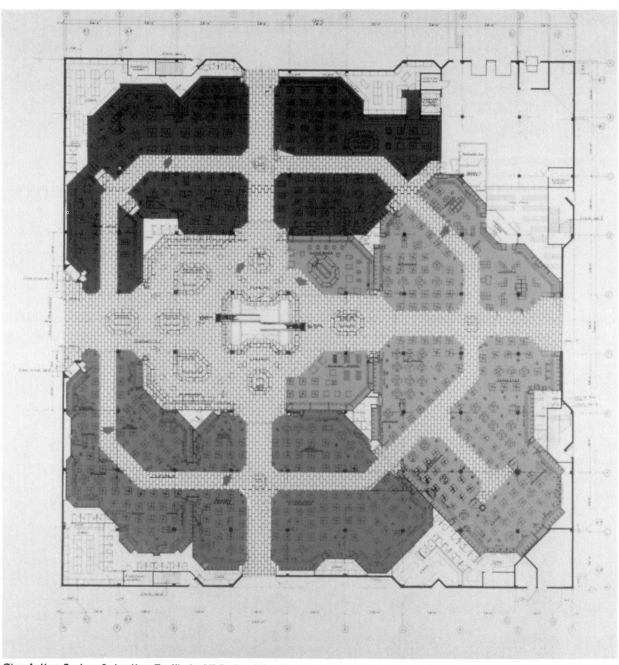

Circulation System Irrigating Traffic to All Parts of the Store
Robinson's of Florida, Fort Meyers, FL
Store Design: Copeland, Novak & Israel

a vital, dynamic interior universe that is constantly changing and constantly adapting itself to changes of fashion. The aisles must provide visual as well as actual, physical access to all parts, and they must do this in a balanced way so that no part is short-circuited or dead-ended.

ADJACENCIES

Adjacencies theory deals with the placement and interrelationships of selling departments within the store plan. Starting from the circulation scheme, the aisles pattern, the calculation of projected customer traffic, and the estimation of the importance of entrances, escalators, and elevators, it is then necessary to locate the merchandise departments so as to solve the following criteria:

1. Impulse versus demand selling
2. Associated, or life-style merchandising, zones
3. Customer convenience and expectations

Impulse departments depend upon maximum customer traffic exposure for their existence and success. The high productivity goals of such departments as cosmetics, jewelry, fashion accessories, men's dress and sports furnishings, etc. must be positioned so that they will profit from the heaviest points of traffic. Generally, they are placed near major entrances and central escalators. These locations are so vital that store management will take extraordinary efforts to quantify and estimate the expected traffic count and to assign to each entrance a percentage factor. For example, if a store has four entrances, the mall entrance might be assigned a 50 percent rate; the entrance from an adjacent parking structure a 25 percent rate; and the others, from surface parking, 15 or 10 percent rate depending upon the shape, capacity, and accessibility of the parking. A central escalator, not surprisingly, would be assigned 100 percent rate. It is the focal point of the store—the hub and concentration of vertical traffic to all of the floors. These estimates lead directly to the selection of department locations, similar to the selection of shelf space within food markets. They are constantly checked and verified against dollar volume and sales-per-square-foot goals. Even locations within a department are hotly contested, as is well known in the cosmetics department, where each supplier and vendor literally bid for a choice position.

Conversely, demand departments will generate customer traffic by their nature, advertisements, promotions, and the principle that the customer selection process is made at home. Their location is accordingly of secondary importance.

Both impulse and demand departments should be located, however, so as to provide a rational mix. This introduces the concept of associated merchandise zones. Similar departments, which appeal to the same target customer and offer exciting options of interselling, stimulating unplanned purchases and suggesting varying merchandise ranges of both style and price, are placed adjacent to one another to create a life-style "world." Thus a men's world, a children's world, a decorative home world, and so on, are formed as larger, homogeneous clusters of departments. Each has its own mood or character, reflecting the character of its merchandise and contributing, as part of the total store, to variety and excitement.

The associated merchandise zones also contribute to customer convenience. Comfort, ease, proximity, and speed of completing the merchandise transaction are fundamental requirements in today's stores. They satisfy the customer's shopping needs, and they make store sales and volume more efficient and productive. In the fiercely competitive retail environment in the United States and increasingly abroad, these requirements underlay the store's renewed efforts to provide service. The customer's expectations are not to be overlooked in this competitive climate. If they are not satisfied,

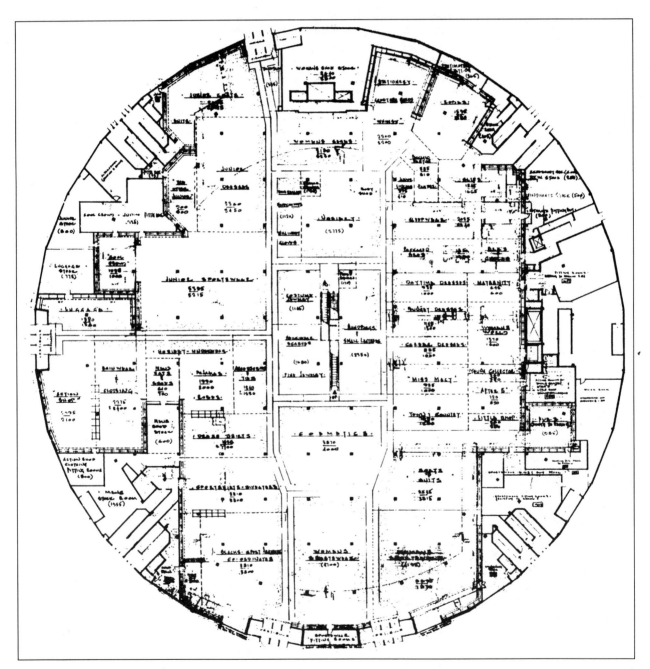

Block Plan Setting Department Adjacencies and Locations
Macy's, Rego Park, NY
Store Design: Copeland, Novak & Israel
From Israel, "Basics of Store Design," *Visual Merchandising*, National Retail
Merchants Association: New York, 1976.

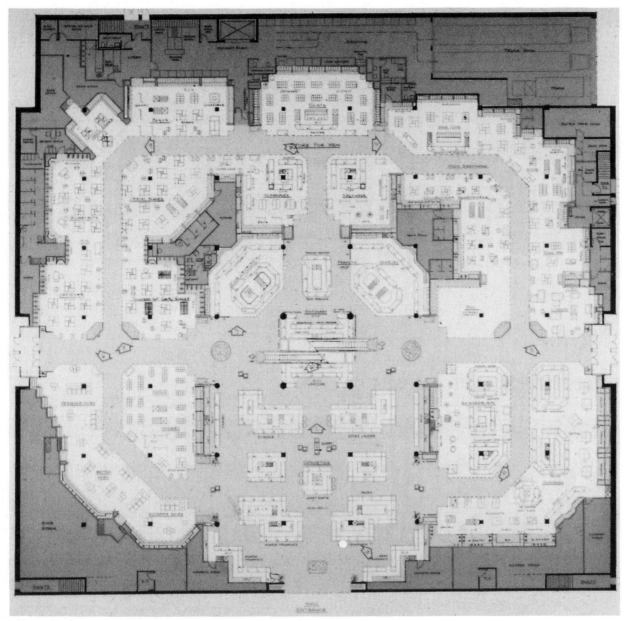

Concept Plan
Marshall Field's, San Antonio, TX
Store Design: Copeland, Novak & Israel

there is indeed the real danger of losing the customer, not just for a single transaction, but forever. As the competition grows, advertises, and seeks to lure the customer to its store by the added value of design, excitement, depth of merchandise assortments, effective pricing, promotions, and all of the other elements of the successful store, these expectations become fixed in the collective consciousness and must be met.

DEPARTMENT SPACE ALLOCATION

As the adjacencies of departments are established, so must their size be plotted. This exercise is normally done in a space allocation plan in which both location, adjacencies, and measured areas are set. In the past, this process was studied in what used to be called a "block plan." Recent practice, however, has eliminated this step and has consolidated it with what is called a "concept plan." The concept plan solves the relationships, adjacencies, and department areas simultaneously by organizing these entities in the context of a circulation scheme with a total design point of view. The complexities of store plans, with their limitless variations of aisle systems, their different configurations according to the store image and design character, require a plan in which every inherent part is composed. The forms, proportions, and rhythms are driven by functional as well as esthetic forces. The shape of the aisle system must produce department spaces that are compact and geometrically correct. Each department served by the major aisle must have an appropriate frontage-to-depth ratio. Deep departments—those exceeding 40 feet—are considered inaccessible and unsatisfactory. The visual excitement along the aisles must be furnished by varied merchandise presentation opportunities and/or repetitive architectural elements that unify and provide continuity. Curved forms might be considered appropriate in a women's dress or lingerie department, suggesting a feminine or sensual mood; rectilinear or polygonal forms might be more appropriate in a men's clothing or home furnishings department. The concept plan must evaluate all of these possibilities and requirements under the discipline of a creative, knowledgeable imagination.

COMMITMENT AND FLEXIBILITY

In the metamorphosis of store design, the flexibility of open planning imperceptibly has changed toward a commitment to a more structured and more complex plan that cannot easily be adjusted or converted to future rearrangements of the major elements. Every time a partition reaches, and is anchored to, the ceiling and floor, it affects air conditioning distribution diffusers, sprinklers, power outlets, lighting fixtures, and flooring materials. Future changes are relatively costly and time-consuming. When these questions were discussed with clients, especially during the 1960s, when this evolution was still at its formative stage, the ensuing debate was comprehensive and soul-searching. Most often these clients, eager to establish a signature interior environment and to outstrip the competition, chose the path of commitment. This debate rarely occurs today. The principle of commitment is the result of a nearly universal acceptance of the overriding need to create a store interior that defines the client's character, quality, and image. The store planner/designer, however, still has the professional obligation to point out the assets and liabilities of this approach, to relate it again and again to the cost objectives, and to recommend modifications and adjustments to those fixed elements that can solve the often conflicting requirements of esthetics, cost, and operations. Today, the acceptance of the principle of commitment is a fascinating revelation of the acceptance of good, strong design as a fundamental attribute of successful, competitive retail selling.

Looked at in another way, the costs of commitment to future, unplanned, and yet inevitable changes to plan and spaces—changes literally assured by the volatility of fashion and the effect of new, enlarged, or reduced business requirements—are not different from the initial investment costs of an increasingly complex interior store installation. Both are part of the cost of doing business and of successfully dominating the market. In this context, the dwindling share of the market by department stores during the 1980s and early 1990s has influenced clients to take a new, penetrating look at the costs of construction and maintenance of their facilities. Perhaps in the future a renewed acceptance of the principle of flexibility will help to contain these costs. Of one thing one can be convinced: Stores of the future will not revert to the monotonous open plans of the 1950s but will find new formulas to achieve excitement of place and control of costs.

PLURALITY AND CONTINUITY

The terms "plurality" and "continuity" encompass a polarity in store planning and design that should be reconciled in varying degrees with the store program and image. Plurality suggests that each department, or associated merchandise zone, has its own unique and special design character. If carried to its logical extreme, this approach would create excitement, variety, and drama—all essential elements of a successful store. It would also be kaleidoscopic, confusing, and disorienting. Store image might disintegrate under the weight of multiple, conflicting individual images. Continuity suggests the use of elements employed throughout the interior spaces that recall by repetition and emphasis an overall, controlled unity of design. Carried to its

Multiple, Conflicting Individual Images
Galeries Lafayette: Existing Cosmetics Department, Paris, France

extreme, this approach could generate boredom and monotony. Good design would embrace the positive aspects of both approaches. In an imaginative and intelligent application, a controlling architectonic element can discipline and hold together innumerable, diverse departmental elements. It is no different from the well-designed shopping mall in which the individual shops, each with its facade and graphics design, are held together by common tectonic elements, such as columns, neutral facias, and ceiling and floor treatment and materials. Today, when stores contain both their own departments and vendors' franchise installations, this technique of unity and diversity combined becomes mandatory. A successful franchiser is proud of its image. In contractual agreements, it will insist upon its rights of individual design. It has its own vocabulary of fixtures, materials, lighting, colors, and graphics, all of which contribute to its success and public image, and these are all zealously guarded. It is the store designer's challenge to incorporate this special ambience into a total interior discipline, to accommodate variety within unity.

This question of individual priority versus total control is very often met, in microcosm, in the design of a cosmetics department. Here each vendor represents prestige, clout, traffic generation, and high sales volume per square foot. Each wants its own identity, created over the years by investing huge sums of money for advertising, packaging, and signage. Each bids for the most favored location. The resolution of these conflicting demands varies according to the strength and the reaction of the department store client. Some will accede to total variety, some will compromise, and some will insist on a total store design system. These designs reflect the character and image of the store. These controversies make life for the store designer complex but ultimately challenging.

Variety within Unity
Galeries Lafayette: Glass & China, Paris, France
Store Design: Walker Group/CNI

PLAN TYPES

Recognizing the nearly infinite variations of store plans in global retailing today, we find it helpful to break them down and describe them.

Open Plan

In an open plan, there is a continuum of open space, defined by enclosing peripheral partitions that separate selling from nonselling or service-supporting spaces. Separations between selling departments are nominal, formed essentially by mobile fixtures, some of which are of greater height in order to provide a degree of definition. Signing and graphics become vital

The Open Plan
Proffitt's, West Town Center, Knoxville, TN
Store Design: Copeland, Novak & Israel
From Israel, "Basics of Store Design," *Visual Merchandising,* National Retail
Merchants Association: New York, 1976.

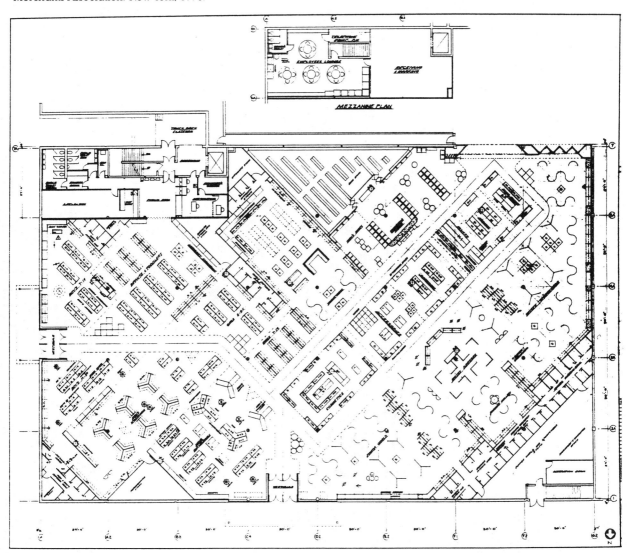

to identify departments and to help orient the customer. Ceilings, lighting fixtures, and floor materials are continuous. Flexibility, visibility, and simple construction are the keys to this type of store plan.

Center Core (or Atrium) Plan

In a center core (or atrium) plan, the central part of the large floor area is defined by full-height enclosing partitions. This converts the central spaces from patterns of fixtures to complete departments with easily identifiable background merchandise and presentation treatments. Two results of this store plan are the greater "use of the cube," that is, the development of full-height merchandise and mood presentations, and the multiplication of the aisle system to move traffic to all parts of the plan, thereby effectively reducing the depth of selling departments and simultaneously maximizing de-

The Center Core or Atrium Plan
Parisian, Huntsville, AL
Store Design: Schafer Associates

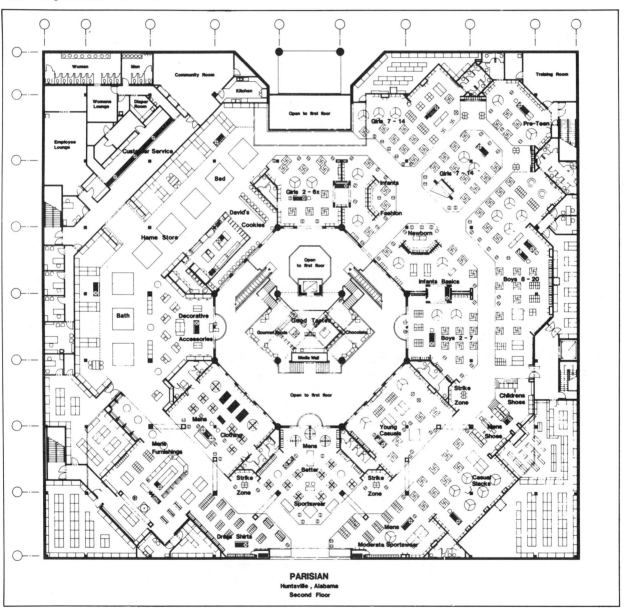

PARISIAN
Huntsville , Alabama
Second Floor

partmental frontage. Generally, the center core is planned around central escalators and encourages the architectural design of an atrium or open vertical court, crowned by a skylight, to produce a memorable icon and symbolic center of the store.

Loop (or Racetrack) Plan

In the loop (or racetrack) plan, a continuous major aisle system is highlighted. In a sense, this plan is a compilation of the open and center core plans. It solves the problem of departmental front-to-depth ratio. It does not require the structural sophistication of the architectural core designs. It assures the movement of traffic throughout the space and is quite flexible and relatively economical. It is used largely by mass marketers and discount operations to force traffic flow to exit at the self-service checkout cashiers.

Free-Flow Plan

In the free-flow plan, which undoubtedly has been influenced by the abstract forms of contemporary, nonobjective art, the traffic flow is forced into an asymmetrical, browsing pattern, leading toward highlighted, important selling areas. It eschews the straight aisle and adds excitement and interest at every turn, generated by the complex composition of curvilinear, amorphic, free forms.

The Loop or Racetrack Plan
ServiStar, Longview, TX
Store Design: Retail Planning Associates, Inc.

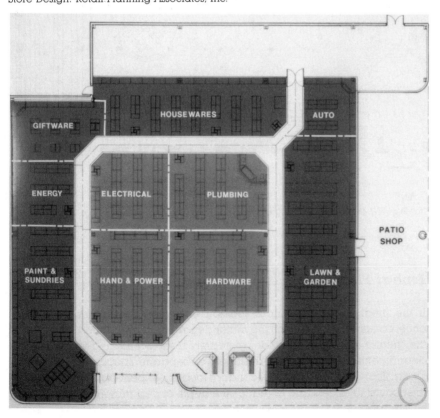

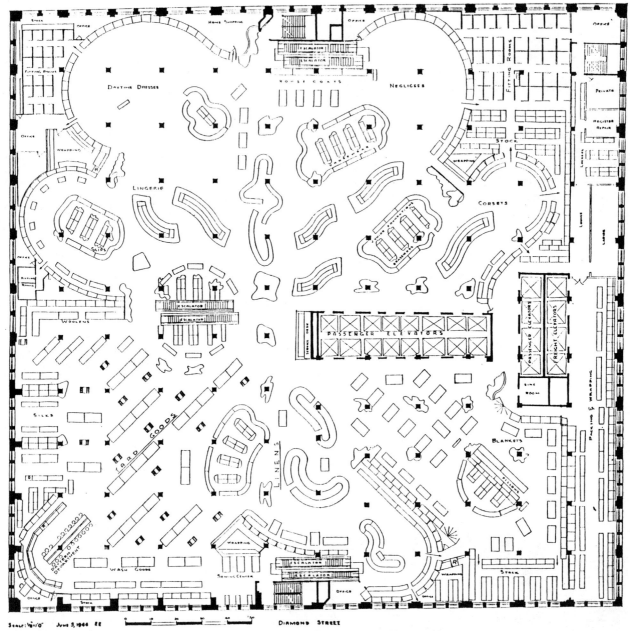

The Free-Flow Plan
Kaufmann Department Store, Pittsburgh, PA
From Parnes, Louis, AIA, *Planning Stores that Pay*, F.W. Dodge Corporation,
Lexington, MA, 1948.

Linear Plan

In the linear plan, a continuous, spacious central aisle becomes a traffic avenue, on either side of which the major departments are placed. Also called the "mini-mall plan," it provides extremely clear access and visibility to all departments, which can be designed as separate spaces. If the departments' floor areas are large, secondary loop aisles penetrate them in order to encourage access and to reduce the depth of department subdivisions. If

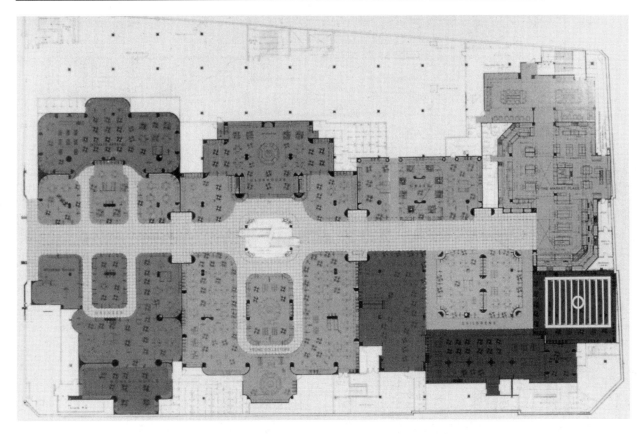

The Linear Plan
Macy's, Stamford Town Center, Stamford, CT
Store Design: Copeland, Novak & Israel

the building footprint is square, one side of the interior can be developed as a service wing to reduce the effective selling depth on either side of the main aisle.

Zone-and-Cluster Plan

In the zone-and-cluster plan, associated merchandise zones are defined by full-height partition systems. Departmental subdivisions within the zones are suggested by clusters of mobile fixtures, generally designed with greater mass and with provisions for lighting. A compromise between the open and center core plans, it provides variety and definitions related to life-style selling, as well as a degree of flexibility. The large scale of the associated merchandise zones reduces the amount of fixed construction elements, resulting in cost effectiveness, especially with respect to the mechanical and electrical building requirements.

Shop Plan

In the shop plan we see the ultimate expression of total variety and individuality. Each department is designed as a separate shop or boutique. Each is structurally, architecturally, and decoratively defined. It is inflexible. It affects each of the structural, mechanical, and electrical building systems and is clearly the most costly of all of the plans, being more appropriate to the large, prestigious, up-scale specialty shops.

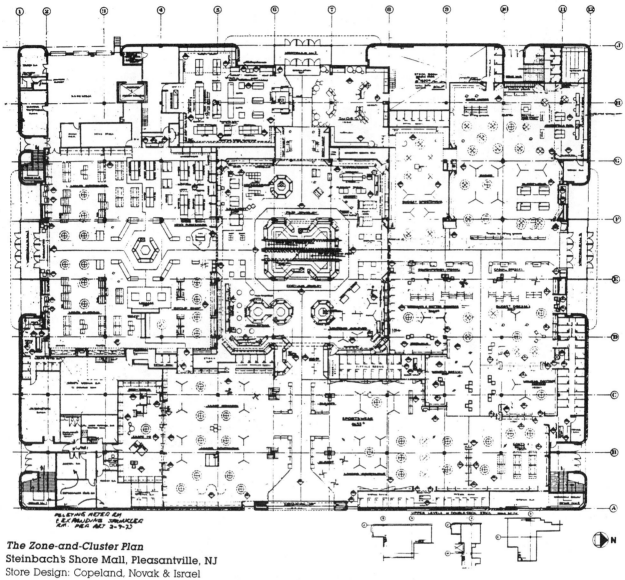

The Zone-and-Cluster Plan
Steinbach's Shore Mall, Pleasantville, NJ
Store Design: Copeland, Novak & Israel
From Israel, "Basics of Store Design," *Visual Merchandising,* National Retail
Merchants Association: New York,1976.

Although the preceding analysis and search for typical classifications are
obviously theoretical, in practice many of the plans are modified and combined according to the building shapes and layerage systems, in an endless
search for innovative reflections of each client's image.

PLAN CONFIGURATION

The plan's configuration, while incorporating the aisle circulation systems
described earlier, is also the result of numerous other factors: the building
footprint; the location of entrances, escalators, and main access points; the
personality and creativity of the planner; and the personality, character,

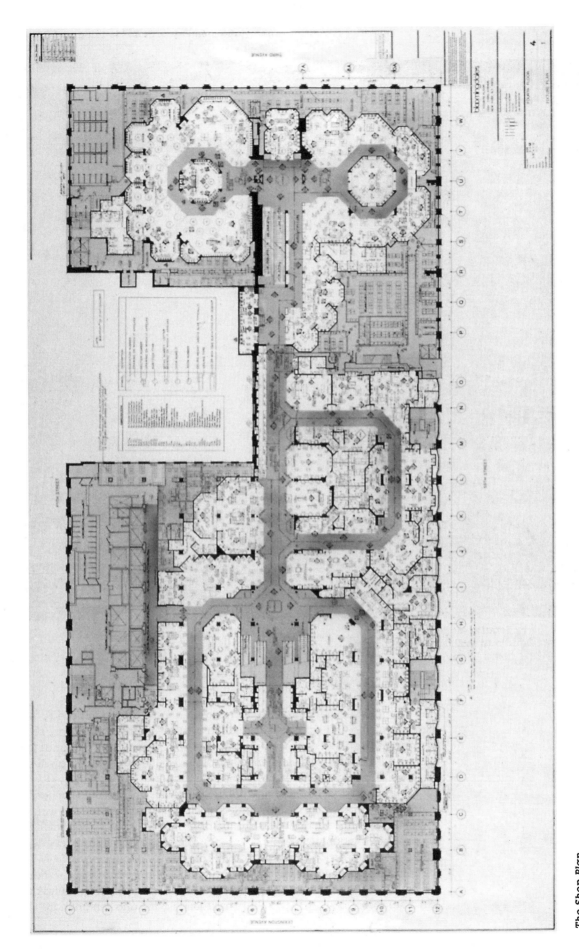

The Shop Plan
Bloomingdales: 4th Floor, New York, NY
Store Design: HTI/Space Planning International

93

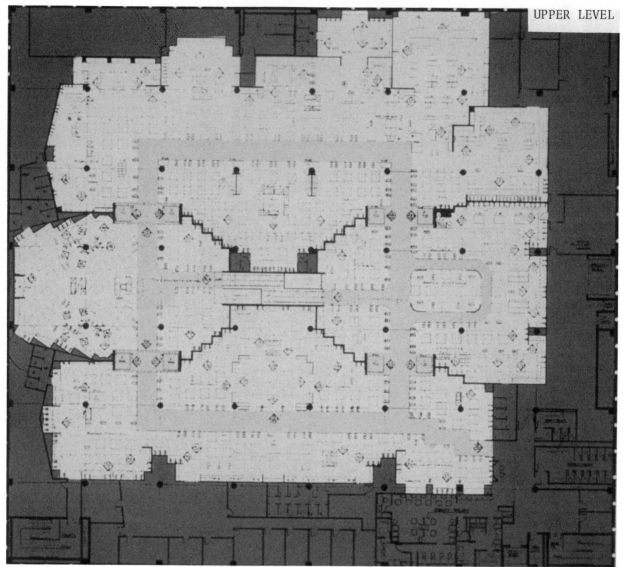

UPPER LEVEL

Multiplying Lineage by Serrated Modules
Carson, Pirie, Scott, Randhurst Mall, Mt. Prospect, IL
Store Design: Copeland, Novak & Israel

and image objectives of the client. In stores featuring large floor areas, the major planning challenge is the handling of large central areas. Those selling departments that are located in the center, responding to demands for customer traffic and identification as established in the adjacency plan studies, require special and often costly design treatments. Historically, one technique was to design the building from the inside out. Theoretically, an ideal adjacency, traffic pattern, and study of selling department shapes would logically form the structural building footprint. In practice, however, this approach led to innumerable problems that in the aggregate far exceeded that of central interior space utilization. Like any undisciplined activity, its success depended upon outstanding planning and design skills, without which often arbitrary and unresolved space relationships led to confusion, customer disorientation, high initial construction costs, and a nightmare for future plan modifications. It conflicted head-on with logical site planning criteria. It impacted structural and architectural criteria, producing extraordinary construction costs and delays. After a few trials, a general consensus emerged that accepted the discipline generated by a more conventional building footprint and structural-column bay system but that exercised all of the imaginative possibilities inside its walls.

Within any building enclosure, the planner has at his or her fingertips a multitude of forms and configurations that can produce a plan that will solve all functional requirements and relationships and that can flow directly into design themes. There is the architectural, masculine strength of shapes generated by straight lines—rectangles and squares. There are curvilinear forms, softening the edges and planes of space, creating contrast, and suggesting sensuousness of the feminine shape. There are diagonals, slashing across space, cutting toward prime target elements. There are polygonal shapes, generating an ideal presentation zone that conforms to the limits of the cone of human vision. Combinations of these shapes, references to the historic or traditional forms, references to contemporary or futuristic art and architecture—all of these are part of the infinite vocabulary of forms, innate in the plan, from which the designer searches to create memorable interior spaces that are special and appropriate to the store's image.

The imaginative composition of plan shapes contributes directly to merchandising opportunities. Lineage, the measurement of partition or fixture lengths, produces merchandise capacity. An alcove based on half a hexagon presents all of its merchandise range in one glance. A section using serrated rectilinear modules multiples lineage and suggests different ways to feature merchandise by style, color, price, and so on. A curved boutique or salon emphasizes itself by contrast and makes its statement as a high-fashion inner sanctum. Selling departments and associated merchandise zones are articulated and defined by the plan configuration.

COORDINATION WITH BUILDING ELEMENTS

The logic of interior plan relationships and organization is controlled and driven simultaneously by their coordination with building elements. In this section, we will review those primary architectural elements that link site and exterior design with the interior plan.

Entrances

The location of entrances is one of the first decisions that the architect and interior store planner/designer must make together. Site conditions such as visibility, easy access from parking, and, in shopping centers, the mall, dictate their locations. Design opportunities, to be studied by the architect, must dramatize the entrance, make it a contrast of openness, glass, canopies, signage, and other materials and forms in relation to the large solid mass of the exterior wall surfaces, a vital symbol of the building, and a memorable icon that pulls the potential customer into the store. However, those locations must also be reviewed, evaluated, and possibly modified with respect to their impact upon the interior circulation system of the plan. It is clearly understood that every important entrance must connect and flow into a major aisle. Every major aisle must be double loaded so that it will provide frontage to selling departments on both sides. Therefore, if the entrance and aisle are

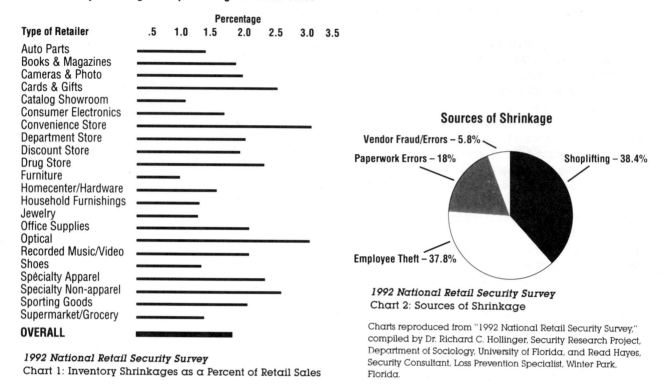

Inventory Shrinkage as a percentage of Retail Sales

1992 National Retail Security Survey
Chart 1: Inventory Shrinkages as a Percent of Retail Sales

1992 National Retail Security Survey
Chart 2: Sources of Shrinkage

Charts reproduced from "1992 National Retail Security Survey," compiled by Dr. Richard C. Hollinger, Security Research Project, Department of Sociology, University of Florida, and Read Hayes, Security Consultant, Loss Prevention Specialist, Winter Park, Florida.

placed too near an exterior wall, that side of the aisle will restrict the proper development of a sales department. If a corner entrance is unquestionably dictated by site and external conditions, then possibly a diagonal aisle system is indicated, which would thrust internal traffic flow toward the center of the floor. The number of entrances is established, not only by questions of visibility and access, but also by building code requirements. It must be remembered that every entrance is also an exit. Exits must be placed so that they will provide direct escape from the building in the event of fire or other disasters. These stipulations often conflict, however, with interior merchandising criteria. Too many entrances tend to disperse and fragment internal traffic, and to reduce opportunities and exposure of impulse selling departments to dominant locations. Too many exits make surveillance complex and provide a field day for potential robberies—the curse of retailing in an increasingly violent society—in which shrinkage from this kind of losses often exceeds sales profits.

Escalators and Elevators

The location of escalators is a function of the location of entrances and of the aisle system. Two major considerations influence their location. The first is that the escalator is the unquestioned center of selling of the plan. Because it is the focus of vertical traffic throughout a multifloor facility, it generates that traffic and becomes the 100 percent location. The second is that, as a direct result of the first consideration, the escalator becomes the symbolic center of the store. Accordingly, it is designed as a strong architectural feature. Open wells or atria give customers an exciting perspective of all of the

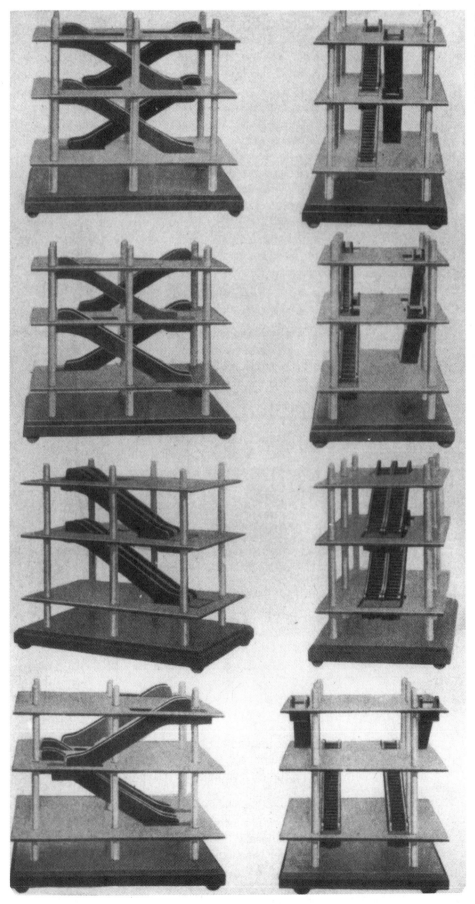

Escalator Configurations:
Parallel and Scissors
or Criss-Cross
From Parnes, Louis, *Planning Stores that Pay,* F.W. Dodge Corporation: Lexington, MA, 1948.

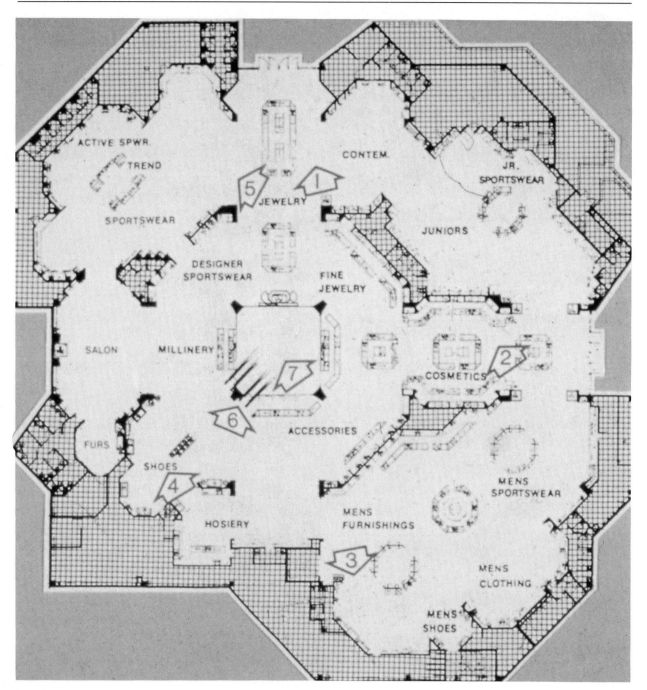

Escalators on Diagonals
Bullock's-Wilshire, Fashion Island, Newport Beach, CA
Store Design: Copeland, Novak & Israel

floors, accentuated by the movement and concentration of people. The monumental space and sculpture of the escalators, often crowned by a sky-light, provide wonderful design opportunities and turn it into a memorable icon (*see color insert*).

Although the entrances influence the location of the escalators on the ground floor, that location must be checked with reference to traffic flow on upper and lower floors. Generally, the geometric center of the building will assure good traffic. However, the escalators should be placed parallel to the long axis of the plan; this will force traffic to penetrate into the larger available areas there and will allow the main aisles to front on several selling departments. Conversely, if the escalators run at right angles to the long axis of the plan, it impinges abruptly on those selling departments and short-circuits the large areas left unexposed. The configuration of the escalators can help or hurt these considerations: A parallel configuration thrusts traffic to one side, tending to isolate the opposite side of the floor; a scissors configuration equalizes traffic flow to both sides. Analysis of traffic flow, while fundamental, might be modified by esthetic judgments, depending upon the style of the interiors and the perceptions of the designer. Mature and sophisticated escalator designs might place them on diagonals, rotate them in a spiral so that each floor entry point is only 45 degrees apart, create flying overpasses, and so forth. A circular escalator structure has been developed by the Japanese, opening up new vistas for design creativity, provided commodious space and cost factors are available.

In contrast to escalators, the location of elevators is of secondary importance. Passenger elevators, generally used by the disabled, elderly, or mothers pushing baby strollers, can literally be hidden, provided they are easily accessible and on hard-floor aisles. Freight elevators should be located completely out of reach of the public. However, loading and staging area lobbies for merchandise should be accessible to the hard-floor aisles for quick distribution throughout the selling floors by means of goods carts. These elements should not interfere with adjacent stockrooms or behind-the-scenes nonselling spaces that require customer access. Whereas economies of construction suggest that both passenger and freight elevators be placed back to back, this is rarely achieved. An additional location factor for the freight elevators is proximity to truck loading and receiving spaces, mandatory in solving space-time-motion requirements. As with all permanent building function elements, elevators should be placed at exterior walls in order to provide open, flexible space availability for selling functions.

Stairs and Toilets

Stair locations are plotted in conformity with building code requirements. Stairs, serving as emergency exit facilities, must be within a designated distance from every point on a floor, measured according to the line of travel permitted by the plan; they must be of a width that will accommodate the number of persons generated by the floor area, calculated on the basis of an allowed square footage per person; they must be accessed by means of fire-rated horizontal passages; they must be protected by fire-rated walls; and they must lead directly to the outdoors, suggesting, therefore, that they be placed along exterior building walls. The resolution of these factors is normally the responsibility of the building architect. However, the store planner/designer must coordinate the interior layout to them and ensure that adjacencies, placement of stock and fitting rooms, and so on, do not conflict. The stair structures frequently lead to the placing of electric risers and distribution panel boards adjacent, since they provide a vertical continuity of space. These equipment closets, requiring constant access for purposes of maintenance, have a similar direct effect on the planning of stock and fitting rooms.

Open or decorative stairs might be located at the option of the store planner/designer. Since they are not requirements with respect to life safety, they become design and convenience elements only.

The location of rest rooms, similarly, is based on convenience. In the past, they were separate facilities for customer and staff. Recently, however, they have been consolidated, as a result of the high cost of plumbing installations and general acceptance by both the public and staff. In current practice, department stores, searching for ways to improve service to customers, are providing quite opulent rest rooms, replete with gold-plated fixture trim, marble vanities, mirrors, and attractive lounges. The vertical placement, or layerage, of rest rooms is based on customer convenience and adjacency to restaurants, beauty salons, and so forth, while at the same time, consideration must be given to staff proximity to locker, rest rooms, and cafeterias. Since rest rooms are part of the permanent building function components, they should preferably be placed at exterior building walls.

Truck Dock

Truck access and loading facilities are primarily functions of the site plan. They must be located with reference to parking areas and traffic lanes. They must not compete or interfere with pedestrian traffic from the parking area to the store entrance. Since they are a large and messy group of elements, they should be screened by architectural walls or landscape devices. They should be adjacent to refuse and garbage collection units. The activity of loading and unloading trucks and of maneuvering dumpsters requires that they be separate from the movement of customer automobile traffic. In addition, topographical contours of the property lead to a logical vertical disposition, so that the truck dock may find itself on a lower or upper level of the store. All of these factors are exterior considerations. The interior store plan, however, requires that the location of freight elevators be adjacent to the dock. The combined areas of truck ramp, dock, receiving and marking, staging, and freight elevator lobby take a large chunk of allocated space. If they are located adjacent to a mall store entrance, this impinges on highly productive selling space; if they are located at an external corner of the building, it projects between public entrances and reduces the access and visibility of those selling departments logically placed in that quadrant. The host of these often conflicting factors requires careful resolution and collaboration by both architect and store planner/designer, who must search together for the best and most efficient plan. In a shopping center, the developer will have a vested interest and will also be a party looking for mutually beneficial solutions. It is obvious that this element is a major factor, another starting point, in a harmonious solution of architectural as well as interior plan and design.

Mechanical Equipment Spaces

Another major space-consuming building component consists of mechanical equipment rooms. This subsection deals essentially with space requirements and locations; equipment data, specifications, systems, and selections are quite beyond the purview of this book. Mechanical equipment primarily includes heating, ventilating, and air-conditioning (HVAC) elements: furnace, boiler, cooler, compressor, cooling tower, fans, controls, and distribution air duct systems. Electrical equipment includes transformers, switch gear, distribution systems, local switch and circuit breaker panels. Many of these elements must be located inside the building; others can be placed on rooftops or penthouses. In order to minimize reductions to net selling space—the ultimate purpose of the store—equipment mezzanines can be provided if floor-to-floor heights of the structure permit them. Recognizing that mechanical equipment represents at least 40 percent of the cost of a store building and that it is a fixed permanent installation, major decisions of location and system type must be jointly made by the architect, the mechanical engineer, the store planner/designer, and the client's facilities manager. Each of these parties brings to the decision-making process an important point of view based on history, talent, and experience.

An example will serve to illustrate the complexities in deciding where to locate mechanical equipment. In a large department store building, this equipment requires a space well over 2,000 square feet—obviously, a large component of the nonselling area. If this equipment is placed on one of the selling floors, it subtracts a large chunk of space from the net selling area. If it is placed in a central rooftop penthouse structure, there is no space loss from the usable building area. In addition, a penthouse for mechanical equipment generally is not calculated as part of gross usable area by many codes and communities. On that basis, there is a space bonus with reference to automobile parking capacity, which is set at a predetermined ratio to gross building area. Offsetting that gain, however, there are two negative factors: (1) Architectural and structural costs are increased because of high loading factors, the additional exterior enclosing surfaces, and their effect upon the forms, materials, and mass of the building; and (2) inflexibility and conflict with selling-space utilization, recognizing that vertical ducts, risers, heavy electrical conduits, and so forth, which may be rationally located directly below the penthouse, will limit the possibilities of interior planning. If escalators, an atrium, and a skylight are planned to be located in the central part of the store, the penthouse might be in direct visual conflict. Other location decisions are possible, of course, and are based on technological developments within the industry. The acceptance of multiple packaged rooftop mechanical units is a recent example. These have the advantages of decentralization, a maintenance asset in the event of a breakdown of a unit. They also directly affect the building's architecture: Higher parapets or screening elements are necessary to avoid having the rooftop structures, machinery, and mechanical devices make the building look like a battleship. By contrast, the provision of separate units, each with its self-contained cooling and air movement machinery, reduces the extent and sizing of the duct distribution network.

This kind of analysis could be extended indefinitely. It is discussed here primarily to show the reader how complex an apparently simple planning decision can be. In practice, a matrix checklist covering these questions is helpful, enabling all professional consultants and the client to make a joint evaluation and decision, weighing advantages and disadvantages of initial cost, maintenance costs, life expectancy of equipment, effect upon structure, effect upon architecture, effect upon interior planning, and effect upon future interior plan changes.

COORDINATION WITH NONSELLING ELEMENTS

While the fundamental goal of the plan is to create exciting space possibilities relating to adjacency, form, and sizes of forward-selling departments, it is also to relate them logically to nonselling elements. At times the location of nonselling behind-the-scenes spaces will govern and drive the location of selling spaces.

WALKERGROUP/CNI
STUDIO I STORE PLANNING SERVICES MATRIX

PROJECT:_____

OWNER: _____

PROJECT NO:_____ DATE OF AGREEMENT:_____

CHECK LIST OF RESPONSIBILITY FOR BASIC SERVICES BY PHASES:

LEGEND
1. Prime
2. Joint (= Lead)
3. Review/Participate
4. N/A (Not Applicable)

PHASE & ITEM DESCRIPTION PHASE I – PLANNING & SCHEMATIC DESIGN PROGRAM	WG/CNI	ARCH	OWNER
1. Furnish layerage and space Allocation Program:	_____	_____	_____
Building Function Areas	_____	_____	_____
Non-Selling Areas	_____	_____	_____
Selling Areas	_____	_____	_____
2. Prepare Time Schedule for Planning, Design, Construction Documents, Bidding, Award and Construction.	_____	_____	_____
3. Provide Statement of Probable Interior Project Construction Cost Estimate.	_____	_____	_____
4. Evaluate Site Plan Elements.	_____	_____	_____
5. Establish Building Function Elements Locations.	_____	_____	_____
6. Prepare Schematic Concept Plans at 1/16"= 1'-0 scale.	_____	_____	_____
7. Calculate planned areas for conformance with Program.	_____	_____	_____
8. Survey existing Conditions.	_____	_____	_____

Matrix Checklist Itemizing Owner-Consultant Responsibilities

Receiving and Marking

The distribution of merchandise within the store begins with unloading the trucks. The merchandise then must be sorted, unpacked, marked, cleaned, pressed, stored, and finally delivered to the selling department itself or its adjacent stockroom. Obviously, the space allocated to these functions depends on the client logistics and the degree of automation and computerized mechanization. The aims are speed and efficiency. If merchandise is held in a receiving mode, it is not exposed to the customer and is not sold. The success of many of the large mass merchandisers and chains is based largely on the incredibly quick dispatch of merchandise from point of fabrication to point of sales. Location is governed by proximity to truck dock as well as to freight elevators. Additionally, wrapping and delivery of sold merchandise must be accommodated in adjacent spaces, frequently located so that they will be accessible to the customer for pick up. The flow of in-bound goods from truck to sales floor must be plotted logically, often in consultation with materials-handling specialists. Carts or inside trucks must be directed from receiving areas or freight elevator lobbies to hard-floor aisles. The wear and tear of this constant movement of internal distribution is enormous and must be carefully considered in the design and selection of durable materials in every part of the store, from freight corridors, doors, base bumpers to selling fixtures. All of the spaces planned for receiving and marking should be isolated from the public and organized to allow visual and physical controls against stealing.

Offices and Personnel Facilities

As discussed earlier, the size of store offices depends on the client's administrative organization, the relationship of the store branch to headquarters and even to such remote facilities as accounting, computers, telephone operations, and so on. The linkage of the branch store offices to customer is done via an area devoted to customer services: opening of new accounts, credit, complaints, layaway, gift wrapping, and payments. Their linkage to staff is done via interviews, hiring, training, providing restrooms, locker rooms, and cafeterias. The size and design character of all of these facilities depends on the store's policy and philosophy. With the increasing attention placed by stores upon customer service and the added value of bright, motivated, and career-oriented sales personnel, these spaces will require increasingly commodious and attractive accommodations (Fickes).

In planning these complexes, several functional criteria apply. They sometimes correspond and sometimes compete with good planning practices, in which the selling space dispositions have first priority. Most of the time, these facilities are placed in the leftover corners of the plan and are fragmented and massaged to fit into otherwise awkwardly shaped spaces. However, the location of the customer services area generates traffic and should be evaluated in terms of how it will enhance business of the departments placed along adjoining aisles. The location of personnel facilities must connect with the staff entrance to the building, with its attendant checkroom and security areas. The staff entrance should not be too prominent and should be placed conveniently to the employee parking area, generally restricted to remote parts of the parking lot so as not to usurp preferred customer parking slots.

Vertical access, if the facilities are located on upper levels, should be comfortable and convenient to passenger elevators. (The use of freight elevators for staff is dangerous and places personnel in contact with inventory storage—a certain temptation to the unscrupulous.) The use of escalators by staff, before or after the store's opening hours, is unnecessary and consumes costly energy. Personnel facilities should include rest rooms that are available simultaneously for customer use. If there are food service elements in the program, the rest rooms become a connector to them and a kind of hub for multiple uses.

CONCEPTS OF DENSITY

The quality and character of a store's interior depend in large measure on the density of selling fixtures. The density factor makes the difference between an up-scale fashion image and a mass merchandiser. Most fre-

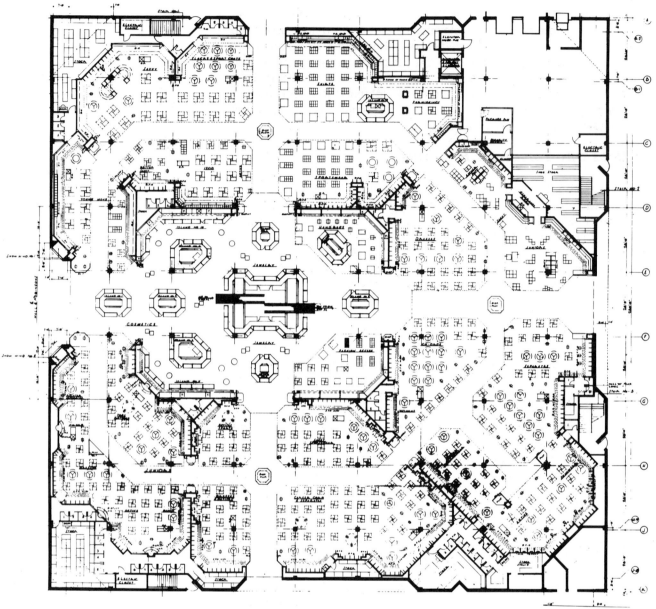

Density: Contrast of Fixtures with Spacious Aisles
Robinson's of Florida, Fort Meyers, FL
Store Design: Copeland, Novak & Israel

quently, however, the store planner/designer has little control over a client's future utilization of space. The approved plans might well indicate secondary aisles of 3 feet between fixtures. If the store is successful, however, and sales volume grows beyond expectations, the demand for more and more merchandise will grow inexorably. Merchandise capacity is directly related to dollar volume objectives and, ultimately, to profit. Who has not fought his or her way through a jungle of fixtures crowded together, literally preventing access to a particular department? Sales promotion campaigns or clearances will inevitably cause this jamming of selling space. One technique that assures the continuity of spatial image is to provide, in contrast to fixture density within a department, a major aisle system of generous and ample width. As the aisle network is the structure and nervous system of the store's interior, so wide aisles will guarantee and literally protect a carefully designed interior from abusive overuse by store management.

Recognizing this tendency of ambitious store buyers and branch managers, enlightened executives will gladly encourage the store planner/designer to provide broad and spacious main aisles. This is similar to providing monumental designs to the escalator atrium or even to dedicating an important central area to the now mandatory grand-piano player. These devices are an inherent part of the store's image. Design is the key to services, to make the store convenient, and to make sure that customers enjoy the time they spend in the store. The formula of density within a department and of luxurious spaciousness in the aisles is a major contribution to this goal. As we will see in Chapter 9, design will amplify this concept and reflect in a variety of ceiling forms and lighting techniques reinforcements to the meaning and power of a well-articulated aisle structure.

ACCESS AND SECURITY REQUIREMENTS

A good store plan strives fundamentally to make every selling department easily accessible to customers. Unfortunately, as a result of our violent society in which both privileged and underprivileged seek to abuse and "beat" the system, stealing has become a major, serious, and frustrating problem for store managers. If the store entrance from a mall is wide open, encouraging and inviting customers to enter, it is also an escape route for the thief. Therefore, we see, in the midst of a monumental, beautiful entrance theme, tacky, narrow and jail-like security devices that are prepared to sound their alarms if magnetic merchandise markers are not officially removed at the appropriate checkout. If the selling fixture is designed to present merchandise in the most dramatic way possible, making a coordinated fashion display all but irresistible, now we see every item of merchandise above a mean price point secured into or upon the fixture by chains, wires, and padlocks. How can self-selection be encouraged if customers cannot try on items that have caught their fancy and especially if there is no salesperson in sight? If the pluralism and interest of a store plan provide alcoves or shops to differentiate classifications of merchandise, or brands, or price gradations, now we are aware that the occasional salesperson has been cut off by physical elements from his or her primary task of surveillance. The paradox is intense. It is a miracle if store operations can resolve the opposing purposes of attracting buyers and of thwarting the illegal removal of merchandise. Statistics show that shrinkage, that euphemistic term embracing theft and unaccounted for administrative errors, exceeds after-tax profits. Who has not seen inner-city stores, even shops on prestigious Fifth Avenue in New York City, with windows protected by metal gratings and steel pull-down shutters? Can these devices of deterrence contribute to improved sales results?

The store planner/designer must be aware of all of these techniques of enclosure, of entrance and exit control, of electronic sensor devices, and of television scanning and monitoring equipment—all sad facts of reality—and search for reasonable solutions.

Entrances and Security Devices
Sibley's, Rochester, NY
Store Design: Copeland, Novak & Israel

SALES COVERAGE

Sales coverage refers to a salesperson's visual and physical control of the area under his or her responsibility. It is clearly related to security and surveillance, but it goes beyond those tasks and encompasses time-space questions. If a salesperson has to travel 500 yards to an "adjacent" stockroom in order to find the proper size and color of an item, how long will it take the salesperson to get back to the customer? Will the customer wait? If a salesperson consummates a transaction with a customer at a poorly located checkout, will the salesperson have lost visual supervision over the rest of the department and therefore have lost several other possible purchases? If the fitting rooms are remote from the forward selling area, will the department suffer losses resulting from the absence of a supervisory salesperson? All of these questions can be partially answered by good, appropriate planning solutions, provided the store planner/designer is familiar with the selling process and knows the proper questions to ask.

CASH WRAP—CHECKOUT PROVISIONS

Checkout facilities—those elements designed to consummate the sales transaction—require careful planning. Store operations must be defined. They directly affect store image, customer convenience, personnel training, computer systems for payment, as well as inventory controls and surveillance. In general, there are three types of checkouts: the clerk cash wrap, the regional cash wrap, and the central checkout.

1. *Clerk cash wrap*: A fairly compressed unit, it is located in a central position within a sales department and is serviced by a salesperson who is not permanently assigned to it but who is expected to roam freely in the department in order to assist customers. Upon completion of a sale, the salesperson leads the customer to the cash wrap, takes and records that payment, and quickly wraps the merchandise. Identification and graphics should be minimal.
2. *Regional cash wrap*: A large unit, it is located so that it can service several adjacent sales departments or regions, run by multiple cashiers and wrappers who are permanently assigned. The number of cashiers and wrappers varies depending on planned or perceived sales activities, the time of day, and the season. The design of the facility should be modular and flexible, allowing for expansion at peak sales periods. Customers should be able to locate it easily; therefore, identification and graphics should be extremely prominent. Since customers will queue up and concentrate there, generous aisle space must be provided.
3. *Central checkout*: A multiple facility, it accommodates the entire store operation. It must be placed at the store's exit. Since it is the only checkout, it must accommodate all customers and all transactions. Generally provided for mass merchandise, discount, and supermarket operations, it is associated with shopping carts and large concentrations of

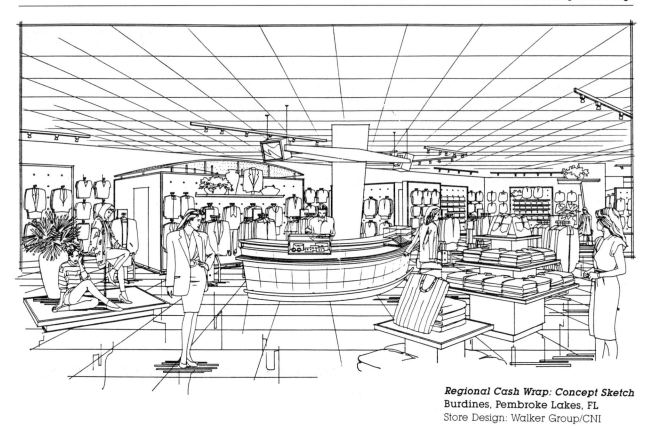

Regional Cash Wrap: Concept Sketch
Burdines, Pembroke Lakes, FL
Store Design: Walker Group/CNI

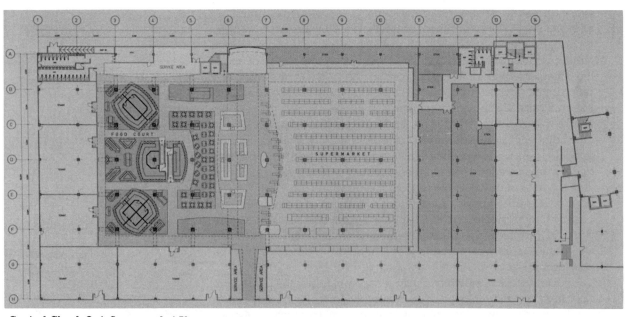

Central Check-Out: Supermarket Plan
Robinson, Seacon Square Mall, Bangkok, Thailand
Store Design: Copeland, Novak & Israel

Central Check-Out: Supermarket
Lucky Stores Prototype, CA
Store Design: Copeland, Novak & Israel

customers. These demand very generous space provisions. It is a final symbol of store image, since it is the last element that the customers remember on their departure, so it should be carefully planned and designed, with compelling lighting and signage.

Each of these types of checkouts carries with it inherent elements of planning. Lighting, power to operate cash registers and computers, telephones and communications systems, credit verification devices, price scanners, and so on, all have systemic and fixed requirements that affect the plan. If the central checkout is used, the planning of building elements must conform without impacting life safety, building code exit requirements, and security against theft. It is obvious, then, that the operational specifications with respect to checkouts have a primary influence on site planning, architectural design, and the resolution of entrances and exits.

FORWARD AND BEHIND-THE-SCENES SELLING SPACE

While sales department space allocations and adjacencies have been reviewed, an additional analysis must be made to establish the ratio of forward to behind-the-scenes area. In this section, "behind-the-scenes" refers to components of selling area and consists of adjacent stock and fitting rooms only. Stockroom requirements are based on merchandise capacity forecasts and are also dependent upon remote warehouse facilities, the efficiency and speed of distribution, and internal handling methods. Recent practice has strongly tended to minimize the stockrooms to "get all of the goods on the selling floor." It is the result of reducing the building gross area because of ever-increasing construction costs, of shrinking the cost of inventory, and of striving for higher sales productivity. Certain exceptions are inevitable: the men's shirts department, for example, still requires ample backup stock to complete pattern and size assortments; domestics necessitates ample stock; the shoe department requires more than 50 percent of its sales area dedicated to reserve stock. Most fashion departments, including women's, men's and children's apparel, minimize stock areas to less than 10 percent of sales areas. The planning of fitting-rooms, which occupy behind-the-scenes space, is based on the philosophy and experience of the store. There is a tendency to provide fewer fitting rooms now than in the past and to group them so that they service adjacent departments. In this event, however, the plans must assure control of entrances and exits in order to discourage stealing. Placing a cash wrap nearby helps provide control and acts as a deterrent. At the same time, provisions should be made for the expansion or contraction of fitting rooms to respond to peak or slack seasonal demands (e.g., swim and beachwear in a sports department). It should be kept in mind that placing fitting rooms and stockrooms together simplifies and unifies the special requirements of lighting and air conditioning. As part of today's store efforts to enhance the service and convenience aspects of selling, fitting rooms are becoming larger and more attractive, with comfortable provisions for seating and for pampering a customer's companion while he or she waits.

8 Architecture

In Chapter 7, a number of considerations that related to interior store planning referred to architectural elements. These were described, however, only insofar as they influenced shapes and locations. In this chapter, functional and esthetic elements of architecture will be reviewed. If this book's fundamental emphasis is on the store itself, it cannot overlook the host of architectural choices, decisions, and opportunities that affect the interior retail environment. If this is to be a reference book for store planners/designers, it cannot disregard architectural matters and must show their interdisciplinary interactions. It must make them aware of cause and effect with respect to building elements and must give them a working understanding of their possibilities. The ideal store client might select one firm to design and build both the building structure and its interiors; in that event, one professional would be the project leader who would guide decision making during the entire project. In reality, this rarely happens. Accordingly, the store planner/ designer must have enough knowledge and understanding of architectural criteria to contribute, as a partner, in order to effect decisions leading to an outstanding and successful installation. Therefore, and in this context, the following sections will deal with architectural elements pertinent only to the store and will not attempt to expound on all of the theories and principles of architecture—a monumental task warranting copious volumes. Suffice it to say that both architecture and store design are human activities that reflect an entire civilization—one that is changing before our eyes.

SITE, FOOTPRINT, AND VOLUMETRIC FORMS

The site generates architectural solutions. An axiom in real estate is that no two sites are identical. Variations in shape, access, topography, soil conditions, subsoil conditions, contextual adjacencies, community zoning and building code regulations, local traditions and construction techniques, climate, taboos, and even expectations all force and contribute to the building form. It is generally accepted that the large retail structure is essentially an enclosed box: Windows and openings, normally considered a major element in architectural design, are undesirable. The interior environment should be totally controlled so that illumination and climate are constant, contributing to the selling experience.

Since the store exterior is a vital factor in its image, its "sign" and signature interfacing with the community, its introduction to the character, quality, and values of its operations, architectural design must face the challenge of how to give the box style a memorable character.

The footprint of the building in relation to the site, although influenced by internal planning and layerage considerations, as discussed in Chapter 7, must conform to regulations governing percentage of land coverage and to its ratio to automobile parking capacity. The number of vehicles required is

The Store as an Enclosed Box
Diamond's, Thomas Mall, Phoeniz, AZ
Architect: Copeland, Novak & Israel

in direct relationship to the gross building area and hence its calculated human occupancy. Obviously, this requirement varies enormously, depending on whether location is in the inner city or on open land or is part of a shopping center. In the latter case, the shape and orientation of the building must be studied so that it will relate well to the shape and efficient utilization of land for parking, traffic access, and movement, and the clear separation of customer from truck movement. Safety and traffic control regulations must be complied with. Frequently, many communities require dedicating a designated percentage of land area to landscaping and green belts, complying with an increasing awareness of environmental and ecological concerns.

The mass or volume of the building, clearly resulting from the number of levels established by the initial program, from the floor-to-foor heights of each of the levels, and from the provision of parapets to screen unsightly mechanical rooftop equipment, must also relate to adjacent structures. A department store, for example, that is seen as a major establishment anchored to and serving a community should dominate physically and symbolically, whether it is freestanding or part of a shopping center.

STRUCTURE

An ideal store interior would be one without columns. During the postwar development of stores, many innovative and complex structural schemes were tried to achieve this—trusses incorporating in their depth nonselling or service mezzanines, suspension systems from rooftop trusses, and so on. Yet, while imaginative, they were also enormously costly and inflexible. Practice today has accepted the fact that columns in a large structure are unavoidable. Experience, trial and error, and structural cost analysis have brought clients, architects, and store planners/designers to plan stores with intercolumniation ranging from 25 to 30 feet. Larger column spaces require costly

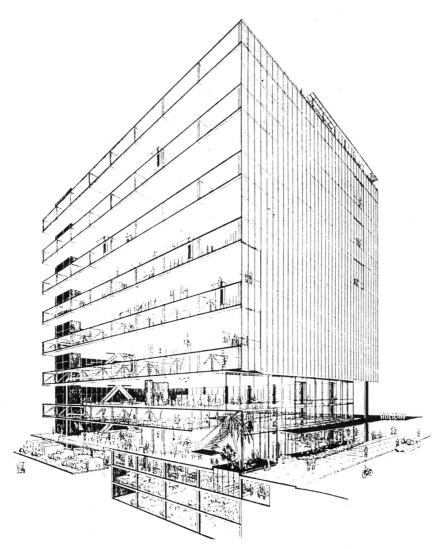

Long-Span Trusses Incorporating a Service Mezzanine: Proposed Projects
Department Store with Overall Ceiling Trusses
Architect: Antonin Raymond & Ladislav L. Rado
From Ketchum, Morris, Jr., *Shops and Stores,* Reinhold Publishing Corporation: New York, 1948.

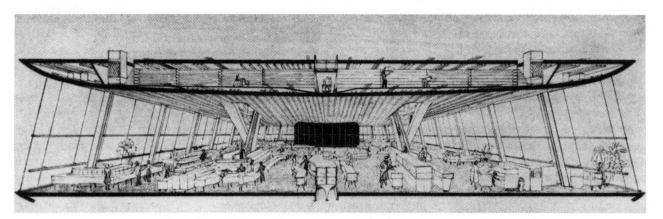

Long-Span Trusses Incorporating a Service Mezzanine: Proposed Projects
Intermediate Stock Floor System
From Parnes, Louis, AIA, *Planning Stores that Pay,* F.W. Dodge Corporation:
Lexington, MA, 1948.

girders with excessive depths. Smaller column bays are unsightly, seriously interfere with flexible interior fixturization, and block visibility. These factors remain relatively constant, even if we take into account a range of variables, depending on the structural system analysis, that is, steel skeleton, reinforced concrete, or prefabricated and prestressed reinforced concrete.

Perhaps an example will demonstrate the formulas used to convert a large department store space requirement into a logical column bay system. Suppose the ground floor program is for 80,000 square feet and suppose that a rectangular footprint is preferred, in order to minimize the large central space zone. Considering the preferred column bay of 28 × 28 feet, we see that

1. 9   bays @ 28 feet + 2 feet* = 254 feet
2. 12   bays @ 28 feet + 2 feet* = 338 feet
3. 254 feet × 338 feet   = 85,852 square feet

This calculation produces an area overage. However, techniques such as indenting entrance elements, recessing the truck dock, and angling, stepping, or curving exterior corners give the architects some leeway in reducing the area to fit the program and in achieving architectural distinction, breaking up the otherwise massive rectangular box (*see color insert*).

It should be noted that an odd number of bays is posited for the short-plan dimension, based on acknowledging that the entrance to the shopping center mall is preferred on the centerline. In this way, the main aisle, connecting the entrance to geometrically central escalators, flows through the center of the column bay and is not intercepted by columns. There are innumerable possible variations to this structural solution. Frequently, the end bays at the building perimeter walls can be reduced or expanded. Odd column placements in these sectors often would be contained by interior peripheral partitions that separate the selling area from stock rooms, fitting rooms, nonselling areas, or support functions. It becomes obvious, however, that the structural grid of the building is the starting point for every subsequent architectural and interior plan and design formulation.

*The 2 feet addition covers thickness of exterior walls, included in calculations of gross area, which, by definition, is to outside footprint dimensions.

Breaking Up The Box
and Achieving a Programmed Area
El Palacio de Hierro, Perisur, Mexico
Store Design: Copeland, Novak & Israel
Architect: Copeland, Novak & Israel
Photograph: Gil Amiaga, NYC

Florida's Store
Burdines, The Gardens, Palm Beach Gardens, FL
Store Design: Walker Group/CNI
Architect: RTKL Associates
Photograph: John Wadsworth

Historicism and Recycling
Marshall Field's, Chicago, IL
Store Design: HTI/Space Planning International
Photograph: Don DuBroff

Escalators as a Memorable Icon
Macy's, Aventura, North Miami, FL
Store Design: Copeland, Novak & Israel

Regional Culture in Search of Identity
Burdines, The Gardens, Palm Beach Gardens, FL
Store Design: Walker Group/CNI
Architect: RTKL Associates, Inc.
Photograph: John Wadsworth

Marble and Differentiating Materials
Rich's, Lenox Square, Atlanta, GA
Store Design: Walker Group

The Low Voltage Incandescent Lamp and Theatricality
Galeries Lafayette, Paris, France
Store Design: Walker Group/CNI
Photograph: John Wadsworth

Classic Period of Contemporary Style
I. Magnin, White Flint Center, Bethesda, MD
Store Design: Copeland, Novak & Israel
Photograph: Marvin Rand

Classic Period of Contemporary Style
Bullock's–Wilshire, Fashion Island,
Newport Beach, CA
Store Design: Copeland, Novak & Israel

Tactile Materials and Textures
Garfinkel's, Landover Mall, Landover, MD
Store Design: Copeland, Novak & Israel
Photograph: Norman McGrath

Visual Merchandising: Use of the Cube
Bamberger's, Livingston Mall, Livingston, NJ
Store Design: Copeland, Novak & Israel
Photograph: Gil Amiaga, NYC

Escalators: The Symbolic Center
Sak's 5th Avenue, South Coast Plaza, Costa Mesa, CA
Store Design: Copeland, Novak & Israel
Photograph: Marvin Rand

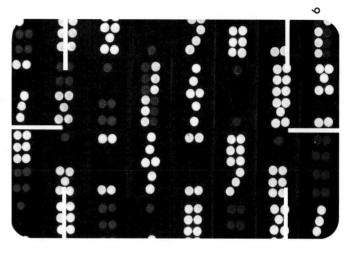

3

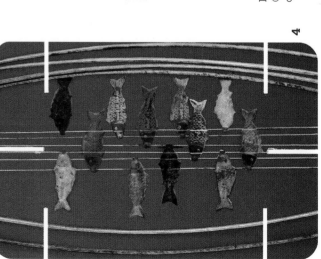

6

Six Images from the Eames
House of Cards Picture Deck
1. Chinese Patchwork Quilt
2. American Indian Kachina Dolls
3. Old Japanese Paper Dolls
4. Toy Japanese Fish Game
5. Ends of Chalk
6. Chinese Dominoes

2

5

1

4

Monumental Center
Marshall Field's, Chicago, IL
Store Design: HTI/Space Planning International
Photograph: Don DuBroff

Left:
**Up-scale, High Fashion
Presentation
Marshall Field's,
Watertower, Chicago, IL**
Store Design:
Walker Group/CNI
Photograph: Don DuBroff

Below:
**Character for an
Electronics Department
Rich's, Cumberland Mall,
Atlanta, GA**
Store Design:
Copeland, Novak & Israel

Right:
Perimeter Design
Bamberger's, Livingston Mall, Livingston, NJ
Store Design: Copeland, Novak & Israel
Photograph: Gil Amiaga, NYC

Below:
Variations of Ceiling Height and Designs
Carson, Pirie, Scott, Randhurst Mall,
Mt. Prospect, IL
Store Design: Copeland, Novak & Israel

Concept Sketch and Photo of Installation
Galeries Lafayette, Paris, France
Store Design: Copeland, Novak & Israel

Above:
Intense, Contrasting Colors
Bloomingdale's, B'way, New York, NY
Store Design: Barbara D'Arcy
Photograph: Retail Reporting Corp.

Below:
Traditional Materials, Harmonious Colors
Macy's, Stamford Town Center, Stamford, CT
Store Design: Copeland, Novak & Israel

Color Reflecting California Life-style
Sak's 5th Avenue, South Coast Plaza, Costa Mesa, CA
Store Design: Copeland, Novak & Israel
Photograph: Marvin Rand

Coordinating Wall, Floor, and Ceiling Materials
Sak's 5th Avenue, New York, NY
Store Design: Copeland, Novak & Israel

Fixture Design Creating a Mood
Harrods: Fragrance Hall, London, England
Store Design: Walker Group/CNI
Photograph: Retail Reporting Corp.

designer · misses

Above:
Signage: Understated,
Classic Fashion Image
Garfinkel's, Landover Mall,
Landover, MD
Store Design:
Copeland, Novak & Israel
Photograph:
Norman McGrath

NEW YORK
BLOCK EXCHANGE

Right:
Brand Name and
Classification Signage
FAO Schwartz,
New York, NY
Store Design:
Walker Group/CNI

Island Back Fixture Top Display
Sak's 5th Avenue, Cleveland, OH

Store Design: Copeland, Novak & Israel

Furniture, Mannequins, and Fixtures
Marshall Field's, San Antonio, TX
Store Design: Walker Group/CNI

Breaking Up the Box and Achieving a Programmed Area
Bloomingdale's, The Falls, Miami, FL
Architect: William Morgan

ENTRANCES

Of all of the architectural elements, none, perhaps, projects the functional and esthetic meaning, quality, and essence of a building more than its entrance. It is the connector between a hostile, outside world and an inner sanctuary designed by humans to express a special use. It is a symbol of welcome and protection. It invites one to penetrate into a chosen and controlled special environment. It celebrates that act of passage.

The various architectural designs of entrances are infinite. Whether they can be found in historical examples, in contemporary works of multitudinous building types, or in diverse expressions of national cultures and religions, the beautiful, delightful, strong, monumental, or intimate variations are limited only by human imagination. For example, contrast the sober yet personalized door of a London terrace townhouse with that of a colonial residence fronting a village green or with that of a bustling, frenetic Las Vegas hotel. Compare entrances of classic temples to Gothic cathedrals and the Crystal Cathedral in Los Angeles. Note how every conceivable building is defined by its entrance. From the port cullis of a medieval fort to the welcoming court d'homneur of a Renaissance palace; from the imperial colonnade of the Supreme Court building in Washington, D.C., to the suave optimism of a stock market; to the triumphal entry arch of a railway station or an airport terminal; to the corporate anonymity of an office building, and, ultimately, to the monumental emblem of sobriety and success of a traditional urban department store palazzo: The list is endless. The entrance is the building.

The Entrance is the Building
Meadowlands Racetrack, E. Rutherford, NJ
Architect: Walker Grad

The Entrance is the Building
Union Station, Washington, DC
Architect: Daniel Burnham
Photograph: Jeff Goldberg/Esto

The Entrance is the Building
Lord & Taylor, Manhasset, NY
Designer: Raymond Loewy
Architect: Starrett & Van Vleck
Photograph: Robert Damora
From Parnes, Louis, AIA, *Planning
Stores that Pay,* F.W. Dodge
Corporation: Lexington, MA, 1948.

The requirements of good design for a store's entrance are equally manifold. The entrance must invite; it must identify; it must protect and shelter; it must project without compromise the mood, quality, and character of the store's operation; it must appeal to its own target customer; it must differentiate from the competition and stand out. And it must be convenient.

The location of entrances already has been reviewed in Chapter 7. It should be restated here, however, Location must both provide the utmost convenience of access from the parking lot and lead to a rational interior circulation scheme. If a corner entrance is indicated by conditions of the site plan, what effect will this have on the interior layout? How is the exterior entrance related to signage and thus to clear visibility from access highways as well as from oncoming pedestrians?

Since the store entrance is a receiving as well as a departure point, it should provide physical and symbolic shelter from the elements—rain,

***Department Store Entrances Related
to Signage***
Diamond's, Tri City Mall, Mesa, AZ
Architect: Copeland, Novak & Israel

Store Entrances Related to Signage
Lechmere, Farmingham Mall, Natick, MA
Store Design: Copeland, Novak & Israel

Doors Celebrating the Entrance
Lazarus, Evansville, IN
Store Design: Walker Group

Entrances Creating a Signature Motif
Burdines, The Gardens, Palm Beach Gardens, FL
Architect: RTKL Associates, Inc.
Photograph: John Wadsworth

snow, wind, sun, cold, or heat. There should be provisions for seating while customers wait for rendezvous or cars. Recent practice has tended to minimize or even to eliminate display windows adjacent to entrances for department stores at shopping center locations because of the inordinate costs of servicing and maintenance and because of security requirements. However, the vital importance of the entrance, particularly as an element providing contrast to the solid, monolithic mass of the warehouse box, should be stressed. See-through windows, for instance, flanking the doors, do not require elaborate and costly props, but they do allow the entire store interior to be seen as a display.

Most geographical regions require double doors and a vestibule to minimize violent drafts and discomfort in the interior zones near exterior entrances. Vestibule design proportions should be ample and comfortable, avoiding the confusion of double-door action and recognizing that customers are often loaded down with parcels, shopping bags, and small children. An ideal entrance would be one without doors—no obstruction whatever to ingress or egress. This is normally achieved in entrances from enclosed malls. For a time, the air door was used for exterior entrances. The air door

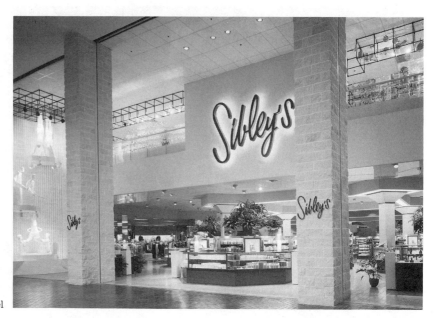

*Mall Entrances Symbolizing Multi-
Level Department Store*
Sibley's, Rochester, NY
Store Design: Copeland, Novak & Israel

Shop Front: The Entrance is the Store
Byck's, Louisville, KY
Store Design: Copeland, Novak & Israel

was no door at all but, rather, a complicated system of forced warm or cool air that would create temperature control by contrasts of air pressure. While theoretically attractive, the system was complex and costly, involving over-head and below-the-surface construction for blowers, ducts, grills, and night-time closure devices. It failed, however, to restrain debris and rubbish from blowing in.

The width of doors must comply with building code exit requirements but should also take into account the customer's comfort. The proper ganging of multiple doors is equally important to avoid confusion and conflict of entrance-exit traffic. If shopping carts are part of the operation, automatically operated doors are a necessity. The choice of door style—frameless, metal, tinted glass, solid—is infinite and should relate to the style and character of the entire building. Changes of level at entrances should be avoided. Steps are a deterrent, a hazard, and a liability. In addition, under the provisions of barrier-free access and the Americans with Disabilities Act, all stairs are required by law to also have ramps or alternate mechanical means of access for the handicapped. These, in turn, require large amounts of space and construction.

All of the components described—canopies, marquises, cantilevered projections, porte cocheres, doors, windows, street furniture, signage, landscaping—provide the architectural designer with unlimited opportunities to create a motif that becomes irresistible—a signature of the store and a wonderful contrast to the warehouse box. Historical reference, regional usages, contemporary or futuristic expressions are all possible, restricted only by the budget and a creative appropriateness to store image.

VERTICAL CIRCULATION

Escalators are the major elements providing customer vertical circulation. Frequently, in the past, they were considered necessary functional equipment and, while located centrally, were literally concealed behind partitions, which were used to provide height and background to impulse-selling departments. During the 1970s and 1980s, however, designers recognized the sculptural and theatrical drama contributed by escalators and the files of shoppers moving up and down to the multiple store levels. Eventually, the concept of the atrium was born. Open spaces surrounding the escalator structure gave a wonderful view, a vertical panorama, of the entire multilevel store with its variety of color, merchandise, and the excitement of people shopping. The force of concentrations of shoppers to stimulate purchases has been well known ever since the advent of the old stoa and town marketplaces. And so the atria reverted to the monumental designs of the late nineteenth century palatial emporiums, which, in fact, required the open well, cupola, or atrium to furnish daylight and natural ventilation. Open spaces, views of multiple shopping levels, natural light streaming through glass skylights, column treatments, and vaulted and domed ceilings contributed to a new and memorable image.

In fact, the escalator-atrium became an iconographic center of the store. If it reduced selling area at the most productive and profitable locations, it also generated traffic and created a compelling feature that increased storewide sales. It became a marketing icon (*see color insert*).

At the same time, the open well has caused considerable concern among life safety advocates. It can be considered an open flue that would activate and spread flames and smoke. Accordingly, most communities require extraordinary protective measures, such as smoke baffles, sprinkler deluge curtains, smoke exhaust fans, tempered glass enclosures, fire access doors, and so forth.

While the atrium is inevitably placed at the geometric center of the store, the arrangement of the escalators themselves is varied. The two fundamental dispositions are parallel or scissors. Each has a dramatic space quality. The selection is based on traffic control and direction; the escalator is a primary mechanism to generate customer traffic flow to every part of every

The Escalator Atrium—

The Iconographic Center
First Glimmerings, 1960s
Diamond's, Thomas Mall, Phoenix, AZ
Store Design: Copeland, Novak & Israel

store level. Depending on the geometric shapes and alignment of the various selling levels, the escalators can be placed at different sectors of a circle and can form a dynamic spiral, bringing traffic to a different arrival point at each level. Often a decision must be made with reference to the transference of traffic from floor to floor: Should the customers have the convenience of riding up or down continuously to their vertical destination, or should they be forced to walk around the well, in that way generating traffic fronting the selling departments at that transference level? Such a decision follows store philosophy, depending on whether customer convenience or commercial exploitation is the primary goal.

In the spirit of monumental space designs springing from escalator arrangements, the Japanese have recently developed an amazing spiral configuration. It displays the essence of drama. It also requires, however, considerably more space. Other escalator design choices involve the tread width, either 2' - 8" or 4' - 0, and the balustrade, either solid or glass.

Stairs are required for emergency exits and are located, sized, and structured to conform with mandatory building code requirements to assure public life safety. Frequently, stairs from an upper level will not interconnect with the ground level but will exit directly to the outside. Sometimes, however, a specific stair will be planned for staff convenience to avoid long walks to and from escalators or elevators; in this case, it must serve doubly for convenience and as an emergency exit. Sometimes the stair tower might be placed outside the major walls of the building box, providing contrasting architectural elements. Sometimes an open stair is indicated in a store design to dramatize the vertical connection between related selling departments placed at adjacent levels; in this case, they do not count as legal exits and can be freely designed, provided sprinkler protection offsets the fire flue effect of its openness.

The Escalator Atrium—
The Iconographic Center
Maturity of Style
Bloomingdale's, Town Center,
Boca Raton, FL
Store Design: Walker Group/CNI

The Escalator Atrium—
The Iconographic Center
Proposed Atrium: Downtown Store Recycling
The Bon Marché, Seattle, WA
Store Design: Walker Group/CNI

The Escalator Atrium—
The Iconographic Center
Influences of Regional Style
Marshall Field's, San Antonio, TX
Store Design: Copeland, Novak & Israel

The Escalator Atrium—The Iconographic Center
Multiple Stories: Dynamic Spiral Configuration
Sak's 5th Avenue, San Francisco, CA
Store Design: Copeland, Novak & Israel

The Open Convenience Stair
Burdines, Miami, FL
Store Design: Walker Group

The location of elevators has been previously reviewed (see Chapter 7). Elevator design is largely based on the standards and details provided by major specialty manufacturers who have developed sophisticated equipment that has been constantly improved over a history of more than 100 years. Since most new stores comprise not more than three or four levels, speed of operation is not a major factor; rather, leveling and door-operating time become critical. Two generic types of installation are available: (1) gearless traction and (2) hydraulic. The first requires a rooftop penthouse structure to house machinery, sheaves, drums, and control equipment. The second requires suitable subsoil conditions to house the supporting piston or shaft, but it does not need overhead space or construction, It is more generally specified in store work because of its relative simplicity and economy of capital as well as operating costs. The design of the passenger cab should be consistent with the style and quality of the entire store, furnished with attractive illumination and directories and using material requiring low maintenance.

The freight elevator has quite different standards based on load, size of merchandise, and safety of operation. A combined passenger-freight elevator is possible but is rarely used in store work, largely because of conflicting safety, convenience, security, and location factors.

ICONOGRAPHY

Memorable, signature elements of architectural design are referred to in this section. These have already been described in connection with entrances and escalator atria, which are major components of the store building that are amenable to special images. However, there are countless other opportunities for imaginative design elements. One example is the integration of signage as part of exterior architectural character. While in Chapter 13 we will explore the challenges and opportunities of signage within the store, this section notes the variety of store names, logos, use of materials, and illumination techniques that contribute to an architectural statement. The store designer should make a significant contribution to this kind of store image, evaluating whether the existing store name and logo used for advertising promotions and packaging are appropriate for architectural adaptation. Examples show the extremes: brilliant compositions in which signage contributes to strong architectural images versus applications of lettering that disregard and violate the architecture, appearing like disorganized, haphazard afterthoughts. Very often the successful development of an architectural sign-image will convince a client to upgrade advertising and packaging in that manner and thereby improve the store's total image.

BUILDING FUNCTION ELEMENTS

Included in the category of building function elements is a large number of permanent elements, ranging from truck dock to stairs, escalators, elevators, rest rooms, mechanical and electrical equipment rooms, vertical risers and ducts; in short, all components that are inherently a fixed part of the building and are necessary by function or building code regulations for its structural and operational integrity. In Chapter 7, we indicated the reasons for locating these elements. It is now important to relate them to architectural design challenges and opportunities. Imaginative and appropriate resolutions will enhance the store building and vastly contribute to its design image as well as to its daily performance. The following are some examples.

- A truck dock, by the logic of site planning, occupies a prominent quadrant of the building. By definition it will be dirty, messy, smelly, and unsightly. Storage of trash and disposables must be accommodated. Intelligent use of screening devices and even of earth berms and landscaping will not only conceal these operations but also will contribute contrasting forms and elements that will enrich the character of the building.
- Stairs must be located according to calculations established by exit code regulations, depending upon occupancy and life safety requirements. Conventionally, these stairs can be located inside the building exterior walls. More imaginatively, they can project outside the walls and develop a rhythmic, contrasting series of towers that convert the warehouse box into a distinguished architectural statement.
- Mechanical equipment requires large areas of louver-controlled openings for fresh air intake and exhaust. Properly located and proportioned, such louvered grills can become an inherent design element of

Forms and Volumes Integrating Mechanical Equipment Functions
Bullock's, South Coast Plaza, Costa Mesa, CA
Architect: Welton Becket & Associates
Photograph: Retail Reporting Corp.

the exterior facades and can contrast with the monolithic appearance of the warehouse box.

• Mechanical engineering evaluations recommend providing a penthouse for central air conditioning equipment. Integrating this structure into the forms and volumes of the building facades or roofscapes gives an added value to the design possibilities. Alternatively, the penthouse can be used as a background for strong and dramatic signing. Conversely, if discrete and separate rooftop mechanical equipment units are suggested, the architect has the opportunity of designing into the building volume screening rooftop elements or extended parapet forms that can enrich the design.

The examples just cited are only an indication of how an enlightened architectural understanding can transform utilitarian components of a building into outstanding expressions of style, meaning, and image. As Louis Sullivan once said, it is not only that "form follows function" but that function generates and inspires form.

SPECIAL FACILITIES REQUIREMENTS

There are a number of specialized spaces within the department store that require special provisions: food service, including restaurants, kitchen, bakery, candy fabrication, retail confections, butcher, baker, delicatessen; beauty salon, spa, health clinic, and gymnasium; computer sales; florist; garden supplies; demonstrations; and so on. Each has specific architectural, plumbing, ventilating, air conditioning, and electrical requirements that affect and are affected by the building structure. Many are governed by special health and public safety regulations. It is important that the store planner/designer organize and control the programs for these spaces at a reasonably early phase of the planning process to assure that their data are fed into the overall architectural and mechanical engineering process at the right time. Delays in this transference of data can be frustrating, confusing, and costly. Such delays are impacted and made probable, since these functions are frequently managed for the department store client by special providers or franchisers, who themselves are not signed aboard until quite late in the project's development. The planning or critical path schedule should highlight these requirements and demand early definition and clarification. Similarly, they should appear clearly on the checklist of responsibilities for all design and consulting partners. For the relatively small square footage involved, a disparate amount of research, design energy, technical detail, and governmental approval time is to be anticipated.

An outline of some of the questions often raised in the planning of a restaurant should illustrate the magnitude of the interrelated components and systems. Location of the kitchen is governed by proximity to the freight elevator for food supply and garbage removal. Sanitary tile kitchen and service area floors may require a depressed structural slab. Multiplicity of floor and equipment drains requires possible clearance and extra space above the ceiling of the floor below. Exhaust flue from the cooking range hoods must have a clear path to the roof above. The public part of the restaurant could be enhanced by windows, if there is an interesting view and if windows can be effectively integrated into the architectural facade design. Restrooms for customer and staff must be provided. All equipment, fixtures, and woodworking details must conform to sanitary code standards to prevent spread of vermin and bacteria. All materials in food preparation and service areas—floors, walls, and ceilings—must be nonabsorbent and washable. Express elevator service to the restaurant floor should be programmed. Should a separate public entrance and elevator to the restaurant be provided for use after store opening hours? Should a separate air conditioning system be planned? (Cooking and food odors cannot be recirculated into the general system.)

As is said, this is only the tip of the iceberg. In practice, these kinds of complex, special occupancies warrant the selection of consultants whose experience is based on their specialized knowledge and mastery of the type of component or system chosen. The selection and approval process is in itself time-consuming and certainly adds considerable time to the entire planning and design schedule.

REGULATORY REQUIREMENTS

A certain index of the quality of a civilization is undoubtedly its extent of government regulations. In America today, the quantity of regulations at national, state, regional, county, and city levels must be at an unsurpassed level. The construction industry is probably at the very center of these forces.

Like the architect, the store planner/designer must have a working knowledge of all of the applicable jurisdictional regulations and codes in the district of a project that govern the design, construction, and occupancy of all building types and that pertain to questions of zoning, life safety, public health, welfare, occupancy and assembly, emergency exit provisions, limitations of size and classification of construction, fire protection, flame resistant ratings of such materials as flooring and wall coverings, sanitary facilities requirements, labor code provisions, Occupational Safety and Health Act, 1970 (OSHA), barrier-free access and requirements, and the still relatively ambiguous stipulations of the Americans with Disabilities Act (ADA).

Enacted by Congress in 1989, the general provisions of Title III of the ADA require that places of public accommodation, which include retail establishments, be accessible to people with disabilities. More specifically, the ADA prohibits businesses from discriminating against these individuals by maintaining facilities that are not physically accessible. Accessibility, under Title III, includes routes and doors into and within the retail establishment: elevators, ramps, wider doors, wider aisles, the arrangement of rest rooms and fitting rooms to accommodate wheelchairs, and the provision of grab bars, improved signage to encourage disabled customers to ask store personnel for assistance, and the modification of telephone installations. Much of the confusion surrounding the ADA concerns readily achieving these barrier-free standards in existing installations. The schedules of priorities and enforcement by the Justice Department for compliance remain untested.

Compliance involves following the requirements spelled out in the Act and the ADA Accessibility Guidelines for Buildings and Facilities. The ADA Accessibility Guidelines provide charts, diagrams, and other specific directives on the interpretation of the ADA rules. Included are technical standards for dimensions and placement of building and site elements, including toilets, sinks, signage, telephones, seating, tables, parking areas, elevators, ramps, and drinking fountains. They also specify the minimum number of accessible parking lot spaces, the number and dimensions of wheelchair spaces in an assembly area, and the required number of accessible telephones per floor. This information is already familiar to architects and designers, since it is outlined in the American National Standards Institute (ANSI) Document A 117-1-1980, the standards of which have been widely accepted and incorporated by most states and municipalities into their own building codes.

Many of the ADA Accessibility Guidelines relate to products and their placement. Sconces and telephones, for example, are not permitted to protrude more than 4 inches into a walkway if the bottom edge of the object is between 27 and 80 inches from the floor. Product catalogues that prominently display the universal handicapped symbol may indicate compliance with ANSI or other codes but not necessarily with the ADA. More and more manufacturers, however, are beginning to publish documents of product compliance, citing specific sections of the ADA Accessibility Guidelines.

The summary on the facing page, prepared by Frank F. Memoli, RA, Professor, Fashion Institute of Technology, illustrates the multitudinous codes and regulations applicable to a store project in New York City, summarized with objectives and the scope of each. All of these express the policy power of the state, which is responsible for protecting life safety, property, public health and welfare.

Many of these codes have crucial effects upon plan requirements, structure, selection of construction systems, and finishing materials. They should be investigated well in advance of the development and approval of preliminary plans.

Another issue that has changed within the last few years is that of professional licensing requirements. Heretofore, any work with structural or public safety elements had to be stamped, sealed, and certified by an architect or a structural engineer. Now the status of the interior designer has changed

SUMMARY OF BUILDING REGULATIONS—
THE CITY OF NEW YORK

ZONING ORDINANCES

In general, zoning ordinances govern or relate to the use of land and the buildings on that land. Zoning regulations must be consulted with regard to the initial permissibility of a retail establishment within a certain geographic location in the city as shown on zoning maps. This body of regulations would also establish such elements as maximum floor area and height, as well as the minimum amount of open land around the project (if the project is a freestanding building or complex) and the amount, type, and location or parking based on the size of the project.

THE BUILDING CODE

For the most part, the building code governs the physical character of the construction of the project to make it safe for the permitted occupancy. Some typical building code provisions include the definition of the overall occupancy classification and the individual spaces within the project (i.e., the functional activities that might take place, such as sales, storage, office, and possibly exhibit, dining, and meeting), and the maximum number of people permitted to occupy the building. Once established, the occupancy classification and the number of occupants would be used to determine such characteristics as the type of construction required, structural capacity, fire ratings, types of finishes used, egress, universal systems, such as lighting and electrical, plumbing, heating, ventilation, air conditioning, and energy conservation. The building code also establishes criteria for activities during the construction process, such as inspections, testing, certifications, and safety for workers on the job site.

LANDMARKS PRESERVATION COMMISSION

The regulations of the Landmarks Preservation Commission pertain to the maintenance of the esthetic integrity of building exteriors and interiors and of certain geographic districts (historical districts) deemed to be historically significant. This is a particularly important consideration pertaining to existing buildings and will seriously impact on what changes may or may not be permitted to the buildings or within the districts. In the City of New York, one must submit applications for work on landmark buildings to the Building Department and the Landmarks Preservation Commission simultaneously and obtain the approval of both agencies.

FIRE DEPARTMENT REGULATIONS

For the most part, the Fire Department is concerned with protection against fire. Toward this end, this governmental agency establishes standards for fire detection, notification, and suppression systems. These include criteria for combustion, smoke, flame, and heat detection; bells, gongs, buzzers, and strobe lights; sprinklers and portable fire extinguishers; the fire department's access to the building; and building evacuation plans.

LOCAL COMMUNITY BOARDS

In the City of New York, there are numerous review boards at the local community level with the authority to examine proposed projects within the geographic boundaries of their particular neighborhood. These boards are composed of local residents who oversee the review process for the purpose of protecting and preserving local standards of community development, safety, density of traffic and population, and land value.

Prepared by Frank F. Memoli, RA, Professor, Fashion Institute of Technology.

radically in many states, under the impetus of new licensing examinations and qualifications (the NCIDQ Exam). The following list of interior design organizations illustrates the numerous professional institutes involved with licensing regulations: Foundation for Interior Design Education Research (FIDER), American Society of Interior Designers (ASID), Institute of Business Designers (IBD), Interior Design Educators Council (IDEC), Interior Designers of Canada (IDC), International Federation of Interior Designers (IFI), National Council for Interior Design Qualifications (NCIDQ), AIA Interiors Committee c/o the American Institute of Architects (AIA).

As a result of this growing thicket of regulations, specialists experienced in the laws and governing codes are frequently brought into the team as consultants: Their responsibilities are the review of plans and details for conformance to code requirements, filing and reviewing construction documents with the governing building departments, expediting the review procedures, and securing approval permits to build. The consultant's fee for these services is more than justified by the saving of time and the elimination of costly misinterpretation of the law.

FLOOR-TO-FLOOR HEIGHTS

Volume and mass of a store, like every other building type, depend upon setting the floor-to-floor heights. This determination is based on several considerations. First, the spatial quality of the interiors: What does the designer consider appropriate to establish a mood? Should the central, open interior spaces be monumental, institutional, or intimate in scale? Second, how does ceiling height affect the selection of appropriate illumination schemes? The higher the ceiling is, the more diffused the spread of light levels. Conversely, the higher the ceiling is, the more wattage is required to achieve designed foot-candle levels. By contrast, a low ceiling requires closer spacing of light fixtures to avoid unacceptable patches of poorly illuminated spaces. Third, do perimeter reserve stockrooms require double-decking or mezzanine construction to augment merchandise inventory capacity? This consideration must take into account the minimum legal height of each level, the depth of construction, and the clearance of the upper deck beneath sprinkler mains, air conditioning ducts, electric conduits, and the depth of the structural tier of beams and slabs overhead. Fourth, especially when the store is part of a multilevel shopping center, the floor levels must coincide precisely with those of the mall to avoid steps or ramp connections.

The historic experience of most stores in the recent past has led to the selection of a floor-to-floor dimension of 18'- 0 to 18'- 6". This has satisfied the conditions enumerated and has worked for most types and sizes of retail operations, from specialty shops to department stores. Given this dimension, one can achieve a maximum ceiling height of 13' - 0 to 14' - 0, depending upon type of construction and the location of the major heating, ventilating, and air conditioning (HVAC) distribution ducts. Since interior design has largely departed from large, high, open spaces toward more humanly scaled spaces and toward the lowering of ceilings at the peripheral walls to emphasize presentation opportunities of the merchandise, these proportions have become almost standard. There are always exceptions, of course. In such cases, if the client and store planner/designer are searching for advanced or totally different concepts of interior space requiring greater ceiling heights and floor-to-floor dimensions, then this proposal should be brought to the attention of the shopping center developer and developer's architect at the earliest opportunity in order to arrive at a rational mutual solution. It must be kept in mind that this kind of special requirement has a direct effect upon the building's cube and, consequently, a major influence on its construction cost.

EXTERIOR DESIGN

Having established floor-to-floor heights and the number of selling levels, the overall height and mass of the structure are then set. Architectural design begins. The mass, the proportions, the sculptural modeling of entrances or exterior corners; the contrast of elements, such as stair towers, entrance treatments, overhangs, cantilevers, or arcades to provide shelter and scale; windows and fenestration where suggested; louvered areas; parapets, cornices, rooflines, roofscapes, and the form and articulation of equipment penthouses; the location, style, and proportions of signage, graphics, and promotional photo projection or video elements; illumination techniques; treatments of walkways, landscaping, trees, earth sculpture, berms, screening walls all come into play. The selection of architectural materials simultaneously enhances and reinforces the forms and style. Materials reflect the character of the store. They might refer to indigenous traditions of a region or create a dramatic, shocking sense of contrast. They must appeal to the taste, expectations, and excitement of the target customer. Contrast the effect of materials—brick, fieldstone, dressed limestone, marble or granite, concrete, stucco, stainless steel, enameled steel, bronze, copper, aluminum, glass—everything on earth is possible, except perhaps for the more fragile woods.

The synthesis of forms and materials creates architectural style. That style also is inspired by, or tilts toward, the historic modes, eclecticism, the international style, postmodernism, regionalism, futurism, or deconstructivism. It must be appropriate, as well as a projection of, and contributor to, the store's image. These are the challenges: Creative solutions are infinite and can lead to buildings of memorable distinction, power, and beauty. Successful solutions are also guided and tempered by constant evaluation and control of costs, as authorized in the project's approved budget.

When the store is an integral component of a regional shopping center, the exterior design is complicated by two questions. Should the store express its own identity, disregard the adjacent design of the mall and its shops, and create a dynamic, contrasting, and conflicting statement? Or should the store integrate and harmonize with the total architectural character? To put these questions in place without rhetoric or a compulsive, stubborn point of view springing from obsessions with individual identities, is to answer them. In the best of both worlds, it is possible to resolve the two extremes. It is possible (and well-designed examples frequently show it) to retain individual signature elements of design and, at the same time, harmonize and relate to the whole. This resolution satisfies the objective of the shopping center developer who is striving to achieve a total, substantial expression in which distinction and dignity of design underline potential acceptance in a community and not so incidentally, commercial success in a fiercely competitive market. It satisfies the major store owner who also wants distinction, character, personality, and success

It is also necessary to note that the exterior design of store buildings, like all major architectural types, is subject to the approval of a host of governing local restrictions. Building codes and zoning regulations obviously apply.

Frequently, the shopping center developer has the rights and power of approval built into contractual agreements. Zoning resolutions, deed restrictions, fine arts commissions, environmental agencies, local community regulations—all of these must be satisfied. Some prestigious towns or neighborhoods require conformance with a historic and desired architectural style to maintain a homogeneous community character. While at times onerous and subjectively restrictive, these controls and design criteria safeguard, enhance, and add value to existing and proposed physical assets.

If a major store is part of a shopping center mall, the mall entrance becomes a major design statement. Most shopping centers have design criteria that specify materials, entrances, show windows, and, above all, signage: location, style, lighting techniques. These apply to all rental retail spaces, except major or anchor stores. In the case of the latter, it is generally accepted that their designs can be special and clearly related to the exterior architecture and interior character. Accordingly the mall facade design is given loving care. Style, materials, the integration of signage, the relationship to the exterior building design, and the dramatic introduction to the store's interior are the essential elements. Most stores take advantage of the climate-controlled features of the mall and present wide, open, doorless entrances.

The width of the entrances relates to the dimension of the total facade, which, in turn, varies according to its position on the mall or mall courts. An open entrance produces a totally barrier-free, inviting, and welcoming statement. Depending upon the facade width, it might be flanked by visual, see-through display windows, by enclosed, dramatic show windows, or by solid materials and eye-level signing. Frequently, the entrance motif or design expresses the number of selling floors of the store and becomes striking and monumental in its scale. In the case of an up-scale, high-fashion retail store, an exceptional design concept might incorporate doors. The statement then suggests exclusivity—"This place is different from the common areas. Only those who belong in an upper-echelon milieu are invited." Such a statement transcends design considerations only and plunges into social and societal implications. It certainly reflects the store as a club, catering to a carefully strategized and identified sector of the market.

COST AND BUDGET CONSIDERATIONS

In Chapter 6 we discussed a general strategy of establishing cost objectives for the major components and systems of a project. Under the criteria noted there, it is important that all aspects of architectural design be kept under control by evaluating and estimating the costs of every decision. This is easier said than done. Most creative designers, whether they are in architecture or other fields, are not conditioned or trained to weigh their ideas and creative solutions against practical cost effects. That is why a team approach is truly necessary in resolving successful solutions. Designers, construction managers, and cost estimators must review every step and implication of the process, preferably under the leadership of a principal in charge who has a working knowledge of all of the details and who can direct the project with a sure hand toward its basic, comprehensive goal and objective. A good budget estimate will provide guidelines for every part of the building, from structure to finish. Each line item is projected on a cost-per-square-foot formula, based on history and experience of similar projects. Computerized data banks provide this background in current practice, modified as necessary by regional cost factors and an assumption of the quality and sophistication of the proposed project.

As indicated in the budget form, in Chapter 6, pg. 70, most well-organized budgets are subdivided into building, mechanical, electrical, and interior elements. Each subdivision becomes the responsibility of each consultant—the architect, engineers, and store planner/designer. Inevitably, gray areas develop that overlap and bridge across these quite artificial divisions. The following are some examples:

- The central escalator elements are part of the building. However, the developing interior designs might elaborate these into monumental atria, incorporating exotic forms and materials, such as skylights, vaulted ceilings, elegant glazed bulkheads, and handrail designs. The surplus cost of these elements, unknown to the building architect at the onset of work, might well be charged against the interior budget.
- Suspended ceilings are part of the building. There is a normal cost spread, depending on the type of suspension system, the acoustic tiles, Sheetrock, or plaster ceiling specified. If the developing interior designs suggest multiple ceiling levels, light coves, vaults, cornices, crown moulds, suspended fins, or light track systems, the surplus cost of these elements, unknown to the architect, will be charged against the interior budget.
- Interior floor-to-ceiling partitions are established by the store planner/designer, based on merchandising and concept plans within the structural building shell. They affect ceilings, lighting patterns, HVAC distribution systems, sprinklers, and so on. They are structural in nature, requiring proper connections to floor and overhead construction. They affect exit pathways, subdividing the planned spaces, and often require alternate escape routes to emergency fire stairs. Who files these plans with the local building department that has jurisdiction? Who secures approvals for applications and permits to build? Is it part of the architectural plan package, properly stamped and sealed? What happens if the store planner/designer is not licensed in the state in which the project is located?
- Hard flooring materials are frequently placed under the architect's responsibility. They are an inherent part of the building and demand careful structural subfloor preparations. If the developing interior designs propose high-cost marble floor inlays or excessive areas of specially designed marble floors, requiring recessed slab preparation, or wood flooring on grade requiring expensive subfloor waterproofing installation, the surplus cost of these elements will be charged against the interior budget.

Such examples can be expanded without limit. They are always potential sources of confusion, frustration, and conflict between the consultants. It is vitally important that the consultants and the client meet at the beginning of the project, discuss these probable ambiguous items, and realistically assign appropriate budgets and responsibilities. Frequently, these assignments have a serious bearing on the time spent by the consultant and accordingly on the consultant's fee for professional services. The responsibilities also have a direct relationship to the consultant's professional liabilities which, in this incredibly litigious society, have a critical impact on fee structures. Only in this way can a harmonious and keenly motivated relationship be established. Only in this way can the outcome be rewarding and successful for all parties, especially the client.

Design

A work that aspires, however humbly, to the condition of art should carry its justification in every line. And art itself may be defined as a single-minded attempt to render the highest kind of justice to the visible universe, by bringing to light the truth, manifold and one, underlying its every aspect. It is an attempt to find in its forms, in its colours, in its light, in its shadows, in the aspects of matter and in the facts of life what of each is fundamental, what is enduring and essential—their one illuminating and convincing quality—the very truth of their existence. . . .

Confronted by the same enigmatical spectacle (the hazardous enterprise of living) the artist descends within himself, and in that lonely region of stress and strife, if he be deserving and fortunate, he finds the terms of his appeal. . . . He speaks to our capacity for delight and wonder, to the sense of mystery surrounding our lives, to our sense of pity, and beauty, and pain; to the latent feeling of fellowship with all creation—and to the subtle but invincible conviction of solidarity that knits together the loneliness of innumerable hearts, to the solidarity in dreams, in joy, in sorrow, in aspirations, in illusions, in hope, in fear, which binds men to each other, which binds together all humanity—the dead to the living and the living to the unborn.*

Design is the art of store conceptualization and includes aspects of architecture, planning, interior styling, decorating, and merchandising. In its broader sense, design is the creative act that organizes a point of view out of chaos. In this sense, God the Father was the primordial designer: "In the beginning God created the heaven and the earth. And the earth was without form and void; and darkness was upon the face of the deep . . . And God called the light Day, and the darkness he called Night." (*Genesis* 1:1,2,5) In this sense, every designer participates in a Godlike act of creation. It is a uniquely personal, noble, profound, and beautiful act.

From these serious and inspirational references, the following major considerations specifically relate to the elements of interior store design.

STYLE

It should be recalled from Chapter 7 that the plan contains within it all of the potentials and possibilities of its spatial form. It is, in fact, impossible to separate the planning from the designing process. One creative mind must direct and give shape to both. In professional practice, this is a fundamental challenge to a project's personnel assignments and staff organization. In a smaller office, one person handles both functions. In a larger office, subdivided out of necessity, efficiency and convenience into "specialists," the designer must oversee the planner to assure that the space and forms suggested by statistical and functional plan solutions embody concepts of style

*From the preface to *The Nigger of the Narcissus* by Joseph Conrad (1914).

Mass Market Merchandising
ServiStar, Longview, TX
Store Design: Retail Planning
 Associates, Inc.

in order to achieve an image that reflects the basic objectives of the project. Both should be under the direction of a principal in charge who has a clear, broad, creative and comprehensive insight into the client's desires—expressed and unconscious—its history, its character, image, and personality, and its mandate to dominate and capture a share of the market face to face with intense retail competition.

An inherent part of this search for a signature image is the formulation of an appropriate style. Style, in this sense, is not to be considered a superficial or arbitrary selection of historic or contemporary design elements; rather, it is the creation of a total atmosphere, an ambience, an environment. It includes architectural and interior design elements that unequivocally express the quality and character of the store. It must also take into account the merchandise in itself and its techniques of presentation, to which they must be subservient. (One rare axiom in store design is that a successful, realized image must include the merchandise in place: Beware the design that looks good before the merchandise is installed. This axiom will be explored in more detail in Chapter 11. Obviously, fixture design also must precisely fit the size and presentation techniques of the merchandise and its package.) It is the difference between a mass marketer, filled up to the ceilings with tons of goods in dense phalanxes of fixtures, compared with an up-scale, high-fashion operation in which mood, decorations, presentation of pre-selected and fashion-coordinated merchandise, suggested by dramatic displays in a luxurious space, immediately set the scene and encourage prestigious, up-scale shopping (*see color insert*). The spectrum and range between these extremes contain every conceivable and infinitely variable modulation of design. This is the essential challenge to the store designer/planner. It is what makes the retail scene endlessly exciting and endlessly renewed. Each project, at every time and every place, is different and demands its own unique, special expression. Each design is also the creature of history, of conditions, personalities, cultural influences, of the spirit of the time, as was shown in Section II, which discussed the history of store design during the last five decades.

The following sections will describe the anatomy of those parts that contribute to a successful integrated style.

VARIETY AND COMPLEXITY

By definition, the department store contains numerous administrative, merchandising, and, consequently, physical parts. Similarly, every store type, except a small shop that is devoted to a specific merchandise category, is physically composed of complex, various divisions of space. Each should physically express a style reflecting and enhancing the nature of its merchandise. Obviously, a menswear department should have a look, a feel, and a character that is right for the merchandise and that is designed to make the targeted male customer comfortable and put him in a buying mood. A women's lingerie department should be quite different—conveying to a female customer the delicacy, intimacy, and sexuality associated with these goods. An electronics or housewares department, or glass and china department would similarly present entirely different selling backgrounds, fine-tuned to appeal to those customers, and to relate to the merchandise

Character for a Men's Wear Department
Garfinkel's, Landover Mall, Landover, MD
Store Design: Copeland, Novak & Israel
Photograph: Norman McGrath

Character for a Lingerie Department
Burdines, Town Center, Boca Raton, FL
Store Design: Walker Group
Photograph: Mark Ross

and its package (*see color insert*). While each department or associated groups of departments should thus have its own ambience, the entire store must still have an overall signature expression. The slogan "pluralism versus continuity" conveys the complex nature of this design challenge. *Pluralism* indicates the diverse elements reflecting the excitement brought together through multiple statements; *continuity* reflects the discipline that design control imposes upon the different parts in achieving that striking, unique overall personality and image.

Frequently, that diversity results from an eclectic design approach. Traditional forms and materials may be right to achieve a clublike mood in a menswear department. Art deco might be an imaginative application of curved and cubistic motifs to suggest a flapperlike, erotic background in a lingerie department. Hi-tech modern seems appropriate and compatible to the merchandise of an electronics department. The synthesis of these conflicting and varied statements is achieved by control over scale, detail, degree of sophistication, continuity of transitional or connecting structural elements, such as ceiling and floor designs, common display backgrounds, enframing neutral components, lighting, and graphics, and a cohesive pal-

Character for a Housewares Department
Steinbach's Shore Mall, Pleasantville, NJ
Store Design: Copeland, Novak & Israel
Photograph: Martin Helfer

Character for a Lingerie Department
Galeries Lafayette, Paris, France
Store Design: Walker Group/CNI

ette of colors and materials. In this sense, the spatial impression of the entire interior environment is symphonic, the harmonic composition of contrasting ideas, rhythms, and tonalities, all of which are subservient to a final, all-encompassing idea.

The development of these design ideas has, in fact, led to a new retail style. It has achieved warmth, glow, and drama. The elements are vast; their combinations and arrangements are literally infinite. The style varies according to the incredible varieties and richness of all of the world's merchandise and cultures. It embraces or eschews regionalism or nationalism. It reflects fashion design cycles. And, in its best manifestations, it seeks to avoid rapid obsolescence: It imposes advanced, imaginative and disciplined elements without a crass exploitation of novelty and gimmicks that will be all wrong, tasteless, and dated the following year.

FRANCHISED BOUTIQUES

The proliferation of franchiser installations on the fashion store scene has been dramatic during the past ten years. Each franchiser brings with it not only the style and brand label of a name and article made glamorous and desirable by all the devices of Madison Avenue advertising, but also its own

Franchised Boutiques: Special Shop Character
Bergdorf-Goodman Men: Polo Shop by Ralph Lauren, New York, NY
Store Design: J.T. Nakaoka Associates Architects
Photograph: Jaime Ardiles-Arce

The Department Store as a Shopping Mall
Galeries Lafayette, Paris, France
Store Design: Walker Group/CNI

special shop character. It is a microcosm of the main store, with its own merchandise, style, decor, lighting, color, graphics, and selling fixtures. It contributes positively to the notion of plurality. It gives to the department store an additional variety and richness, which are so inherently a part of the excitement of shopping. (More recently, the franchiser has begun to install his or her own stores, thus becoming an overt competitor to the department store in which he or she first established his image and following.)

The designer, while respecting these assets of variety, is charged with incorporating multiple boutiques into the whole, without generating the chaos of a flea market. In this respect, the department store is becoming more and more like a shopping mall. The designer has at his or her disposal a whole vocabulary of architectural forms and materials that can cohesively integrate the variety into a disciplined space continuum.

INTEGRATION OF FIXTURIZATION

Fixturization is analyzed in Chapter 12. It is vital to note under design considerations at this time, however, how the selling fixture should be incorporated into the total design concept. There are many types of fixtures: floor fixtures, perimeter fixtures, special fixtures subdividing departments; fixtures for merchandise hanging, frontal projections, shelving for folded goods; fix-

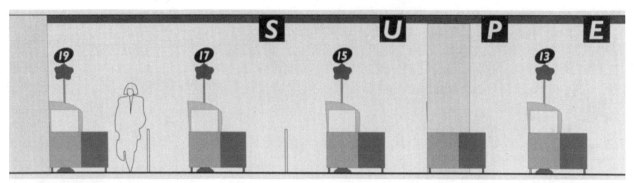

Integration of Cash Wrap with Design
Robinson, Seacon Square Mall, Bangkok, Thailand
Store Design: Walker Group/CNI

tures for boxed packages or for the presentation of a single, rare crystal sculpture. Materials used for fixtures are similarly myriad: stainless steel, copper, brass, aluminum; enamelled or vinyl-coated metals; special alloy metallic finishes; glass; lacquered or natural finished woods; plastic, plexiglass, acrylics. Composite clusters of modular fixtures, flexible changeable systems, fixtures containing their own lighting devices—every variety has its use and selling purpose.

The designer, understanding the innumerable functions and types of fixtures necessary for a store's operation and realizing that the merchandise presentation and design style must relate to the individual character of each department, must manage and organize them so that they conform and integrate with the entire store. The designer must oversee their plan placement and density, in order to comply with merchandise capacity requirements and also to maintain variety, interest, and good traffic flow. The designer must be aware of the different heights of the fixtures and group them so that they are agreeable in their volumetric, vertical composition. Special fixtures, such as cash wrap facilities, are large and bulky in scale (See the concept sketch in Chapter 7, page 108). He or she must determine whether these should blend into the materials and design of a department or whether they should contrast, be prominent in order to encourage the quick finalization of a sales transaction, or be the same throughout the store in order to present a uniform, quickly identifiable, institutional character. Since fixtures, and the merchandise they house and present, constitute a dominant part of the store's interior, their organization, design, and selection are fundamental to successful, total store design. They should not be left as an afterthought or, perhaps worse, to the selection and placement by merchants, manufacturers, or unimaginative technicians.

PERIMETER TREATMENT

Of the three primary surfaces of a store's interior—the perimeter, the ceiling, and the floor—the perimeter is an inherent part of merchandise presentation. It is directly the result of the plan configuration. As was traced in the planning development of stores over a span of five decades, contemporary plans have manipulated traffic aisles and perimeter partitions so as to multiply the lineage and exposure of merchandise and to produce a dramatic identifying background treatment for literally every selling department.

Perimeter Design
Burdines, The Gardens,
Palm Beach Gardens, FL
Store Design: Walker Group/CNI
Photograph: John Wadsworth

That treatment, by its combination of merchandise, merchandise presentations, signage, and illumination, serves to attract and pull the customer through the department and to maximize the selling efficacy of its perimeter, which is remote from its frontage on the aisle (*see color insert*).

Traditionally, the perimeter consisted of a tier of merchandise at its lower level, a lighting or containing element just above the merchandise, and a superior decorative wall treatment at its upper level, often with artwork, graphics, and signage that identified the department. In current practice, this conventional tripartite zoning structure has given way to a much more imaginative exploitation of the cube. Fixture hardware incorporated in the construction of the partition system runs from floor to ceiling, allowing totally flexible arrangements of hanging, double and triple hanging or face outs, or combinations of hanging, face outs, shelving, and coordinated presentation elements. With the development of specialized, dramatic lighting systems, the former valance or cornice, which concealed the lighting, has disappeared. Theatrical accent or wash lighting techniques can be attached to, or incorporated into, the ceiling design. The result of this revolutionary transformation of the perimeter has been a fresh evaluation of the scale or height of the merchandized partition and a new opportunity to lower the ceiling plane in order to concentrate attention on the merchandise itself. In turn, this new flexibility has permitted the arrangement, height, and configuration of the ceiling to vary according to design concepts and to humanize the entire scale of the interior. The ultimate result has been a totally new

Perimeter Design
Marshall Field's, San Antonio, TX
Store Design: Walker Group/CNI

Perimeter Design
Bullock's-Wilshire, La Jolla Village Square, La Jolla, CA
Store Design: Copeland, Novak & Israel
Rendering: Richard Rykowski

WATERFALL
Average Quantity of
Garments Per Post: 48

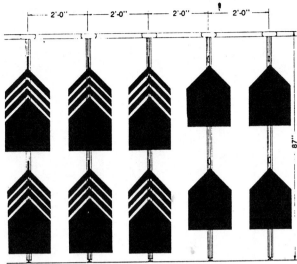

FACE OUT & WATERFALL

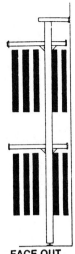

FACE OUT
Average Quantity of
Garments Per Post: 46

**POST FACE OUT WITH
STRAIGHT HANGING**
Average Quantity of
Garments Per 4'-0" Section: 94

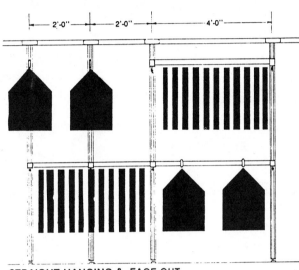

STRAIGHT HANGING & FACE OUT

**STRAIGHT
WITH HANGRAIL FACE OUT**
Average Quantity of Garments
Per 4'-0" Section: 96

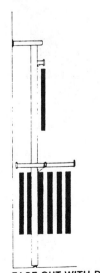

FACE OUT WITH DISPLAY
Average Quantity of Garments
Per 4'-0" Section: 49

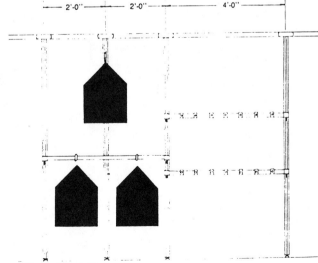

• Compatible with
universal ½" slotting
• Unique new oval hangrail

ROD DISPLAYS
6 or 7 Rods Per
4'-0" Section

Fixture Hardware Incorporated in Partition Construction
From deChiara et al., *Time-Saver Standards for Interior Design and Space
Planning*, McGraw-Hill, Inc.: New York, 1991.

147

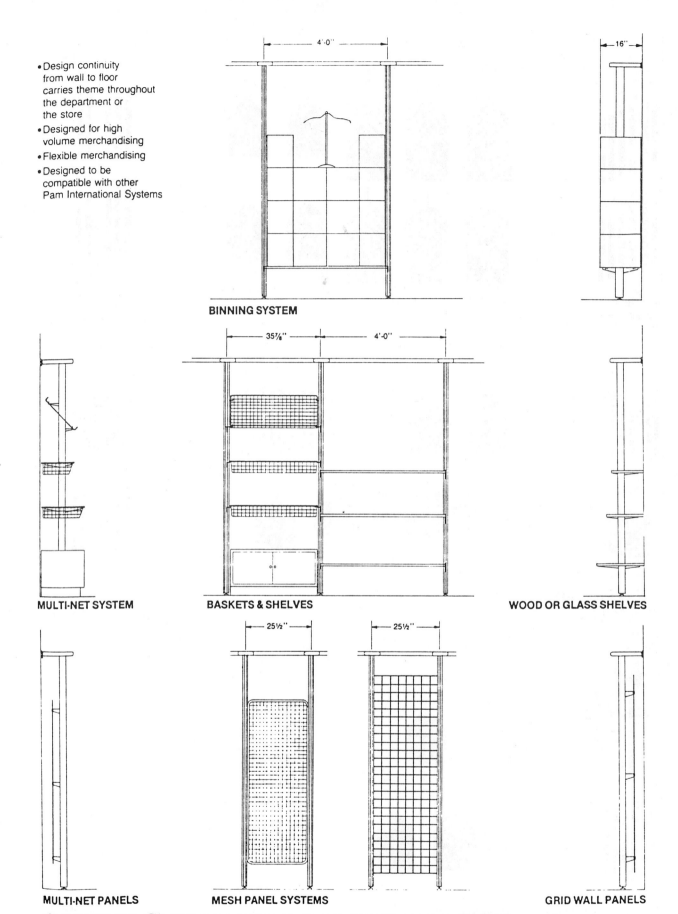

- Design continuity from wall to floor carries theme throughout the department or the store
- Designed for high volume merchandising
- Flexible merchandising
- Designed to be compatible with other Pam International Systems

4'-0"

16"

BINNING SYSTEM

35⅞" 4'-0"

25½" 25½"

MULTI-NET SYSTEM

BASKETS & SHELVES

WOOD OR GLASS SHELVES

MULTI-NET PANELS

MESH PANEL SYSTEMS

GRID WALL PANELS

- All Multiples/Systems 2™ upright posts are engineered with easily changeable post covers (Pat. Pend.)
- All metal components are coated with a durable, long lasting, baked on epoxy powder finish.

Fixture Hardware Incorporated In Partition Construction

From deChiara et al., *Time-Saver Standards for Interior Design and Space Planning*, McGraw-Hill, Inc.: New York, 1991. Reprinted with permission from the publisher.

store look in which merchandise presentation drives the design and dominates everything.

Certainly, traditional components still have their use, functionally and artfully applied: cornices or curtain walls or cabinets to highlight and enclose parts of the perimeter and to contrast with the more flexible parts; fins and dividers to segregate styles, color or classifications of merchandise within horizontal runs; pegboard or slatwall screens, or perforated panel systems to provide ever more flexible arrangements of merchandise; graphics, signage, and brand name identifications; dramatic, imaginative visual presentation systems, light sculpture, theatrical accent lighting. They constitute an entire vocabulary of "display" ideas to reinforce and coordinate merchandise and design into a dynamic striking life-style expression and, above all, to stimulate sales.

CEILING TREATMENT

The ceiling (from the French word *ciel*, meaning "sky" or "canopy") surface of a store represents its single largest element. It, together with the floor, encompasses the entire selling area. However, unlike the floor, it is seen totally, at one glance, visually interrupted only by floor-to-ceiling partitions providing lines of articulation that permit changes of level, form, or treatment.

Basically, the ceiling is a relatively lightweight material suspended from the building overhead structure by a system of steel rods and channels. The three major materials used in stores for ceilings are plaster, Sheetrock, and acoustic tiles. Plaster is seldom specified today because of its relatively high initial cost but especially because it is a wet trade requiring several time-consuming applications and because of its effect on interior humidity, which delays the work of all other trades. Sheetrock, properly installed, presents the smoothness of plaster, is quite rapidly installed, and lends itself to decorative and painted finishes. Acoustic tiles are available in a multitude of types, styles, patterns, and finishes. They are inherently modular and reveal either joints or metal supporting "tees." They are quickly installed and prefinished, thus eliminating the need for on-site painting or decorating. Overseas, a fourth material and system have been popular, comprising an arrangement of prefinished metal fins, panels, and louvers that are clipped to a supporting and suspending structure and are largely open to the space above. Quite surprisingly, the acoustic qualities of the ceiling are not viewed as an important factor in most stores. On the contrary, the sound of people and movement, particularly the sound of the cash registers ringing, adds an important dimension to a store's excitement.

The function of the suspended ceiling is to form a finished overhead surface and to separate the designed space below from the utilitarian zone above, the plenum, which contains the mechanical systems: HVAC ducts, sprinkler lines, plumbing and sprinkler pipes, electrical conduits, and so forth. In addition, it houses lighting fixtures and devices, HVAC distribution diffusers, and sprinkler heads. The coordination of these components is a task of both the building architect and the store planner/designer. (An accepted rule of thumb is that the mechanical-electrical systems of a store building comprise about 40 percent of total building costs. In this context, containing this complex array of servicing components is truly a major exercise.)

Metal Ceiling System
Burdines, Miami, FL
Store Design: Walker Group

Variations of Ceiling Height and Designs
Davison-Paxon, Perimeter Mall, Atlanta, GA
Store Design: Copeland, Novak & Israel

As indicated earlier, during the 1970s and 1980s, designers became aware of the dramatic contribution of the ceiling to a total store ambience. Concurrent developments of the plan, perimeter presentation concepts, visual merchandising, and the idea of a store as theater reinforced this recognition and transformed the look of the store. Variations of height; lowered ceilings at the perimeters to eliminate purely decorative wall treatments above the merchandise zone and to concentrate attention on flexible layers of merchandise; direct light troffers, indirect light coves, vaults, domes, stepped planes culminating in a skylight or dropping down in scale to enframe shop fronts as stylized proscenia, beams, fins, suspended grids incorporating lighting track; metal ceiling systems—all of these elements contributed to an explosive richness and variety of design (*see color insert*).

Simultaneously, these new ceiling designs opened up infinite possibilities for new concepts of lighting. Instead of a uniform lighting system, the changes of heights and treatments led to a variety of lighting effects that reflected the functions and identities of the different parts of the store. Ceiling sections over the aisles could allow minimum light, contrasting with adjacent highlighted selling departments and, in effect, borrowing light spillage from them. The principle of chiaroscuro became part of a new theatrical vocabulary. Aisle lighting could be achieved by relatively low energy levels using fluorescent light coves. Fronts of departments could be intensely and dramatically lighted to focus attention on displays and the color, texture, and style of the merchandise. Departments appealing to high fashion, or ad-

Variations of Ceiling Height and Designs
Sak's 5th Avenue, South Coast Plaza, Costa Mesa, CA
Store Design: Copeland, Novak & Israel
Photograph: Marvin Rand

Chiaroscuro: A New Theatrical
Vocabulary
Bamberger's, Livingston Mall,
Livingston, NJ
Store Design: Copeland, Novak & Israel
Photograph: Gil Amiaga

Variations of Ceiling Height and Designs
I. Magnin, White Flint Center, Bethesda, MD
Store Design: Copeland, Novak & Israel

vanced ideas, youth, or electronics, could have individualized design expressions in which the imaginative integration of ceiling forms and specialized lighting fixtures would contribute to a sense of excitement and variety. Introduced in department stores, this technique was quickly adapted by every retailing type. As an example, even the previously humdrum food supermarket now changed: Fresh produce was emphasized by dropped trellises containing incandescent lighting; meats were dramatized by lighting of correct intensity and color to make the products irresistible; delicatessen and prepared foods were similarly identified by cohesive design elements. The supermarket became an exciting specialty shop appealing to varied tastes and appetites, glamorizing the weekly shopping chore, and certainly increasing sales volume.

Supermarket: Department Emphasis by Ceiling
Concept Perspective
Robinson, Seacon Square Mall, Bangkok, Thailand
Store Design: Walker Group/CNI

Supermarket: Department Emphasis by Ceiling
Lucky Stores Prototype, CA
Store Design: Walker Group/CNI

INTEGRATION OF VISUAL MERCHANDISING TECHNIQUES

Chapter 14, describing opportunities of visual presentation systems as part of the perimeter treatment, leads to all other aspects of presentation throughout the store. The growth and indeed dominance of visual presentation is one of the great phenomena of current store designs. Designers must have a clear and creative working knowledge of all of the systems and components available, and, if not commercially available, the ability to design them in a way that is consistent with the store's overall character. As in design, they must make provisions for a diversity of department expressions and still achieve a total store style. They must locate in the plan important points for major presentations, visualizing in their mind's eye the customers' pathway and providing strategic statements to lure customers through the aisle system, to stop them, and to make them buy. These major presentations are, in effect, interior show windows: glass enclosed or backed by a unified architectural treatment or, by contrast, varied according to merchandise content and fashion directions. The selection, location, arrangement, and height of selling fixtures on the floor directly influence the placement of visual presentation elements, which offset a boring uniformity of volumes and which animate and coordinate promotional selling opportunities.

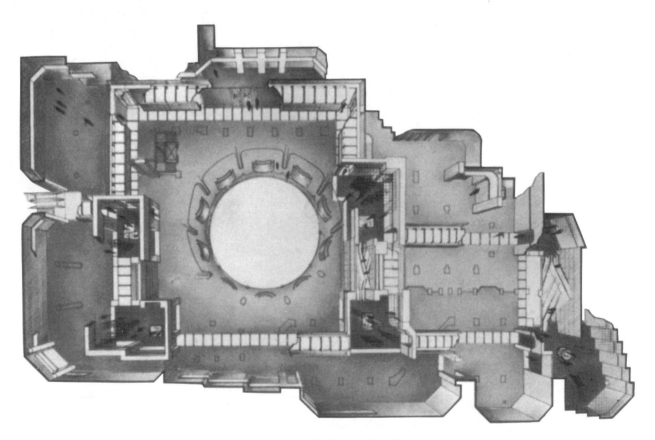

Plan Generating Location of Major Presentations: One-Point Perspective Plan
Galeries Lafayette, Paris, France
Store Design: Copeland, Novak & Israel

Visual presentation is an entire curriculum in itself. It incorporates many disciplines and concepts. An entire industry has developed to serve its needs. Many of the major elements will be reviewed in Chapter 14. At this time, it is vital to refer the store planner/designer toward the new and growing directions. Store design must integrate and breathe into it renewal, imagination, and pertinent style.

ELECTRONICS

The electronic revolution has brought into the store two groups of facilities and equipment that have, in turn, revolutionized retailing. The first includes all of the technological aids in providing customer services. Everything from the cash register itself, with its linkage to the computer to validate a customer's purchase and constantly to update inventory control; to rapid price and data-scanning equipment at the cashier; to moving, switching, and automatically delivering merchandise carriers to adjacent stockrooms; to materials-handling systems and controls at the warehouse; to telemarketing; to electronic substitutes for coupon clipping; to frequent-shopper identification cards and subsequent gifts or discounts; to establishing customer fashion preferences, sizes, colors, and so on; to filing, retrieving, and coordinating the data with currently available inventory; to video scanning projectors and monitors to deter shoplifting and to implement security measures; to a host of developing and future devices to make selling faster, more pleasant, efficient, and profitable—all of these have been reviewed in detail and, in fact, fall outside the scope of this section.

The second, however, includes audiovisual electronics, the video, which has become a vital, major element of visual presentation. Video has brought into the store motion, sound, special programs, promotions tied into marketing, advertising, and displays—all of the advances of striking electronics technology from Madison Avenue (Van de Bogart). This development has challenged the store planner/designer and the visual merchandiser to integrate these devices imaginatively into store design. From point-of-purchase at the fixture level, from focal major presentations, from coordination with merchandise displays, to arresting video walls—all of these elements are competitively vital and provide an entirely new dimension, indeed a whole new universe, to creative and advanced ideas of store design. Television has invaded the retail store. Many stores have established in-house production facilities to link sales campaigns with a face-to-face encounter with the customer. Multimonitor displays, called "video walls," have provided incredible variety and power to sales presentations and have brought into the store all of the impact, artistry, and potential of cinematography.

INTEGRATION OF GRAPHICS

Just as a total design concept must integrate within it ideas of fixturization, of operating equipment like cash wrap facilities, of visual merchandise techniques, and of audiovisual electronics, so, too, it must consider and incorporate into it notions of graphics systems. Like so many of this book's compartmentalization of elements, graphics will be analyzed in some detail in a later chapter. Without being redundant now, however, it seems pertinent to

Video Invading the Store
Burdines, Town Center, Boca Raton, FL
Store Design: Walker Group
Photograph: Mark Ross

Integration of Signage and Architectural Design
Joseph Magnin, Fashion Square, La Habra, CA
Store Design: Skidmore, Owings, & Merrill
Photograph: Retail Reporting Corp.

draw attention to those elements that the designer must relate to and that he or she must enfold in the interior design package.

A fundamental signing philosophy should be reviewed and established with the client. It should define the extent of identification signage. Should every selling department have a major sign? Should each category or classification within a department be identified? Should brand name signs be provided? If so, should brand names use their characteristic logos, or should they be unified storewide? Questions such as these should be answered and then programmed into a graphics checklist. Nothing is more frustrating than for the store designer to omit in his or her proposed elements the necessary signage and then to see other consultants, sign manufacturers, or in-house visual merchandisers appear at the last moment, just before store opening time, and stick up a multitude of signs that disregard or overpower the exquisite details of perimeter or fixture treatments. Understood up front, the style, scale, typography, and composition of signs can reinforce and enrich the entire environment. As a general rule, the higher the quality of the store is, the fewer the required signs. If an interior is well designed and well integrated with merchandise presentations, it will project its special character spontaneously and dramatically. Yet the added value of a well-known and desirable brand name cannot be overlooked. In a cosmetics department, for example, the name, logo, and package are fundamental to competitive, intensive sales. Defining the typography is also necessary to good design. Very often it is established by the store's packaging and advertising, and becomes an extremely valuable attribute to its total image. Very often an imaginative interior signing proposal, seen as an integral part of an exciting interior space design, will influence a client to upgrade and revise the entire logo type and packaging image.

COST AND BUDGET CONSIDERATIONS

Imposing a pragmatic discipline on a designer and forcing the designer to understand the cost effects of intangible efforts are, perhaps, the most difficult tasks for the store planner/designer principal in charge. A designer is born and trained to create imaginative, striking, advanced, and new design concepts. At best, he or she is hazy about the costs generated by all of the interrelated, complex elements of plan, perimeters, fixtures, ceilings, electronics, signage, lighting, and so on. The project principal fears clipping the designer's wings. Yet the ultimate responsibility is to the client—to bring the project in on budget. The solution to this delicate and ever-recurring challenge is what makes the difference between success and failure. The demand is for psychological insight, skill, comprehension, experience, inner strength, diplomacy, and a clear understanding of all of the implications and objectives of the project. Controls can be applied by personal direction or by systemic, elaborate, line items of computer-generated data. In the final analysis, this resolution is what makes design firms successful, based on outstanding personal qualities and a warm, highly motivated office staff.

10 Colors and Materials

As defined in *The American College Dictionary*, color is "the evaluation by the visual sense of that quality of light—reflected or transmitted by a substance—which is basically determined by its spectral composition. It is that quality of a visual sensation distinct from form."

Undoubtedly, more has been written about color and its psychology than any element of interior design (Chidilwa). The very definition, by its prolixity, indicates the ambiguous nature of what surrounds us every day. Cut to its essence, however, there are no rules concerning color selection. Everything is possible. It is a matter of taste, style, and a subjective viewpoint that achieves the objectives of a project. Decoration is the handmaiden to design. Ideally, both disciplines are indissoluble but, in the larger office practice, they are separated into discrete specialties. It is absolutely vital that their conceptual process and development be totally integrated so that the resultant style of the store interior becomes a seamless synthesis of form, color, and materials. The following analyses relate the theory of color and decorations to the design of stores.

COLOR THEORY

Although there are no rules, there are several accepted notions in color design. Terminology is often loose and even conflicting. As in music, language attempts to describe a different medium—one that conveys an idea, emotion, and mood directly to the senses. The following statements, if not theoretically comprehensive or definitive, are generally understood in store design practice.

1. Every color in the spectrum has three characteristics.
   a. Hue is the actual color.
   b. Lightness is the shade of the color: the amount of white or black mixed with the hue. It is frequently called value.
   c. Saturation is the intensity or vividness of a color.
2. Similar colors are adjacent on the color wheel, such as red and orange.
3. Contrasting colors have three colors on the color wheel between them, such as red and green.
4. Complementary colors are on opposite sides of the color wheel, such as red and blue-green.
5. Colors are infinite. All are combinations of the three primary colors— red, yellow, and blue—mixed with varying degrees of white and/or black.
6. There are three basic approaches to the composition of colors, or a color scheme:

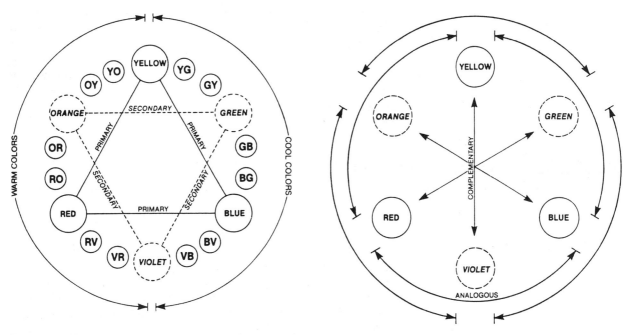

Diagram of Color Wheel

    a. *Monochromatic.* The use of one color modulated by variations of intensity, texture, pattern, and material.

    b. *Harmonic.* The use of similar or adjacent colors, modulated to produce a dominant mood.

    d. *Contrasting.* The use of opposing, intense colors, to project a bold, dynamic, and dramatic scheme.

7. Texture describes the tactile quality, perceptible to touch, of a surface. There are innumerable degrees of texture, from high gloss, piano, polished, to glossy, to satin, to eggshell, and to flat finishes.

PSYCHOLOGY, AMBIENCE, AND THEME

The color spectrum is organically linked to human responses: The cool end—violets, blues, greens—has a quieting, tranquil influence; the warm end—yellows, oranges, reds—tend to stimulate and excite. The cool colors are associated with evening, sky, natural verdure; the warm, with blood, sun, the tropics, flowers. The selection of a color palette in a store should be made to support its total image and design theme. Intense, bold, and contrasting colors tend to project a popular quality appropriate to mass merchandising. Muted, grayed, and harmonic colors have become historically and traditionally associated with up-scale merchandising. Many retailers have established a color palette that is carried through in every department. Contrast, for instance, Bloomingdale's and Macy's: the former has strong, contrasting colors and contemporary materials dominating the merchandise and projecting a bright mood of New Yorker chic; the latter has harmonious colors and traditional materials that are subservient to the merchandise, giving a sense of stability and continuity (*see color insert*). Contrast a Limited with The Gap with a Banana Republic. Each has developed its own style, color palette, and relationship to merchandise. At the same time, color must be appropriate to the merchandise itself. Compare the warm, clublike, traditional colors in a men's department, which enhance the textures, and brown, gray, and blue colors of men's apparel; to the white, apricot, pink, taupe colors of a women's lingerie department, which provide a sensuous relationship to the skin tones of the merchandise; to the charcoal color and stainless steel texture of an electronics department, which projects the mood of an adult toy world, like the inside of a Porsche.

REGIONAL AND SEASONAL INFLUENCES ON COLOR

Color in a store is also conditioned by location. Regional and national traditions of design have a far-reaching impact. Local customs, taboos, and design influences should be understood (e.g., black is universally shunned in most American stores because it symbolizes death. By contrast, in the Orient, white is the symbol of death). The merchandise itself is different: The urban, natural fabrics shown in a store in the North are intrinsically different from the cottons and light man-made fabrics worn in the South; the life-style of Florida or California is different from that of the Southwest (*see color insert*). Color should be used appropriately, taking these factors into consideration. A successful color scheme in New York would look and feel all wrong in Florida, Paris, or Singapore. In addition, seasonal merchandise moves require colors that are appropriate to dramatic changes. It is important that a color scheme enhance the presentation of top coats in winter and beachwear in the spring and summer without the need for a major, costly redecorating job, which would disrupt operations and sales.

CYCLES, STYLE, AND FASHION

Color is extremely susceptible to cyclic influences and changes, which are in themselves the result of diverse cultural forces. A museum retrospective of Matisse paintings might have a profound effect on color and decorative schemes for several years. An entire decorative industry might develop its color and style in that direction. Led by interior design magazines, prominent spokespersons, and critics, flooring materials, carpeting, drapery and upholstery fabrics, wall coverings and wallpapers, even accessories such as bedding and linens, will follow a prescribed, dominant, coordinated color system. If that system is built around dusty pink colors, for example, woe to the decorator who wants a color scheme of yellows: It will be literally impossible to find good coordinated selections of fabrics and materials during that cycle.

Whites, which are always popular, might be the fashion rage following the popularity of a book that referred to and described life in the Viennese secession period. Color styling of automobiles is a strong, if subconscious influence. Blacks and rally greens are in; metallic bronze is out. Fashion design is always ubiquitous. The very concept of rapid obsolescence, built into our industrial culture, demands frequent cyclic changes of color. A boom period or an economic recession has an intangible but clear influence on color moods in fashion apparel, in residential interiors, and, consequently, in retailing.

The historic styles imply the need for special color palettes. Contrast empire, country French, Adams, Biedermeier, Georgian, and Williamsburg: Each recalls and suggests a distinctive color scheme. Contemporary design is more open to innovation, undisciplined by tradition, and totally the result of strong individual design tastes and directions. The style of a store, which reflects its personality and image, establishing a subliminal but striking identity that is totally distinct from its competition, appealing to its targeted customer, and expressing its position in the price spectrum, depends largely on its color statement. Color, more that any other element of design, carries an emotional impact. It envelopes; it dominates; it conveys mood and character; it is art in space.

EFFECTS OF LIGHTING AND SPACE PERCEPTION

Color reacts to and affects lighting. Dark colors absorb, light colors reflect. A color selected under natural light will look amazingly different when placed under incandescent or fluorescent light. It is necessary for the designer to select a color palette under light conditions that are as close as possible to those that will exist in the actual proposed space. Illumination engineers have developed empirical tables that establish room factors based on color intensities. If a dark color scheme is established, more wattage and footcandles are required to render the space agreeable and to highlight the merchandise. If a dark floor is specified, its absorption of light tends to produce a shadow effect at the ceiling and to make the space feel poorly lighted. Additional up-component light sources are required to achieve a cheerful ambient space effect. Cool colors tend to turn ceilings gray and unpleasant; warm colors tend to radiate warm reflections on ceilings.

It is quite well known that dark and intense colors seem to bring a wall surface closer and seem to reduce the size of a space. Light colors, by contrast, seem to open the size of a space. An understanding of these perceptions allows the decorator to improve and modify an awkwardly proportioned space. On the other hand, the use of intense color at a strategically placed wall will generate excitement and tend to pull a customer to it (*see color insert*). The evaluation of these often conflicting effects is perhaps the most important challenge to the designer, who must reconcile and impose upon them an overall style consistent with the search for a tasteful, imaginative, appropriate, and unforgettable store image.

COLOR, MATERIALS, AND MERCHANDISE

Color in its relationship to merchandise presentation is complex. Many stores will insist upon showing merchandise against a light background. The point of view in this case is that every color, texture, and pattern of goods will show up in contrast and that the light surface will reinforce the illumination level. On the other hand, some clients will encourage the use of dark backgrounds to create theatrical, dramatic contrast to their merchandise. Everything between these two extremes is possible. However, the choice must also take into consideration the nature of the merchandise itself: What will enhance the presentation of women's dresses might do nothing for china or glassware. Contrasts of texture as well as of color come into play. With color behind shoe displays, values and hues that prevent the visual sculptural definition of the shoe, dominated by tones of brown and black, should be avoided but also must accommodate the fashion colors of shoes of every conceivable hue. What works? Many stores have specified a mirror background to finesse the question and coincidentally to multiply the display visually; however, just as many other stores strongly believe that mirrors cheapen a shoe presentation and veto its use. A similar debate occurs with respect to china and glassware. One client may love mirrors or high-gloss backgrounds, suggesting a contemporary design approach; another will insist on traditional dark, velvetlike textures for contrast. There are no pat solutions. This is the difference between a measurable science and the art of design.

FLOORING MATERIALS

Decorative and design resources provide literally infinite choices for flooring materials. There are two major classifications:

1. *Hard Flooring*. Included is everything from stone to wood to plastics: granite, marble, slate, travertine, terrazzo, prefabricated composite stone tile, crab orchard flagstone, brick, ceramic tile; parquet wood, strip wood, plastic impregnated wood, wood veneer; vinyl tile, composite vinyl tile, linoleum.
2. *Soft flooring*. Essentially carpeting: broadloom, strip, individual rugs; natural wool or man-made fibers; loop or cut pile, textured (mooresque), single color, woven, or printed pattern; contemporary or traditional; glued down or installed over undercarpeting.

Each of these two classifications has countless subdivisions, all related to style, quality, technique of installation, wearability, maintenance, and cost. The selection must satisfy three fundamental criteria:

1. Maintenance, wearability, and projected life, depending on whether it is planned for high, moderate, or low traffic locations.
2. Cost in relation to the approved budget.
3. Appropriateness and the achievement of style and character.

In addition, many of the hard-flooring installations require structural and architectural preparation. Marble flooring of conventional thickness, placed on a screed subfloor requires a recessed structural concrete slab. The cost of that special preparation may well be transferred from the building to the interior budget line. Marble flooring of reduced thickness, on the other hand, can be installed on the standard concrete slab by the adhesive method. This marble, however, is limited in the size of the flagging by the structural limits of the material. Wood flooring, placed on grade level, requires special water or damp proofing, under slab protection. These costs are high. Without the preparation, however, the floor will inevitably buckle and deteriorate.

If marble floor flags crack because of improper installation, if mortar joints between ceramic tiles crumble because of improper materials specifications, if wood flooring buckles because of the omission of expansion joints, these defects are traceable to judgmental errors of the store planner/ designer. If, as is highly likely, they become the cause of frustrating, long-term cross claims and lawsuits initiated by a disgruntled client, not only is the designer professionally liable, but also the designer undoubtedly will lose goodwill and the client. If one estimates the cost of replacing a large area of a defective floor in an ongoing retail operation, which would involve the removal of selling fixtures and of merchandise and the shutting down of an entire department, with consequent loss of business, the numbers multiply enormously. It is a very serious, sobering responsibility.

Flooring, as suggested earlier, is an element that bridges the architectural-interior designer responsibilities. Many states in America recognize the designer's role and have enacted professional qualifications and licensing certification requirements. Professional liabilities and responsibilities result. The rather frightening, negative possibilities described in the hypothetical scenarios above attest to the fact that the interior designer must exercise stern judgment in the selection procedure, constantly evaluating esthetic, functional, practical, and budgetary criteria.

WALL MATERIALS

Most store partition systems are of dry wall or Sheetrock construction. Surface finish becomes a dominant component of ambience and style. An entire catalogue of design materials indicates the scope and range of possibilities:

Masonry
Stucco, craftex
Wood paneling, mouldings, planking
Metal sheeting, mouldings
Acrylics and plastics
Perforated paneling
Grid systems, treillages
Structural or back-painted glass
Mirrors
Pegboard, slatwall
Wall covering fabrics
Wallpapers
Paint

The range includes the entire vocabulary of architectural and interior design materials and systems. A design study for a typical wall elevation would include a composition of many of these materials. Each category summarized above contains a multitude of various choices; for example, are the wood paneling and mouldings contemporary or traditional? Is it natural finish or colored lacquers? If natural finish, is it high gloss or flat?

Is the wood natural, bleached, stained, or analine dyed? Are there metal trims and accents? Are the panels slick and joined flush, or are they embossed or sculpted or patterned? How do the finishes relate to or suggest the forms, proportions, scale? Does each department have its own special design of form, materials, and colors, or is there a principle of unification and continuity throughout a floor and throughout the store? These questions merely suggest the complexity of design judgments and selections. Of one thing only is there any certitude: Painted Sheetrock walls are out. The surface

Color Lacquer Wood Paneling
Neiman-Marcus, Beverly Hills, CA
Store Design: Eleanor Le Maire Associates
Photograph: Retail Reporting Corp.

design and treatment in competitive stores today, incorporating the elements of merchandise, presentation, graphics, video, and so on, must be texturally rich, varied, and compelling.

FIXTURE MATERIALS

Similar questions with regard to material and finish are pertinent to selling fixtures. The entire universe of architectural, decorative, and furniture fields is available. Several additional factors, however, govern. The materials and finishes must harmonize with and enhance the merchandise being presented. They must be distinctive and help identify a brand name or classification. And, while distinguishing each brand, they must all conform to a holistic storewide quality and character. A selling fixture is mobile by definition. It is also flexible. Thus, the variety, mobility, and flexibility must all work together. Uniform fixture styling or finish is archaic. But every fixture must be able to stand alongside any other in the store and be harmonic, an inherent part of the total style and image.

DECORATIVE ACCESSORIES

Although this chapter is titled "Colors and Materials," it is necessary to refer to all of the other decorative elements that contribute to the store's ambience. Without attempting to describe in detail an entire curriculum of interior design (in former times, of "decorating"), it is important to recognize the role played by the following components:

Furniture
Furnishings
Decorative accessories
Lighting fixtures
Artwork

Furniture provides functional, convenience, and mood-inducing attributes to the store's interior. One example is the seating in a shoe department, which should satisfy the functional requirements of selling. It may be composed of individual chairs, sofas, settees, or benches. The arrangement and mixture of these should contribute to the interaction of salesperson and customer, allowing a degree of privacy and proximity to both displays and reserve stock. The seat itself, while comfortable, should offer the proper support and ease of intermittent sitting and standing. The style of the chairs, as in a restaurant, is a major factor in expressing a design concept; for example, in a ladies' dress depart-

Furniture: Essential Arrangements in a Shoe Department
Gimbel Brothers, Philadelphia, PA
Store Design: Copeland, Novak & Israel
Photograph: Retail Reporting Corp.

*Furniture: Essential Arrangements
in a Shoe Department*
Shillito's (now Lazarus), Louisville, KY
Store Design: Copeland, Novak & Israel
Photograph: Marvin Rand

Seating Groups in a Fashion Department
Sak's 5th Avenue, Cleveland, OH
Store Design: Copeland, Novak & Israel

Chandeliers to Accentuate Style
Bonwit Teller, Eastchester, NY
Store Design: Copeland, Novak & Israel

Artwork to Enrich Interior Design
Gimbel Brothers, Philadelphia, PA
Store Design: Copeland, Novak & Israel
Photograph: Retail Reporting Corp.

ment, the provision of a few seating groups, lounge chairs around a coffee table, discretely located near the entrance to fitting rooms, makes it convenient for the shopper, comfortable to her friend or escort, and a symbol of the store's concern for the customer. (Recent practice in men's fitting rooms provides comfortable space, chairs for the companion, and a dignified atmosphere completely different from previous planning, which minimized the room size and furnished a built-in bench slab for changing clothes.) Similarly, a plush or spartan provision of furniture in the fitting room reflects the client's attitude toward its customer's comfort and sense of well-being—all aids to the shopping experience and sales performance.

Furnishings include upholstery materials, curtains, draperies, and window treatments. Each of these classifications adds richness, depth, color, pattern, and softness to what might otherwise come across as a hard-edged, brittle design.

Decorative accessories include a wide range of elements: lamps on countertops, or in fitting rooms; planting; small furniture pieces; framed pictures—original prints, reproductions, posters; bric-a-brac. All of these help humanize the store and transform it from an impersonal, institutional, commercial space to one that recalls the variety and richness of a fine home.

Lighting fixtures include wall sconces and chandeliers. They must be integrated with the design and the lighting. They do not necessarily provide footcandles of illumination, but they do highlight, accentuate, and add conversational impact. They might be contemporary or in a surprising, contrasting period style. Decorators have innumerable resources at their disposal, limited only by taste and budget.

Artwork includes a whole universe of painting, photography, tapestry, and sculpture. Each medium must be selected to enrich and animate the space. For example, a painting might be selected, framed, and hung on a wall, or it might be a commissioned mural or a trompe l'oeil. The drama, appropriateness, and style are not merely appendages to the other elements of design and/or merchandising but also add richness, depth, distinction, and a special signature to the store. Some enlightened communities have stipulated that a designated percentage of new construction costs be allocated to artwork. This requirement has not only forced a client to invest in artwork, but has established in those communities a high competitive standard of esthetic excellence, enhancing their culture and civic reputation.

Except for flooring materials and designs, all of the other categories in this chapter represent a rather small component of the interior budget; yet,

Commissioned Artwork to Give Character
Burdines, Sarasota, FL
Store Design: Walker Group
Photograph: Otto Baitz

Commissioned Artwork to Give Character
Lazarus, Columbus, OH
Store Design: Walker Group/CNI

budgeted they must be. If not included at the beginning of the project, they
surely will never be included. This kind of error of omission can severely pe-
nalize the successful fulfillment of a store design and ultimately disappoint a
client who is seeking a special, distinctive image. The interior designer's experience, skill, sophistication, taste, and understanding of esthetics versus
commercial functionalism in retailing will add value, richness, and an unforgettable character to the store.

11 Fixturization

The selling fixture is the fundamental element that unites design, merchandise, image, and graphics in a retail environment. It is the essential building block. As defined, it is selling equipment that has been designed to display, present, and store merchandise.

CAPACITY REQUIREMENTS

The type, size, and quantity of fixtures are the direct result of a merchandising program. Before an appropriate fixture is designed or selected, it is necessary to go back to the statement of strategic merchandise goals and to analyze the projected dollar volume. The store's total dollar volume is, in turn, itemized by selling departments. Each selling department subsequently develops a schedule of capacity requirements, further subdivided by classifications of merchandise. The capacity or inventory is the result of converting dollars into units of merchandise, the SKU's (store keeping units), each unit representing a retail price and reflecting also its annual turnover. In addition, a judgment is made to determine the percentage of merchandise in reserve stock and on the selling floor. In most current stores, the great percentage is on the floor, in full view of the customer. Total high costs of store inventory, together with improved technologies of moving goods quickly from manufacturer or supplier to warehouse and ultimately to the store itself, have influenced most retailers to minimize the reserve stock allocations. There are, however, many exceptions. Men's shirts, women's shoes, linens, glassware and china, and lamps are examples of classifications that require considerable adjacent backup stock: It would be physically impractical to place all sizes, styles, patterns, colors, and so on, on the selling floor. Prestige fashion stores still prefer large reserves of their stock in order to retain a spacious, open density of floor fixtures and in order to allow space for coordinated presentations, arrangements of seating, and a feeling of luxury.

Once the number of units of merchandise (the SKU) on the selling floor is determined for each classification, it becomes possible for the store planner/designer to study the fixturization. Part of this process involves a judgment of placement: What classifications can be housed at the perimeter; what classifications can be housed on the floor? What should be positioned up front, on the main traffic aisle? What is the preferred adjacency of classifications? Part of the process requires a knowledge of how the goods are best presented: hanging, face outs, folded on shelving or in binning, in manufacturer's packages or open, or in coordinated combinations of all of these. Only after these retailing judgments have been agreed to, both by client and store planner/designer, can the fixture layout, selection, and design be started. It should also be remembered that adequate space must be allowed for special promotional and visual presentation opportunities, for

WalkerGroup/CNI
320 West 13th Street New York New York 10014 USA
(212) 206 0444 FAX (212)645 0461 Telex 220867

© copyright WalkerGroup/CNI 1991

MERCHANDISE CRITERIA QUESTIONNAIRE

CLIENT _____   NO. _____   ISSUE DATE _____

LOCATION _____   FL. _____

1. Who is the Target customer? _____

2. What is the price architecture within each merchandise category? _____

3. What is the preferred adjacency of the merchandise category to category? _____

4. What merchandise generates the most transactions? _____

5. What merchandise generates the most profitability? _____

6. How often do you organize sales per year? _____

7. How many promotions do you organize per year? _____

8. How many fitting rooms and cash wraps are required? _____

9. What other support functions are required (i.e., stock, offices, lockers?) _____

10. What type of customer conveniences are required (i.e., seating, toilets?) _____

In terms of assisting you in filling out the attached merchandise capacity criteria sheet consider how many units of merchandise will fit on the basic fixture component.

Hanging per linear foot/meter   Shelving per linear foot/meter   Showcase per linear foot/meter

Questionnaire for Merchandise Criteria

cash wraps, furniture groupings, and other highlighted constructions or features to give excitement and drama to the department.

Fixturization is generally subdivided into wall systems and floor fixtures.

WALL SYSTEMS

Wall systems include full-height perimeter partitions and varied-height subdivisions between departments or zones of merchandise. In America, the most popular system is of Sheetrock and stud construction, known as dry wall. Supporting hardware fixture elements, concealed, metal-slotted wall standards, are fastened to metal (or wood) studs and permit the carrying of hang rods, face outs, shelving, and other merchandise presentation units by means of brackets that clip into the slots and that can be completely adjusted in various vertical positions. Thus, the wall becomes the selling fixture (see Chapter 9, page 144). In addition, divider fins, mouldings, paneling, cabinetry, and other kinds of design, visual presentation, or decorative embellishment can be applied to the wall. Overseas (and in America during

WalkerGroup/CNI	MERCHANDISE CAPACITY CRITERIA		PAGE
330 West 13th Street New York, New York 10014 (212) 206-0444 FAX (212) 645-0461	CLIENT	JOB NUMBER	ISSUE DATE
© copyright WalkerGroup/CNI 1992	LOCATION	FLOOR	

Area Requirements				Number of Units Required						Fixture Capacity Requirements						
Department/Sub-Department Name	Selling Area	Fitting Room Area	Stock Area	Selling			Stock		Total Number of SKU's Required	Units per Feet/Meter	Total Linear Length of Hanging	Units per Feet/Meter	Depth of shelf	Total Linear Length of Shelving Required	Total Linear Length of Showcase Required	Preferred Type of Fixture Presentation
				Hanging	Shelving	Showcases	Shelving	Folded		Hanging	Required	Shelving				

Merchandise Capacity Criteria

Design Elements Applied to a Wall System
The Broadway, Glendale Galleria, Los Angeles, CA
Store Design: Robert Young Associates
Photograph: Retail Reporting Corp.

the 1970s) another system is available in which metal slotted or channeled uprights, anchored to floor and ceiling, receive snap-on, prefabricated, and prefinished infill panels. Quick installation time is the asset of this system. However, the rather mechanical repetition of the uprights and the hard-edged quality of the prefinished panels limit freedom of design expression. The selection of the methods of construction, heights, forms, and materials of the perimeter lead directly to an integrated system of merchandise and design elements—a dramatic background to interior sales space.

FLOOR FIXTURES

Floor-selling fixtures include a vocabulary of different types, which are analyzed below according to two subdivisions of convenience: islands and loose fixtures. They are generally fabricated as interchangeable modules to allow for total mobility, which permit limitless arrangements and clusters. They are manufactured off-site and are prefinished. They are designed to different heights, depending on merchandise requirements, so as to produce a controlled effect when placed side by side. All possible combinations must be anticipated, since they are moved from time to time, seasonally, or as selling and presentation techniques change. Forms, style, materials, and colors are as variable as the designer's imagination; while they should reflect each department or classification of merchandise in a special way to reinforce pluralistic images in the department store, they should also be compatible with one another in any arrangement.

Floor Fixtures:

Modular Mobility and Variety
Carson, Pirie, Scott, Chicago, IL
Store Design: Niedermaier Design
Photograph: Retail Reporting Corp.

ISLANDS

A selling island describes a composition of back fixtures, clerk aisle, and counter line. It is based on the salesperson assisting the customer in selecting and/or trying on merchandise, and completing a transaction. Generally, the back fixture is at eye level, designed to present displays above merchandise storage (in drawers or shelving). It also contains facilities for the cash register and cash wrap. The counter line consists of showcases, self-selection units, and counters. It might be uniform or a mixture of each. Showcases have many variations: They can be all glass for complete display; they might be of shallow glass display with storage below, as in jewelry; or they can have various depths of glass, depending on the scale of the merchandise and the preferred method of presenting it. They can be built of welded metal frame construction, with solid wood end panels, or of museumlike glass-to-glass detailing, as in a vitrine. Self-selection units are similar in design and construction to showcases, but they omit the glass enclosure to permit the customer to handle the goods without sales help. Counters are enclosed boxes

Selling Island: Composition of Elements
I. Magnin, White Flint Center, Bethesda, MD
Store Design: Copeland, Novak & Israel
Photograph: Marvin Rand

Selling Island:
Alternate Sketch Compositions
Architect: **Kenneth C. Welch**
From Ketchum, Morris, Jr., *Shops and Stores,* Reinhold Publishing Corporation: New York, 1948.

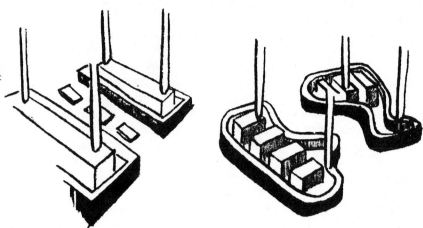

Jewelry Showcases with Special Display Components
Bamberger's, Livingston Mall, Livingston, NJ
Store Design: Copeland, Novak & Israel
Photograph: Gil Amiaga

with concealed stock facing the clerk aisle, and a solid-top surface that allows for point-of-purchase displays or the appraisal and trying on of merchandise. In addition, there are corner infills of special treatments, and fillers between showcases and columns, depending on the composition and configuration of the island.

LOOSE FIXTURES

Loose fixtures include an infinite variety of special fixtures: tables, gondolas, garment racks, glass binning, clusters of multiheight cubes or cylinders, display platforms, and special structures designed to provide optimal presentations for a host of merchandise items, from apparel to pots and pans to crystal ware, to linens, to books, to television sets (*see color insert*). The list is endless and is constantly changing. It is as variable as all of the material items that contribute to America's high standard of living. It varies also with the culture and life-style of nations and regions. Ultimately, it reflects and presents everything that people use. It is the business of an entire industry.

Variety and Functions of Fixtures
See-through Definition of
Escalator Well
Rich's, Perimeter Mall, Atlanta, GA
Store Design: Walker Group
Photograph: Retail Reporting Corp.

Variety and Functions of Fixtures
Stylized Shop Front Containing Flexible Fixture Hardware
Sak's 5th Avenue, Cleveland, OH
Store Design: Copeland, Novak & Israel

THE FIXTURE INDUSTRY

The selling fixture can either be custom designed and built or selected from manufacturers' stock catalogues. If it is custom designed, it can be precisely engineered and detailed to produce results that are totally consistent with and reflecting all merchandising, structural, stylistic, and image requirements. Comparative costs, however, must be considered in relation to the budgetary allowances. A custom-designed fixture will generally cost more than one selected from a stock catalogue, unless competitive bidding conditions at a carefully selected time in the market induce attractive prices. The catalogue fixture is limited by size, profile, shape, construction, materials, color, and finishes, based on the manufacturer's economic production schedule and its projected evaluation of the demands of the market. On the other hand, catalogue fixtures are the result of trial and error. A custom-designed fixture, while a specific, creative part of a total store design viewpoint, might be untested, structurally weak, or unproductive. In recent years, the store fixture and display industries both have recognized this paradox

Variety and Functions of Fixtures
Merchandise Presentation in a High-Fashion Setting
Bergdorf-Goodman Men, New York, NY
Store Design: J.T. Nakaoka Associates Architects
Photograph: Jaime Ardiles-Arce

and have provided continually improved, creative, innovative products that
are available in a short time, that are competitive, and that reflect style and
fashion trends. As with so many elements of the store, an evaluation and balance must be drawn. The wisdom of selecting appropriate fixture options
from both resources will lead to stores of quality and style, built within budgets related to sales plans and return on investment, and beating the competition with compelling style and productivity.

MATERIALS, FINISHES, LIFE, AND MAINTENANCE FACTORS

Materials and finishes of the selling fixture are countless. Construction might
be of wood cabinet work, metal, glass, or plastic. Surfaces and finishes range
from exotic wood veneer, color lacquer, plastic laminate, zolotone (or tex-

tured, spattered); to stainless steel, chrome, brass, bronze, anodized aluminum, enameled steel, vinyl-coated steel; to clear, polished or sand-blasted plate glass, tinted glass, tempered glass; to Plexiglas, acrylic, thermo laminate and preformed composition plastic. Combinations of materials and finishes in a single fixture or in a system of modular fixture units are obviously possible, limited only by function and imaginative design.

The fixture is generally constructed to last from 7 to 10 years. Although its cost is amortized or written off by most stores after 7 years, it remains in use far longer, for as long as it maintains structural integrity and presents merchandise according to accepted standards of a constantly changing fashion industry—sometimes as long as 20 years and occasionally even longer. In this context, the initial capital investment, based on quality construction, materials, finishes, detail, and workmanship, must be weighed against its life expectancy and projected maintenance costs. Maintenance is itself a major consideration. Everything in the store requires maintenance: architectural elements, ceilings, mechanical equipment and systems, flooring, walls and partitions, and the selling fixtures. The air in a store is initially filled with dust and other pollutants: the movement of people stirs up the air and deposits other foreign matter; the movement of merchandise on carriers, racks, or trucks—handled by careless service personnel—smashes into corners and creates unimaginable damage; shopping carts in self-selection stores; chemicals within the merchandise; chemicals and detergents used in normal operations; movement, wear and tear. All of these impact on maintenance. Since maintenance is an operating cost, rather than an initial or capital cost, its effect on operating profits is felt every day. Poor maintenance, resulting in an unkempt and run-down look, is a sure way to indicate a lack of care and attention by store management. It is a sure way to alienate the customer and to lose business.

12 Lighting Design

Lighting design is a discipline concerned with the chemical and physical process of converting electrical energy into light. It balances the scientific measurements of energy against the esthetics of creating functional, appropriate, and exciting methods of lighting architectural elements and interior spaces. Since light has an emotional and functional impact on the interior store environment, it is necessary to provide a general overview of those fundamentals of illumination theory that contribute to store design objectives. Stated boldly, without light there can be no store: All of the elements discussed in this book—mood, design, color, materials, merchandise presentation, and sales performance—could not exist. Good lighting design is one of the major components of the store's overall design.

ENERGY

Electrical energy is converted to light by heating a metal filament or gas contained in a sealed bulb or tube, causing incandescence or a glow. The amount of whiteness of a light source is described as color temperature, measured in Kelvin degrees, ranging from 6000 K (blue) to 1500 K (red), or from daylight to cool to neutral to warm. There are other ratings to describe the color rendering attributes of a source. These spectral energy distributions indicate the degree of color distortion on an object—in the store and on the merchandise. The actual appearance to the eye, together with the effect of adjacent colors, are fundamental considerations.

A lumen is the amount of light emitted by one international candle. A footcandle is the measurement of a unit of illumination on a surface or object equivalent to that produced by a standard candle at the distance of 1 foot. A watt is a unit of power generated by a current of 1 ampere flowing across a potential difference of 1 volt. These designations are vital to an understanding of the efficiency of a light source. Lumens per watt to produce a designated footcandle reading are the essential measurements in lighting efficiency. However, using energy effectively is a complex process and is only the starting point to achieving a successful design. Footcandles are no longer the major criteria. Ambient lighting levels describe general illumination, which should be adequate to allow the customer to identify and appraise the value of the product. Accent, or task, lighting directs attention to detail, motivates purchases, leads customers through the space, and provides a theatrical atmosphere. The ratio of accent to ambient lighting is an important measure of contrast when one is seeking a varied and dramatic mood. A variation of light intensities reinforces the pluralistic design approach in the store and helps produce a special identity for every discrete part, as well as for the whole.

LIGHT SOURCES

There are three major lamp classifications: incandescent, fluorescent, and high-intensity discharge. Each has advantages and disadvantages. The design selection must take into account the following criteria:

Color rendition
Energy consumption
Efficiency
Application
Lamp life
Maintenance

Incandescent

Color rendition in incandescent lighting approaches natural outdoor sunlight. It is warm and flattering to both fabrics and skin tones. Its filament radiates a concentrated point source of light that casts shadows, enhances the three-dimensional forms of merchandise, and defines textures and tactile values. In a word, it generates sparkle. It is similar to light in most residences, restaurants, and theaters. It is an important attribute, particularly in a customer's selection of apparel. (The color of a dress or a coat selected in the store should not change drastically in the home or in other customarily frequented places.) Much of its electrical energy is converted to heat. Accordingly, its lumens-per-watt efficiency is relatively low. In application, since it is

Incandescent Lighting Scheme
Bonwit Teller, Eastchester, NY
Store Design: Copeland, Novak & Israel

a point source, the fixture can be minimal in size and inconspicuous. It tends to lose intensity with use and has the shortest lamp life of the three classifications.

There are numerous basic lamp types, each of which has its purpose and use (de Chiara et al.):

General purpose
Accent or projector
Low voltage
Tungsten-halogen

Each is generally available in different wattages and accordingly can be laid out in flexible patterns, depending on ceiling heights and distribution curves. Maintenance is relatively simple. Lamps in open aperture fixtures can be replaced from the floor with a "cherry picker" device.

Fluorescent

A fluorescent light consists of a glass tube coated inside with a phosphor and containing a metallic gas, generally low-pressure mercury vapor. Electric current causes an interaction between the phosphor and gas, emitting light. The chemical composition of the gas determines color. Many varieties are available, traversing the entire spectrum from daylight to warm. Of the three classifications, fluorescent is the most efficient. A greater percentage of the electric wattage is converted to light; less to heat. Since the tube is linear, it emits continuous or diffused light. Shadows are nearly eliminated. The space appears uniformly lighted. There are various wattages, generally related to the length of the lamp. Until quite recently, the large lamp length required fixtures of at least 2 feet and generally 4 feet in length. The fixture dominated the ceiling as a result and had to be carefully laid out so as not to conflict with the architectural design. Conversely, its linear configuration made it ideal for use in light coves or in troffers for wall washes.

Commercial developments of the PL or compact lamp, mounted vertically, now approach the incandescent usage in a high-hat type fixture and provide general illumination from a pinpoint source, combining the efficiency of the fluorescent with the small-scaled aperture of the incandescent.

Fluorescent lamps have a much longer life than do incandescents, and they also deliver a higher percentage of their rated output for longer periods. To the advantage of lower-current consumptions costs are thus added the benefits of reduced maintenance and less frequent lamp replacement.

High-Intensity Discharge (HID)

The high-intensity discharge (HID) family includes mercury and metal halide. They are more efficient than incandescent and less efficient than fluorescents. Their lamp life is comparable to fluorescents. They are concentrated point sources, like incandescents, and provide both tactile definition and sparkle. While the metal halide lamp has fairly acceptable color rendition, it tends toward the cool end of the spectrum and has an unflattering effect upon skin tones. HIDs lost favor during the 1980s, when state regulations limited wattage per square foot in order to conserve energy. They have been used largely by mass merchants, discounters, and supermarkets. Newer commercial developments of energy savings and low-voltage incandescents, as well as compact fluorescents, have preempted the HIDs from most fashion-oriented stores.

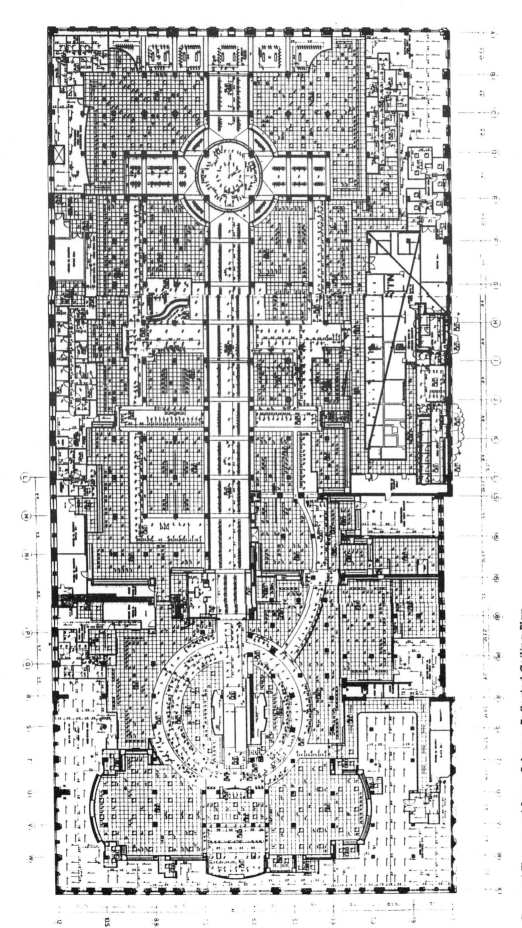

Compact Fluorescent Lamp Scheme: Reflected Ceiling Plan
Bloomingdale's: 2nd Floor, New York, NY
Store Design: Walker Group/CNI

LIGHTING FIXTURES

The lighting fixture contains the lamp's electrical connection, holds and supports the lamp in place, and directs the light source toward surfaces or objects by means of physical or optical elements. It is designed essentially to conceal the light source or glare by means of rings, baffles, or lens. While these devices tend to reduce lamp output, other components such as spectral high-finish reflectors can concentrate and direct the light source and consequently improve its efficiency. Fixtures can be surface mounted, recessed, or suspended from a ceiling. They can be monopoint or attached flexibly to a linear, energized channel called a light track.

There are innumerable types of lighting fixtures. Their design and manufacture constitute a major industry. They serve every conceivable light source and purpose. They are available in every possible style, from a period chandelier to a contemporary, small-aperture recessed high hat, to a theatrical spot or drama light clipped to a suspended light track, complete with barn door and color filter attachments. The term "application," mentioned earlier under "Light Sources," embraces this multitude of designs and should also be considered in relation to architectural and interior design opportunities. Not all lighting fixtures that look and function alike perform alike. Variations in efficiency result from the manufacturer's quality control and the selection of appropriate reflective materials. Standards of workmanship, as well as a mastery of the photometric characteristics of light emission, contribute to effective lighting. The same fixture type, applied to the same light source, can have a cost ranging from one to ten, according to each manufacturer's precision of design, specification of materials, quality of workmanship, and marketing appeal.

The November 1993 issue of *Visual Merchandising and Store Design* (VM & SD) magazine contains a special section titled "The Source for Lighting." It is an up-to-date directory of lighting manufacturers and their products, listing and illustrating many of the fixtures and applications described in this chapter. It supplements the general theoretical data presented here, and clearly indicates the incredible varieties of lighting fixture designs that have revolutionized and transformed lighting techniques in the store during the past 10 years.

CEILING BRIGHTNESS AND HEIGHT

The smaller the fixture's aperture, the stronger the brightness, if unshielded, and the darker the ceiling appears in contrast. This has a direct effect upon the ambient quality of the space. Even if adequate intensity of light is projected onto the working plane, where most of the merchandise is presented, the overall quality of the space will appear dark and unpleasant. This can be minimized by washing the ceiling with indirect light, produced by light coves, reflectors mounted on selling fixtures above normal eye level, or suspended luminaires. These elements contribute to what is known as the up-component of light. The dark ceiling effect is also in contrast to exterior, natural brightness and can produce a negative, blinding reaction for customers when they first enter the store.

Ceiling height determines the spacing of lighting fixtures. A light beam spreads according to its distance from the source, widening with increasing distance. Accordingly, lower ceilings require closer fixture spacing. This principle should be evaluated by the designer. Lower ceilings provide an intimate, more human scale and direct attention to the merchandise presentations, particularly at perimeter partitions. However, they require additional fixtures and light sources, which generate heat and which consequently required additional air-conditioning provisions, thereby compounding energy requirements. The effects of this on total store wattage, air cooling tonnage, and total project costs can be explosive.

WALL WASHES

Bathing full-height partitions with light is another method of providing an ambient light level. It is similar to other elements of up-component lighting. It creates the illusion of a brighter interior without increasing intensity or foot-candle level. It can be achieved by valances that conceal indirect light sources, by troffers or coves that throw light down from the ceiling, or by fixtures provided with special optical lenses or reflective surfaces that are designed to wash the wall with light.

MERCHANDISE LIGHTING

Selecting appropriate light sources and their most effective placement related to merchandise is complex. Each broad category of merchandise requires a lighting technique that accents and dramatizes its quality. Hanging garments require relatively continuous light sources located so that they will illuminate the front of the garments and their sleeves, not their shoulders, to assure that customers' shadows do not interfere with the presentation, and to eliminate the possibility of glare in their eyes. Glassware, china, and gifts are most dramatically defined by a combination of incandescent and fluorescent lighting fixtures. With glassware and crystal, incandescent light projected down toward the center of their concave forms will cause brilliant sparkle and highlighting. Additional up-lighting from bases or shelving accents the beauty of their presentation. Merchandise on multiple shelving can be lighted by special reflectors placed under the shelves' front edge. Opaque glass shelves can be formed to allow up-lighting as well. Shelf lighting is complicated, if its flexibility is demanded, requiring costly and intricate interconnections to vertical electric supply conduits. Fitting room lighting should be similar to that used on the selling floor, modified by the requirements of flattering the customer and of avoiding vertical light projections that produce unnatural shadows. Innumerable lighting techniques, fixtures, and devices have been invented for imaginative displays and visual presentations in order to furnish theatrical contrasts of intensity.

PRINCIPLES OF DRAMATICS

The store-as-theater concept was born during the early 1970s. As described in Chapter 3, under "Lighting Design," several forces emerged simultaneously. State regulations to conserve the use of energy during a worldwide

Wall Wash Lighting Techniques
I. Magnin, South Coast Plaza, Costa Mesa, CA
Store Design: Walker Group
Photograph: Norman McGrath

shortage of oil and to limit wattage for every building type restricted stores to a total cap of about 3 watts per square foot. This practically eliminated the incandescent light as a source for general illumination. It forced store designers, however, to search for new ways in which to use the fluorescent lamp and to integrate it into architectonic design forms in the ceiling instead of by the repetitive, overpowering patterns found in commercial, large-scale fixtures. This search was aided by new technological breakthroughs, such as the incandescent light track, compact fluorescents, and low-voltage incandescent lamps. The notion gradually emerged that uniform lighting was no longer a valid goal. Variations of light intensity to reflect different functions and tasks were understood to create an entirely new store look, with dramatic variations of effect. Aisles did not demand high levels of light. The fluorescent lamp could produce more than adequate illumination for the customers' passages: Dropped ceilings, coves, troffers, and similar elements would articulate the ceiling and define zones of circulation. The less efficient incandescent accent light, used in the front of the selling department, would create a dramatic contrast. The combined average of watts per square foot would allow the engineering of the entire store to conform to the stipulated limits. The principles of contrast, modulation of light and shadows—chiaroscuro—gave new insight into the dramatic possibilities of space design in its fullest sense. They permitted the variation of ceiling heights consistent with different lighting criteria, the imaginative use of indirect light coves, troffers, vaults, domes, soffits, trellises, beams, and any other ceiling element that would contribute to dramatic space design, to different lighting schemes engineered to the specific identity of each department, and to the pluralistic expressions that made the entire store theatrically exciting.

NATURAL VERSUS ARTIFICIAL LIGHT

One would have thought that energy restrictions, together with the relatively high operating cost of electric current consumption, would influence store owners and designers to reintroduce the use of daylight into retail buildings. Certainly fenestration would add a new element of architectural interest to the store-warehouse box. But there are multiple disadvantages. Controlled artificial light, given the sophistication and excitement of so-called enlightened illumination design, cannot be matched by the variations and uncertainties of natural light. Changes of weather, early twilight during the winter months, glare, the difficulty of penetrating into the inner space zones of the large store, the problem of silhouetting merchandise by back lighting from windows, loss of heat, maintenance, repairs, and security—all of these conditions dominate. Even the occasional use of clerestories or skylights increases the problem of light control. The technique of providing the selling surface directly under a skylight, for example, with effective light during nighttime hours (when the store is most active), has remained an unsolved design challenge.

CAPITAL INVESTMENT VERSUS OPERATING EXPENSES

With lighting, more than any other element of the store's interior, comparing the initial cost with operating expenses is of crucial importance. High operating expenses can impugn all of the design and performance criteria initially accepted. Capital investments can be hypothecated or mortgaged over the anticipated life use of a facility. Expenses, on the contrary, are ongoing and have a direct annual effect on profit or loss. The selection of light sources and fixture quality must therefore be carefully evaluated with regard to esthetics, function, maintenance factors, initial cost and operating expenses. A balanced evaluation must be reflected in the project's original budget, in a comprehensively understood agreement between client and store planner/designer.

13	# Graphics

Graphics, in relation to store design, has two purposes: to make the identity of the client so clear that it becomes the yardstick against which its products, behavior, and actions are measured; and to instruct, lead, and help customers make their purchases. Everything that an organization does must be an affirmation of its identity. That identity must be visible, tangible, and ubiquitous. The products that the client sells must project its standards and values. The store must be a physical manifestation of its identity. Its communications materials, from advertising to catalogues, from its name to its logo, from its informational signage to its point-of-purchase pricing, sizing, and description of merchandise contents, from its packaging to the markings on its delivery trucks, must have a consistent quality and character that accurately and honestly reflect the entire organization and its aims. All of these are palpable, they are visible, they are designed. Their design is a significant part of the store's image and personality; their visual style affects its position in the market.

Identity is expressed in the names, symbols, logos, colours and rites of passage which the organization uses to distinguish itself. . . . At one level, these serve the same purpose as religious symbolism, chivalric heraldry or national flags and

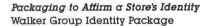

Packaging to Affirm a Store's Identity
Walker Group Identity Package

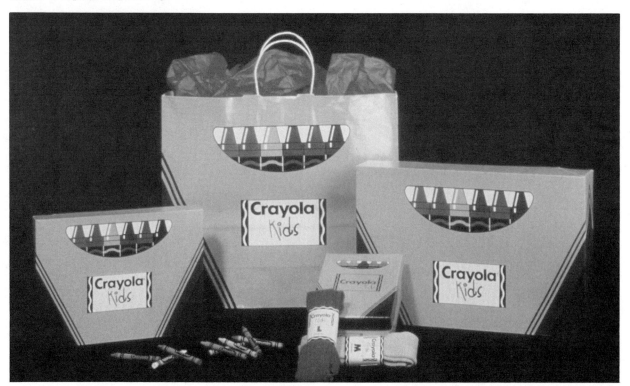

symbols: They encapsulate and make vivid a collective sense of belonging and purpose. At another level, they represent consistent standards of quality and therefore encourage consumer loyalty.

We are entering an epoch in which only those corporations making highly competitive products will survive. This means, in the longer term, that products from the major competing companies around the world will become increasingly similar. Inevitably, this means that the whole of the company's personality, its identity, will become the most significant factor in making a choice between one company and its products and another (Olins).

The following subsections describe the application of graphics and signage to the design of stores.

SIGNING OBJECTIVES

In a store, signing has as its objectives the answers to the following questions: What is it? Why should I buy it? How much does it cost? The manner, style, extent, and integrity of the answers contribute to the store's personality. As a general rule, the greater the extent of signing, the less the store's quality,

Bold Signing Identifies a Department
Macy's, King Plaza, Brooklyn, NY
Store Design: Copeland, Novak & Israel
Photograph: Henry S. Fullerton, 3rd

measured on the spectrum of popular or mass to up-scale marketing. In a self-service store operation, without any sales clerks to help customers in evaluating or purchasing, every item must be described with absolute clarity. In a high-fashion operation, the impact and drama of a merchandise presentation will influence the purchase, with sales clerks available to assist customers.

SIGN DESIGN

The name and logo of a dominant exterior store sign are the first welcoming symbol to customers. It might be familiar to them as a result of newspaper, magazine, or television advertising or by direct mail pieces and seasonal catalogues. The scale and style of the logo, however, must work effectively in relation to the architectural design of the shop front or building. The famous Bloomingdale's "B," or the star in the Macy's mark, are examples of appropriate application of a subconsciously accepted symbol. Frequently, however, a logo, familiar to customers over a long period of time, with historic and cultural associations also, may not work in its architectual application. In this event, the designer is responsible for proposing a new format, which, in fact, may bring a new, striking image to the entire store operation; it may communicate the idea that the store is indeed updating and improving its style, contents, and service. The harmonious integration of architectural design and sign lettering is the clear goal. Furthermore, the utilization of the logo for innovative and imaginative packaging becomes an additional asset.

Integration of Architecture and Logotype
Ohrbach's, Woodbridge Mall, Woodbridge, NJ
Architect: Copeland, Novak & Israel

INSTITUTIONAL SIGNS

In the old days of retailing, a customer was greeted by a mission statement, prominently displayed, that presented the philosophy and purpose of the store's founder. It was a grand moralistic and visionary text, embodying principles of enlightened merchandising, social and community responsibility, and great integrity. Couched in florid Victorian prose, it was a sobering welcome, probably as meaningless as the Boy Scout pledge, but imbuing the would-be shopper with an aura of tradition, good purposes, and a feeling that continuity and values were always up front. Alas, that soul-bearing statement has now virtually disappeared (except, of course, in corporate annual reports). Vestiges of it, however, remain, even in supermarkets, where a farewell message might reassure customers even as they are making their way through the checkout. Even clear-cut directions to the various aisles convey some of the old institutional concern for customers' comfort and shopping convenience. Basically, however, it is the overall ambience—the design and merchandising presentations—that convey the message. Design is the message.

DEPARTMENT SIGNS

Identification of the content and location of various departments or lifestyle zones has always been of concern to store management. In the past, as illustrated in Section II, uniform, regimented sign panels were typical. They were ceiling mounted, projected from columns, or attached to prominent unifying elements. They were cut out of wood, etched or silk-screened on glass, and occasionally internally illuminated. Most stores today argue that a well-merchandised and displayed department is self-evident and self-identified. A programmatic overall strategy is necessary to reflect this viewpoint and to develop an overview that expresses a management style while simultaneously making it quick and easy for customers to orient themselves.

CLASSIFICATION AND BRAND NAME SIGNS

Within a department judgments similar to those made with respect to identifying various departments are necessary. In a large department, like men's wear, there are numerous divisions, from furnishings to shirts to clothing to designer shops. Each requires clear identification, which it is not always possible to project by merchandise presentation or displays. Therefore, the imaginative incorporation of brand name signs into interior design elements is important. These names are selling tools, associated with a long history of marketing and advertising, and clearly help a store establish a distinctive difference from the competition. The very fact that they consist of diverse typefaces reinforces the rich plurality of effect but also provides the designer with a challenge to create an organized and imaginative pattern and scheme. The arrangement, articulation, and scale of wall elements, for example, can enhance or limit their application. Unless the coordination of interior design elements with sign requirements is addressed at the outset of the design process, unsatisfactory and chaotic solutions will inevitably occur. The consistency and quality that are so vital in creating an accurate reflection of the store's identity will be lost. This problem is unavoidably magnified by a frequent division of design responsibilities and even of political opposing points of view within a client's management organization. The store planner/designer must be strong and candid in establishing a program that is satisfactory to all parties, and must develop and ultimately monitor it creatively.

POINT-OF-PURCHASE SIGNS

Point-of-purchase signs include a potential hodgepodge of numerous ticketing, pricing, sizing, and promotional information signs placed at the selling fixture. Like brand name signs, if these are forgotten during the design process, their chaotic clutter will conflict with an overall store style and will undoubtedly mitigate and destroy the aim of an organized, total esthetics. Each fixture should incorporate required signing attachments. All of the potential clutter of mismatched sizes, colors, materials, and forms should be avoided by standards set for typeface character and size, for size of the printed sign board, and for unifying color and materials control. Since these signs are placed at the point of purchase, immediately seen and read by customers, their importance to the total design aim cannot be overstated. A whole hierarchy and set of uniformly designed standards should be prepared. Since this represents an activity that is not normally provided either by the store planner/designer or the visual merchandiser, it would make sense to select a graphic design consultant. Such a signage program should be made an extension of customer service, must carry adequate information for value-conscious and hurried customers, and should reflect a client's design standards. It must respond to extremely varied and hurried demands from merchandise buyers. It should also take advantage of new computer technologies.

Blending Design and Identification Elements
Bullock's Northridge, Los Angeles, CA
Store Design: Welton Becket and Associates
Photograph: Retail Reporting Corp.

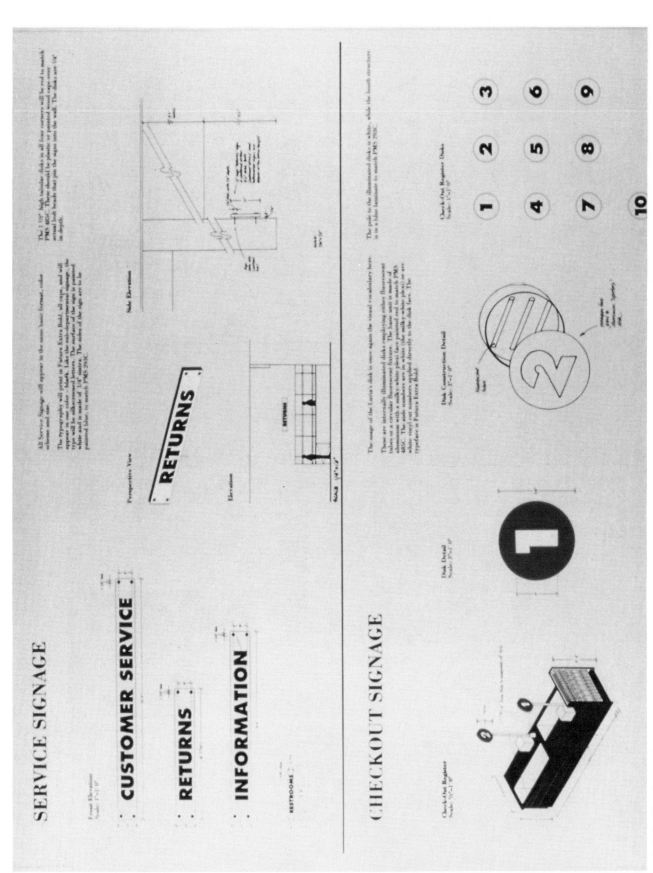

Point of Purchase: Hierarchy of Standards
Studies for Graphics Programs
Store Design: Walker Group/CNI

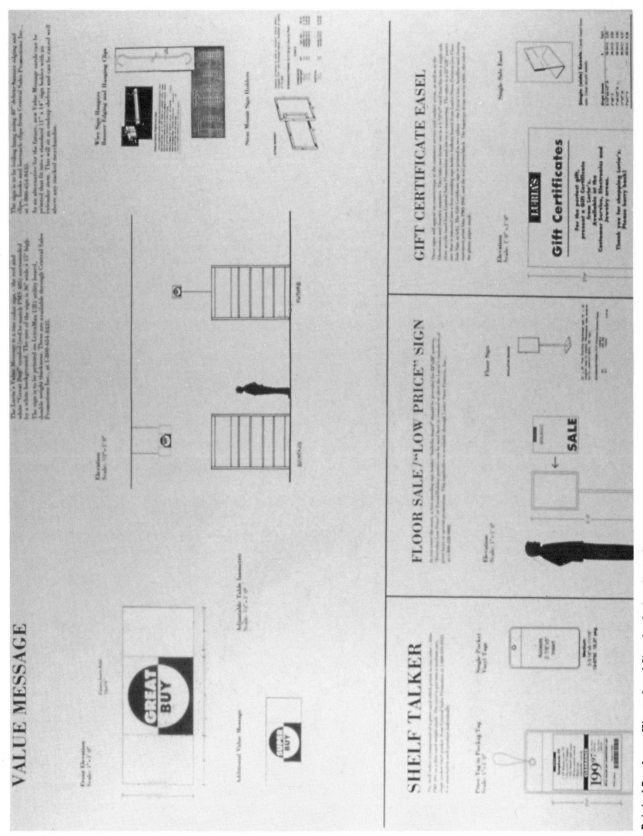

Point of Purchase: Hierarchy of Standards (continued)
Studies for Graphics Programs
Store Design: Walker Group/CNI

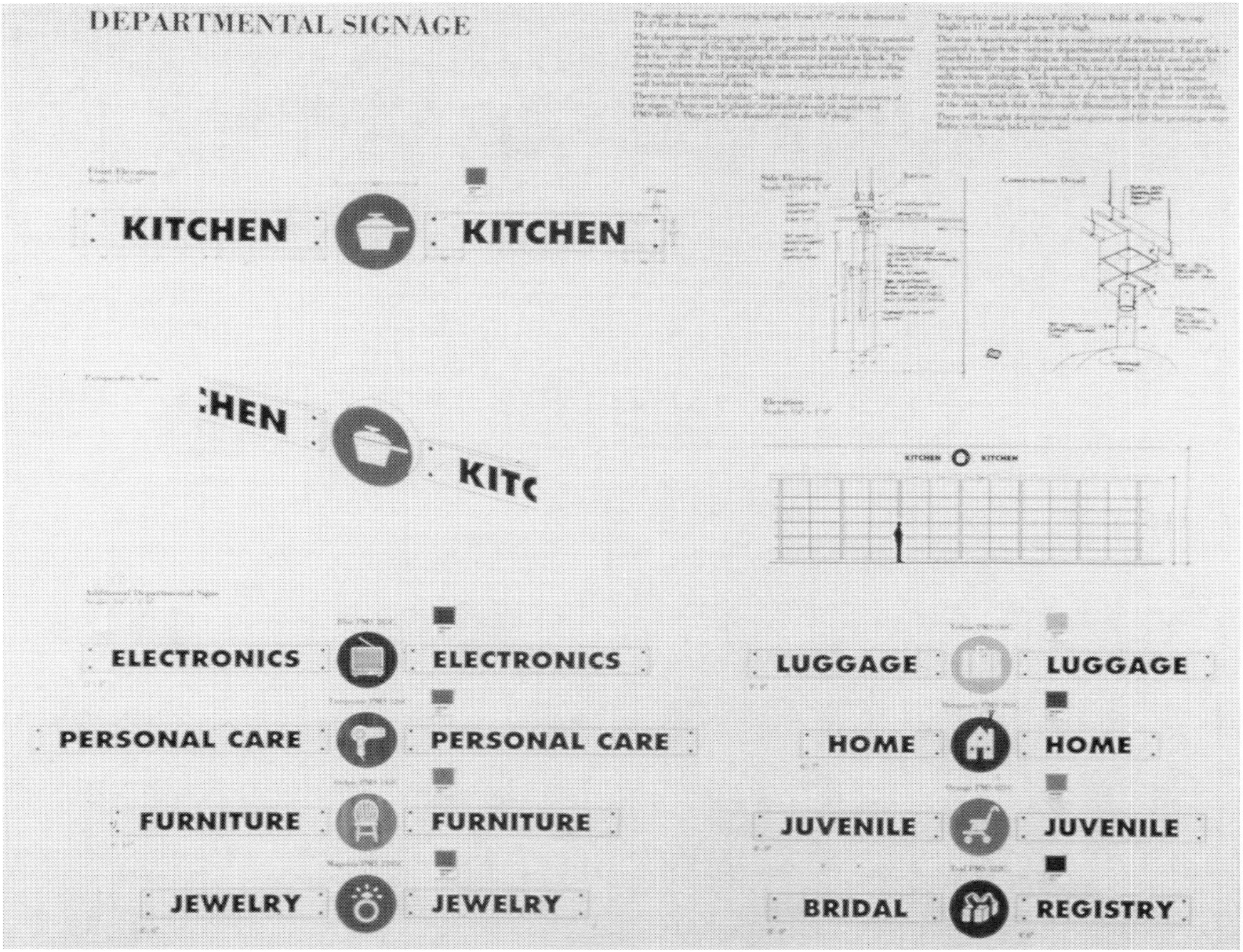
DEPARTMENTAL SIGNAGE
KITCHEN
KITCHEN
HEN
KITC
ELECTRONICS
ELECTRONICS
PERSONAL CARE
PERSONAL CARE
FURNITURE
FURNITURE
JEWELRY
JEWELRY
LUGGAGE
LUGGAGE
HOME
HOME
JUVENILE
JUVENILE
BRIDAL
REGISTRY

Point of Purchase: Hierarchy of Standards (continued)
Studies for Graphics Programs
Store Design: Walker Group/CNI

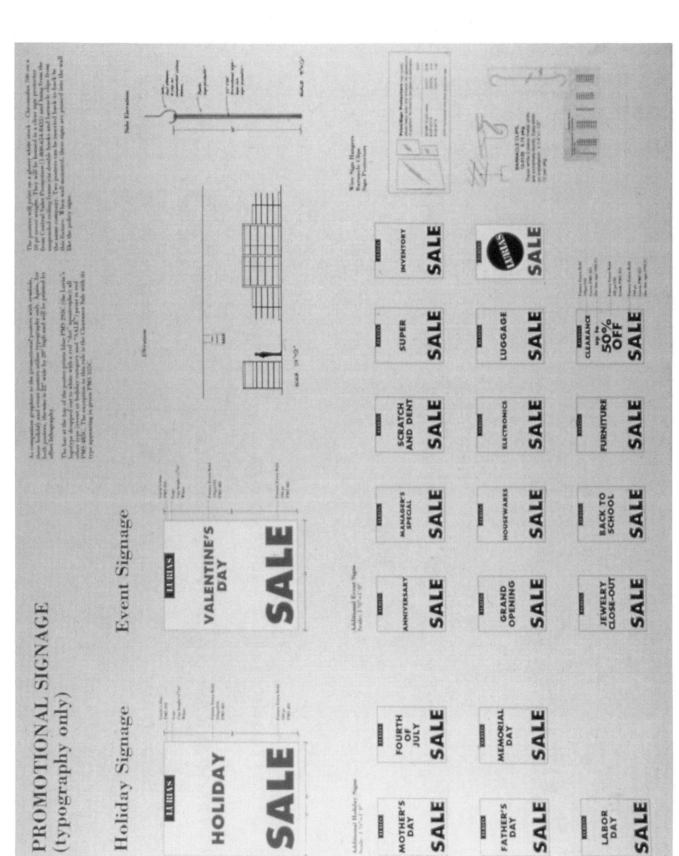

Point of Purchase: Hierarchy of Standards (continued)
Studies for Graphics Programs
Store Design: Walker Group/CNI

200

***Point of Purchase: Hierarchy of Standards** (continued)*
Studies for Graphics Programs
Store Design: Walker Group/CNI

201

GENERAL INFORMATION SIGNS

In addition to department and merchandising signs, there is another category that includes general messages—everything from directions to up-down escalators, to an entrance (or exit), to designated parking lot, to customer service centers and offices, to rest rooms. An inherent part of the store's interior, these functional and utilitarian signs should also conform to overall standards of design, typeface, size, color, and materials, and to the use of clear, legible, graphic symbols. Placement and a hierarchy of sizes contribute to design control and to a consistent visual style.

COMPLIANCE WITH THE AMERICANS WITH DISABILITIES ACT

Mandated provisions of the Americans with Disabilities Act (ADA) have been reviewed under "Regulatory Requirements" in Chapter 8. The ADA includes many recommendations to provide accessible signs, specifically tactile signs for identifying permanent spaces and elements such as elevators, escalators, and rest rooms. Such signs should have a nonglare finish, with the text contrasting with the background. All letters must have a designated width-to-height ratio. Letter heights are specified for overhead and tactile signs. Tactile signs must include both raised letters and Grade 11 Braille. International symbols for accessibility, parking signs, and emergency-rescue areas for disabled persons must comply with details of size, location, and illumination.

American National Standards Institute (ANSI) codes currently are being revised to include or exceed ADA standards. Once they are adopted as standards by the local, state, and federal governments, they will govern every new and renovated facility.

SIGN PLACEMENT AND SIZE

The location and size of signs are dependent upon design characteristics. Department identification signs should be placed at the front of the department, at a height that makes it visible from a considerable distance. Accordingly, the letters should be large. The exact size is not only a question of legibility, however, but of design standards and objectives, consistent with all of the other elements of the store's interior: Is the image bold, commercial, promotional, arty, classic, discrete, or understated? Answers to these questions are infinite and can be resolved only by intelligent and imaginative graphics design. Classification and brand name signs are generally placed at perimeters, partitions, valances, curtain walls, or paneling. Since they are read at closer distances within the department, the size of the lettering can be reduced, the degree similarly dependent upon the quality standards. A major design and identification decision is necessary to determine whether uniform type size and material of the letters for all brands should be established or whether each vendor might retain its own unique and varied logo. As with color, there are no rules; only indications, directions, traditions, and reactions to cultural and cyclical standards (*see color insert*).

Signage: Understated, Classic Fashion Image
Bloomingdale's, Boca Raton, FL
Store Design: Walker Group/CNI

SIGNAGE SYSTEMS

Should there be a system of signage in the store? This question can be answered by an illustration of two contrasting approaches. The first would clearly establish a unifying technique, applying an overall controlling standard of typeface, size, material, placement, and so forth, for every department, or section of the store. This type of approach tangibly reflects a corporate identity, similar not only in every department, but also in every store that is built. It imposes on the customer a subliminal response to order, organization, and purpose. The second would absolutely deny a unifying systemic approach: It would apply a discrete graphics design for each department to reflect a separate, varied merchandise content and life-style. The nature of each department would inspire a graphics design that was immediately, strikingly appropriate and expressive. The first approach provides harmonious control but also uninspired dullness; the second, while exciting and pluralistic, projects the disorder of a flea market. Obviously, there are endless gradations of approach within these polar opposites. As in every component of the store's interior, the store planner/designer must test the alternatives in a creative way in order to resolve the essential criteria of continuity and variety. There are no pat solutions. This is what makes store design a challenging and constantly changing field.

Vehicle Markings

PACKAGING

Solutions to the interior signing program should also be integrated into the store's packaging. Everything from shopping bags, to labels, to boxes, to paper should incorporate the name, logo, color scheme, and design thrust. Surveys have revealed that there is incredible advertising value in a shopping bag that is seen by thousands of people every day. The same advertisements are flaunted daily by a store's vehicles, boldly showing its colors, graphics, and image.

TECHNOLOGICAL DEVELOPMENTS

Signage and graphics make up an industry that has been at the cutting edge of new technologies. It has developed signing ideas and opportunities of amazing variety, all of which are designed to communicate identity and data with novelty, imagination, and excitement. A summary of some of the new notions and devices indicates the mind-boggling range of possibilities:

Vertically rotating triangular vanes showing three images
Computer program-controlled carving of 3-D signs
Full-matrix electronic display with remote control broadcasting
Modulated design of low-wattage lamps for electronic images
Video monitors that integrate computer animation for multimedia
    presentations
Optical fiber multicolor illumination device

Animated fiber optic signage
Integrated fiber optics and inflatable media
Reproduction and blow-up screen-printing techniques
Moving image lightbox
Flexible neon rope light
Neon-programmed animation system
Multi-neon-color changing system
Color-size identification attachments to hanger tops

All of these are available to implement, animate, and brighten the signage messages in a store. Imaginatively and creatively applied, the designer now has new vocabularies and dimensions

Visual Merchandising

Display derives from the French word *deployer*, meaning "to unfold," which refers undoubtedly to the folding and unfolding of fabrics and apparel presented on a table surface. Chapters 3 and 4 have described the birth of the visual merchandising profession and its revolutionary influence on store design. This chapter describes its elements and objectives.

Visual merchandising is the presentation of merchandise at its best; color coordinated, accessorized, and self-explanatory. Display is the pizzazz—the theater, the sparkle and shine that surrounds a presentation of merchandise and makes the shopper stop, look and buy what has been assembled with care and offered with flair.

If ever something was needed to distinguish one store from another, to make one specialty shop seem more special, more unique, more tuned into what the market wants . . . that something is visual merchandising and display.

Merchandise presentation is set on a stage or platform or on a rug. The mood is established, the customer is immediately involved with the merchandise . . . wherever the customer goes, there is merchandise on display: on counters, on ledges, on and off columns, or back walls, over hang rods, hanging down from the ceiling, spread out on the floor.

Graphic presentation of merchandise takes the place of signs and printed or spoken explanations. The merchandise presentation has become more involved, more exciting, more challenging and more stimulating. Display and fashion are so closely intertwined that the health of one depends on the well-being of the other (Pegler).

STORE EXTERIOR

The window trimmer was the original displayer. Today, the design of shop fronts, freestanding or shopping center anchor store buildings, incorporates the display window into its architecture. The various window types summarized below must take into account the size, scale, and frontage of a building, as well as the merchandising mix and philosophy of presentation. Like the architecture itself, the style, composition, and presentation of merchandise in the window are encapsulated images of the store's personality: They can welcome shoppers and draw them in or discourage entry; they can theatrically accentuate a single fashion mannequin and proclaim its up-scale high-fashion identity; or they can pile together clearly marked and priced assortment samples of every merchandise item in the store. Each display technique focuses on potential buyers, their position in the market, their lifestyle, and their purchasing power. Just as eyes are windows to the soul, then the windows of a store are the store. In addition, the windows should be designed to accommodate the merchandise—jewelry, shoes, ladies' sportswear, housewares, electronics, furniture. Each type of merchandise requires appropriate vertical position relative to eye level, size, depth, and lighting techniques.

Windows are the Store
Bally of Switzerland, Atlanta, GA
Store Design:
HTI/Space Design International

Windows are the Store
**La Boutique Van Cleef & Arpels,
Honolulu, HI**
Store Design:
J.T. Nakaoka Associates Architects
Photograph: David Franzen

CLOSED-BACK WINDOWS

Enclosed windows offer the greatest dramatic opportunities for display. They are miniature stages. They permit dramatic contrasts of lighting and complete control of the presentation subject. They require the time and money of relatively elaborate props and of imaginative skills of the display artist. The annual costs of design, service, and maintenance become major budget items. While the investment is easily justified on a vital, busy street, where competitive positioning and the showcasing of a flagship store's prestige are important factors, it is not considered feasible or viable in most shopping centers, where shoppers go directly from their automobiles to a store. Occasionally, however, the mall entrance of an anchor store will feature the dramatic, enclosed display window. By contrast, individual shops fronting the mall can make a dramatic statement effectively with this display treatment and present a special, distinguished image. The servicing cost factor is, of course, still present.

OPEN-BACK WINDOWS

With the open-back window (also known as the visual or see-through window), the entire store is the display. The panorama of various departments and the excitement of hordes of shoppers seen at a glance contribute to vi-

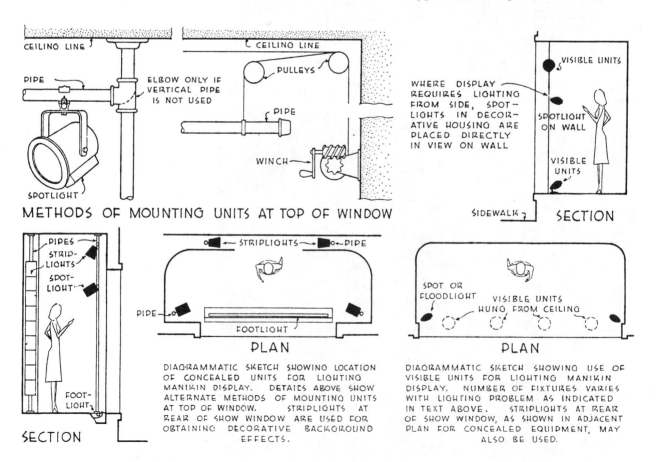

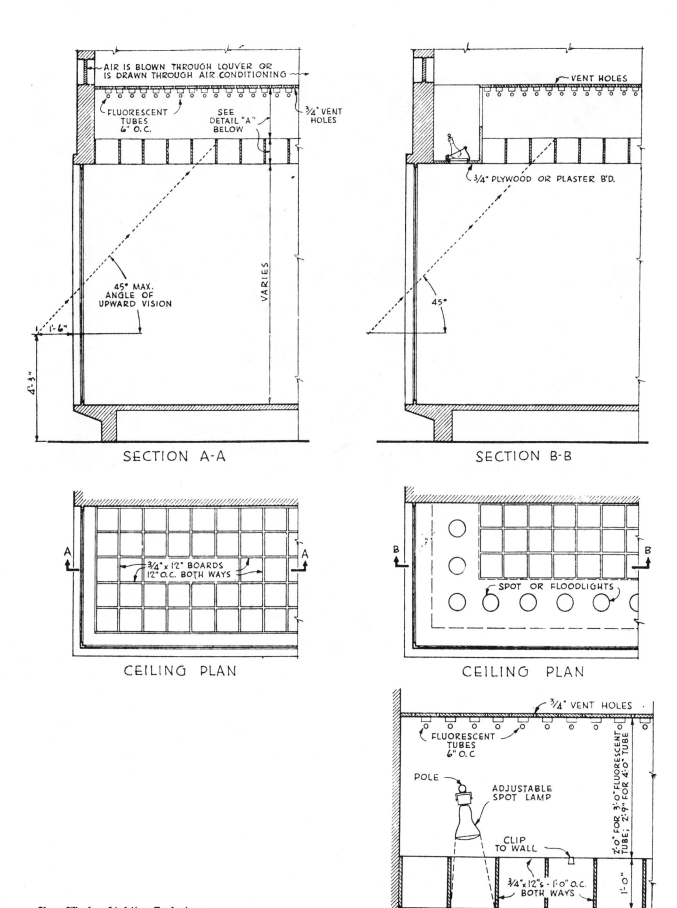

AIR IS BLOWN THROUGH LOUVER OR
IS DRAWN THROUGH AIR CONDITIONING

FLUORESCENT
TUBES
6" O.C.

SEE
DETAIL "A"
BELOW

3/4" VENT
HOLES

45° MAX.
ANGLE OF
UPWARD VISION

VARIES

1'-6"

4'-3"

SECTION A-A

VENT HOLES

3/4" PLYWOOD OR PLASTER B'D.

45°

SECTION B-B

3/4" x 12" BOARDS
12" O.C. BOTH WAYS

A   A

CEILING PLAN

B   B

SPOT OR FLOODLIGHTS

CEILING PLAN

3/4" VENT HOLES

FLUORESCENT
TUBES
6" O.C

POLE

ADJUSTABLE
SPOT LAMP

CLIP
TO WALL

3/4" x 12"s - 1'-0" O.C.
BOTH WAYS

2'-0" FOR 3'-0" FLUORESCENT
TUBE; 2'-9" FOR 4'-0" TUBE

1'-0"

DETAIL "A"

Show Window Lighting Techniques
From *Time Saver Standards*, F.W. Dodge Corp: New York, 1946.

The Store as Display with Foreground Features
Winkelman's Tel-12 Mall, Southfield, MI
Store Design: Jon Greenberg & Associates
Photograph: Retail Reporting Corp.

sual impact and identity. The result of this display technique is an overriding need to make the entire store attractive, dramatic, and distinctive. A case could be made, possibly, for the historic influence of this type of window display in triggering all of the revolutionary design trends and concepts that are the subject of this book: Interior store design is revealed; design is at once a competitive tool.

The store as display can also be supplemented and dramatized by the use of mannequins, props, and even selling fixtures that serve as foreground features to the open store. Sometimes screens and panels can create an intermittent background to them, producing in this manner the advantages of both the closed- and open-backed window. There is infinite flexibility with this technique; the extent, position, and style of the background treatment changes with the content of the display. The most critical disadvantage of this technique is the loss of perimeter merchandise space, background treatment, and, concurrently, merchandise capacity; but this is dependent on the lineage of window relative to interior department areas. An evaluation must take into account this kind of loss versus the cost savings of investment for elaborate display elements and of servicing and maintenance. While appropriate dramatic lighting for this type of window display is an inherent part of the interior illumination design, care must be taken that high-contrast, high-intensity spotlight fixtures do not create distracting glare problems for shoppers in the vicinity of the windows.

The Store as Display with Foreground Features
Petite Sophisticates Prototype, Beverly Center, Los Angeles, CA
Store Design: J.T. Nakaoka Associates Architects
Photograph: Paul Bielenberg

SPECIAL WINDOWS

In addition to the two basic types of window displays just described, there are many other special window treatments, limited only by the nature of the merchandise displayed and the creativity of the designer. They range from the shadow box type, to the horizontal strip, to the multistory window wall. They can be flush, recessed, or projecting. They have infinite variations of form, scale, position, depth, continuity, or discontinuity, all of which are expressed according to merchandise size, color, character, plan configuration, style, and possibilities of composition in contrast to opaque architectural materials of the shop front or store building. They might be closed or open backed. They require specific, special attention to dramatic and appropriate lighting design.

STORE INTERIOR

"Wherever the customer goes, there is merchandise on display. . . ." (Pegler)
The following itemization summarizes the visual merchandising possibilities
of some of the major elements of the store interior.

ISLAND DISPLAYS

The tops of island back fixtures, elevated to eye level or above, are natural
stages located in convenient central positions, generally between the primary store entrance and the escalators, thereby guaranteeing exposure to
heavy customer traffic. Also, because of relatively high ceiling dimensions in
the store's center, there are unrestricted opportunities for attenuated and
bold presentations. These might take the form of semipermanent props, such
as overscaled bowls of floral arrangements (real or artificial), or of groups of
full-height mannequins, dressed and accessorized to promote the current
fashion trend, or of avant-garde sculptures and constructions intermingled
with fashion merchandise statements. These opportunities dominate and
can suggest a fashion mood for the entire store in the most imaginative and

Island Back Fixture Top Display
Macy's, Rego Park, NY
Store Design: Copeland, Novak & Israel
Photograph: Henry S. Fullerton, 3rd

theatrical terms. They have the same importance as exterior window displays and can create an overpowering, enveloping awareness of the store's fashion identity (*see color insert*).

The upper portion of the back fixture is constructed like a shadow box display, of modest height, and internally lighted. Its function is to dramatize and highlight the merchandise being sold within the island itself. Thus, it contrasts and supplements the bold storewide fashion expressions placed on the tops, and provides imaginative, coordinated presentations associated with specific merchandise and its packaging (e.g., in a cosmetics department). It also reinforces the presentation techniques of the island showcases. At normal eye level, it is frequently seen with identifying brand name signage.

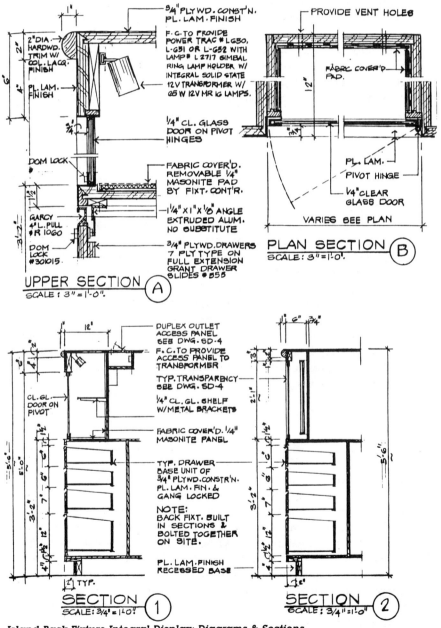

Island Back Fixture Integral Display: Diagrams & Sections
From de Chiara et al., *Time-Saver Standards for Interior Design and Space Planning*, McGraw-Hill, Inc.: New York, 1991. Reprinted with permission from the publisher.

SHOWCASES AND COUNTERS

As described in Chapter 11, there are various types of showcases—some full glass, some half glass, some shallow glass. The full-glass configuration generally allows for a combination of inventory arrangements, together with suggested item presentations. The half-glass configuration is similar but scaled down to display smaller items. The shallow-glass configuration is more specifically designed for precious items, like jewelry and perfume; although a large assortment can be presented, it is generally artistically arranged with forms and carefully composed buildups or inserts that isolate and glamorize the units—often works of museum-quality art in themselves.

The corners of showcases and counter islands often present special display opportunities in contrast to the selling lines. These might be the equivalent of shadow box displays, towerlike vitrines, or multiheight pedestals that expose selected merchandise for customer handling and appraisal. The solid, enclosed counter generally provides a surface for customer-salesperson interaction, as well as a place for varied point-of-purchase presentations.

DISPLAY PLATFORMS

Elevated platforms, normally placed strategically at the front of departments or against end-wall partitions separating departments, provide mannequin display opportunities. They vary in height from a few inches to perhaps 18 inches. They should be large enough to provide compositions of from two to three mannequins plus accessories and props. They should be designed to be seen clearly in contrast to adjacent floor surfaces in order to prevent customers from tripping or smashing into them. Their tops should be interchangeable to allow for diverse fashion statements and also to allow for fastening and stabilizing the mannequins and props. Since these features are exposed to customers (and children), secure measures must be taken to avoid falling mannequins or material, with consequent frustrating and costly damage liability lawsuits.

ENCLOSED DISPLAYS

Glass-enclosed displays are show windows in the store's interior. These are of major importance and are generally placed at the entrance to a fashion world, for example, a men's department. They are keynote statements, combining fashion ideas and a mood, that present the quality and market position of that department. Part of a strong architectural design, with intense, dramatic contrasts of light, made more special by the enclosing and reflective properties of glass, these interior windows contribute enormously to the excitement and sense of theater of the store. Like exterior show windows, they are relatively expensive to furnish and maintain, and so are provided only at key, strategic plan locations.

The application of see-through glass screens to partially enclose a free-standing, centrally located department or to form a stylized, symbolic

Glass-Enclosed Display in a Store Interior
Macy's, Dallas, TX
Store Design: Copeland, Novak & Israel

Glass-Enclosed Display in a Store Interior
Marshall Field's, San Antonio, TX
Store Design: Walker Group/CNI

Glass Screens: A Stylized Facade
I. Magnin, South Coast Plaza, Costa Mesa, CA
Store Design: Walker Group

Glass Screens: A Stylized Facade
Bloomingdale's: 4th Floor, New York, NY
Store Design: HTI/Space Design International
Photograph: John Wadsworth

façade to major departments fronting the traffic aisles creates other display opportunities and challenges. As with open-back windows, the merchandise and the ambience of the entire department become the display. However, highlighting this with an occasional mannequin or with accessories and props adds to the punch and envelops the customer in a continuously enfolding sequence of exciting fashion statements.

PERIMETERS

The background of a department, the perimeter, which combines merchandise, presentations, interior design elements and graphics, is important for drawing and leading customers to the rear. Studies have shown that this sector of a department gets minimum traffic and exposure, in inverse proportion to the density of fixturization and depth of the department. Therefore, every visual presentation technique helps increase the productivity of this space, where opportunities for showing large quantities and many classifications of merchandise exist by virture of the perimeter height. There are limitless design and visual presentation variations: single hanging, with shelves or ledges above for vignette merchandise displays, double or even triple hanging right up to the ceiling; compositions of shoulder hanging and face-outs; combinations of hanging, face-outs, shelving, and binning; props, grids, neon sculpture, panel systems, mannequins, or bust forms. Color, materials, forms, graphics, contrasting light intensities all contribute to effective and dramatic utilization of the relatively high wall surfaces.

COLUMNS

There has always been considerable controversy surrounding the use of columns for merchandise presentation or display. One school of thought proclaims the necessity of keeping columns clear, minimizing their visual importance, allowing a view of the store interior to flow without interruption. The other sees the vertical structure of the column as a bonus, an opportunity to pile up merchandise and to exploit the height advantage for displays. As is the case of most contrasting viewpoints, a middle ground frequently is reached. An occasional column, properly located at the entrance to a department, can be the structural matrix for a marvelous, full-height display that literally forces customers to come up for a closer view. Too much fixturization and merchandise hanging from the columns block things up physically and visually. Certainly, the column is an effective structure for hanging Christmas or seasonal decorations, and it has been used imaginatively and dramatically in this way since the birth of retailing. The column also can be creatively used for banners, plaques, streamers, and so on, related to special storewide events and promotions.

END PANELS

Partitions separating departments and projecting forward to major traffic aisles provide an important background for display application. Because of

The Column as Matrix for Display
Hudson's, Lakeside Mall, Detroit, MI
Store Design:
Morganelli-Heumann & Associates
Photograph: Retail Reporting Corp.

the depth of merchandise and of its fixtures, an end panel to these partitions is not less than 5 feet wide. It offers, therefore, dramatic opportunities for both interior design and display statements. Frequently, the store planner/designer takes these surfaces as repetitive architectural elements and, by their forms, rhythms, and interest of texture and materials, creates a strong connecting structure in order to bind together the diverse statements of the individual departments. However, the value of these surfaces as background for mannequin platforms, furniture, and visual presentation groupings should not be overlooked. The synthesis of strong architectural rhythms and of theatrically lighted displays provides one of the most dramatic opportunities for outstanding design in the store.

End Wall Display Opportunity
Sak's 5th Avenue, Pittsburgh, PA
Store Design: Copeland, Novak & Israel

POINT OF PURCHASE (POP)

The term "point of purchase" covers numerous devices that present merchandise to the customer directly, at arm's length, at the point of purchase. It
includes everything from a glove form on a countertop, to a holder for ear-
rings, to a hat form, to rotating carousels displaying necklaces, to ladies' ho-
siery in egg-shaped containers. It reflects the myriad varieties of merchandise in the store. It is frequently designed, manufactured, and distributed
without charge by the vendor of a product, and has been accurately and
expressly designed to present the merchandise, often in its package, in the
most efficient way, based on research and development over a long period
of marketing history and experience. Although it is an efficient device for
selling an item, the combination literally of thousands of different types of
items in the store leads to uncontrollable clutter and discontinuity. It is one of
the many responsibilities of the visual merchandiser to control this potential
mess, to limit its free use, and to consolidate the different designs and presentation techniques into one style and one coordinated system. This takes
discipline and constant editing. Each buyer is anxious to get the maximum
quantity of sales items on display at every turn; if the buyer is allowed, he or
she would bury showcases and self-selection fixtures under a forest of unre-
lated sales presentation devices. Store design, in its effort to reflect an orga-

nized identity of the entire store, must organize these POPs, select appropriate locations for them, and refuse their wildcat growth. The "mom and pop operation," the "schlock" store, which welcome "free" and limitless installations, attest to what can happen if design is submerged under commercial exploitation.

ELECTRONICS AND ANIMATED LIGHT

Technological developments have been reviewed in Chapter 13. Many of these have profoundly influenced the possibilities of transmitting animated messages through display. An entire universe of possibilities has been revealed just in electronics and programmed animation systems. Reference has been made to video and the video wall, which integrates computer animation for multimedia presentations. This is an incredible selling instrument! It offers a dramatic way in which to project fashion stories, sight, and sound from the studio into the epicenter of selling. Coordinated with fashion advertising on the printed page, as well as on television, the impact in the store of all of the arts of cinematography and fashion design is enormous. The imaginative and clever integration of multiple television monitors into the architecture, store design, and merchandise presentation elements of the store adds a new dimension to store design.

Similar opportunities open up for dramatically coordinating into the elements of a store's interior design all of the other electronic and animated

Neon Light Sculpture
I. Magnin, San Francisco, CA
Store Design: Walker Group

light media briefly catalogued in "Graphics" by supplementing conventional but static display compositions with computer-animated images and sound; with modulated, changing images of incandescent lamps; with programmed color changes of neon light sculptures; with reproductions and photo blowups, with constantly changing, abstract, lighted multicolor, fiber optic images. The store now can be the center for overpowering, beautiful, timely, sales effective expressions of "total art."

MANNEQUINS AND DIMENSIONAL FORMS

The history of mannequin design is a wonderful footnote to the development of visual presentation in the store. (See the bibliography.) From wax to papier-mâche to plastics, the technological improvements in fabrication, stability, style, and accuracy of reproducing the human figure have kept pace with the consumer revolution, the popularization of fashion, and the complexity of store design. The mannequin is a universal accessory to lifelike projection of fashion styles; yet, inevitably, debates recur about its value in the store. It is a cyclic debate—the sensual reproduction of human form in realistic postures versus abstract three-dimensional forms that employ the avant-garde attributes of contemporary structures and sculptures. Like so many of these in-house disputes, there are advantages to both techniques. Both forms can be intelligently and dramatically intermixed in the store to tell the "story" properly.

SELLING FIXTURES

In Chapter 11, the structure, design, and varieties of selling fixtures were outlined. It is the visual merchandisers who must breathe life through the art of selling into these fixtures. It is they who must direct the assortment and placement of the merchandise: the composition of colors; the coordination of apparel tops and bottoms; the method of folding, binning, or hanging; the accessorizing to suggest various life-styles; and the highlighting at the fixtures with vignettes, dimensional forms, and props. They must help the merchant animate the selling fixture to induce sales. They must create compelling sales stories—whether it is fashion apparel for women, men or children; coordinated china, glassware, and silver in irresistibly stunning table settings; or the bed, dressed to suggest erotic fantasies. They must be culturally aware of all of the styles of town, country, suburbs, of important events on stage, concert halls, or in museums, of politics, of prominent personalities, of new book releases, of world affairs, which capture the endlessly changing fashion spirit of the moment and which make the structurally static selling fixture into an active, truly silent salesperson.

FURNITURE AND PROPS

Decorative furnishings are valuable supplements to visual presentation. A stagelike setting of mannequins, with groupings of chairs, tables, lamps, and

Dressing the Self-Selection Fixture
Rich's, Lenox Square, Atlanta, GA
Store Design: Walker Group

Dressing the Self-Selection Fixture
Sak's 5th Avenue, Pittsburgh, PA
Store Design: Copeland, Novak & Israel

French paintings, can immediately dramatize a fashion statement. An occasional sales table, whether it be in modern, Biedermeier, or Chippendale style, can highlight a merchandise promotion or special item. The contrast of furniture and fixtures softens the hard-edged and contemporary feel of the store interior and also, by association, conveys the warmth and beauty of customers' residences (*see color insert*). The use of armoires, multidrawer chests, or hutches with variegated bins gives surprising and unlimited opportunities for display. The references of furniture to historic traditions or to expressions of various civilizations can immediately project a mood and a fashion style. All of these make a distinctive statement and reinforce the quality of a store's personality.

SYNTHESIS

As is apparent from the brief summary in this chapter of the role of visual merchandising, the connection between its discipline and that of the store planner/designer is vital. It is more than a connection; it is a partnership. Both are concerned with the successful creation of a store with competitive force and special identity; each, however, approaches that task from a different perspective. The visual merchandisers work up to animate and dramatize the merchandise; they appeal directly to the customer; their point of departure is the merchandise, its sales appeal, its identity, its dynamic and ever-changing expression of style and store character. The store planner/ designers are fundamentally concerned with the complex planning and design of the store's physical structure; they work down from the matrix and container of the merchandise, striving to achieve a memorable total store image. Their interdependence is total.

Examples should illustrate this synthesis. During the store planning process, it is vital that both partners share decisions that concern location, structure, and character of major display elements—all of those described in this chapter. These decisions affect many architectural and mechanical equipment elements. The location and design of special display lighting obviously follow. The degree of intensity and contrast with the general ambient light level affects total wattage and, ultimately, energy requirements. During the design development stage, with reference to treatments of perimeter partitions, a shared point of view is absolutely necessary to establish criteria for showing merchandise inventory, its display, and accessorizing, the signing serving it, and consequent lighting techniques. These criteria take into account size and placement of signs, height of partitions, and the height and modeling of ceiling planes. The location and treatment of display platforms adjacent to main traffic aisles affect flooring materials. The placement of full-height glass screens, to symbolize a shop front for a selling deparment, affects not only lighting patterns but the location of air conditioning diffusers and sprinkler heads. If the visual merchandisers, who are familiar with a store's advertising graphics and colors, recommend a special color, or even a color scheme, to project a store's identity, then the store planner/designers must intelligently apply it to those elements of the interior that can effectively embody it.

The visual merchandiser is the artistic soul of the store. The store planner/ designer is the director of a comprehensive team of specialists, all of whom are seeking to integrate all of the elements into an outstanding total tectonic store design.

IV PROCESS

15 Anecdotes

It seemed to me, after having analyzed and described the theoretical elements of store planning and design, that a fitting conclusion to the book would be a series of personal reminiscenses. By "Process," then, I mean that I will reveal a different perception of the design evolution. While it is absolutely vital that theory and the elements of design be understood and mastered by a practicing store planner/designer, there is still another obstacle that must be surmounted in order to achieve the creation of a successful store—the interactive relationship of client and consultant, the complex psychology involved in interpreting and realizing often ephemeral wishes and goals. I had often heard my partner, Peter Copeland, say that a good designer must first of all be a good psychiatrist. Understanding the clients' dreams and wishes, often contradicted by the realities of operations, budget commitments, and construction, is fundamental and primary to mutual success. I thought, then, that a series of personal anecdotes—sometimes humorous, ironical and paradoxical; sometimes vicious, rude, and gross—would be an amusing but insightful cap to a serious subject and would give to it a touch of personal history. Sometimes these stories indeed contradict the position of theoretical concepts. But the mix—the combination of theory and personal experience—would give this book a deeper realism and a quality based on a profoundly complex synthesis of physical building and interior design parts, and of the psychology of people in positions of power—the clients.

The anecdotes that follow are vaguely chronological in their sequence and in this way reflect my development as an artist and a man. As will be apparent, I shall protect the identity of both clients and stores. The incidents, personalities, organizations, and decision makers are real, not fictitious, but I shall describe them only by first names and nominal locations. The diligent reader will undoubtedly recognize them; perhaps they will elicit a chuckle and a fond memory. Hopefully, the presentation of these anecdotes will provide a human counterpoint to the more objective sections of the book but, more important, will illuminate esthetic, moral, business, and psychological judgments, which I shall try to summarize. I have used a first-person, narrative style in order to provide warmth and a more human view into the design process in the client's hallowed inner sanctum.

FIRST BEGINNINGS

One of my first project assignments was the store design of a new suburban postwar branch unit of a large Southern chain that is located in a sleepy backwater city in tidal North Carolina. The owner's son Bill and I were both officers out of the navy, contemporaries in age, and just starting our careers. The responsibility to produce a fine new store, a postwar model in this relatively provincial community, was an intense challenge to both of us. Our common military heritage was a bridge that connected us, despite our totally different backgrounds and that produced instant warmth, respect, and friendship. Bill and I would sit during the evenings at his rolltop desk overlooking the street floor of the hot, old downtown store and debate and search for solutions to literally every component of the proposed new store. Each of us was a novice in our respective fields. The friendship enabled us to debate, formulate, and resolve everything from architectural design, plan adjacencies, lighting, fixtures, color, and display (at that time, visual presentation was unknown). Each of us, in this all-consuming dialectic, was learning our trade. We picked apart every conceivable solution. It was an unexpected and fruitful experience. It provided a solid underpinning to both of our careers. It also, not coincidentally, provided a long-lasting designer-client relationship with many other divisions of the chain and was an important contribution to my firm's growth.

MISTER JACK, I

Mister Jack was the aristocratic scion of one of America's first retailing families. As chairman of a dominant New York department store empire, he ran the business with an iron hand. His word was uncontested law. He was the captain of the ship, dictatorial, without recourse.

Our firm had developed a good, continuing relationship with this client. I was the principal in charge of several units, working very hard with the in-house staff, which in itself was very large, bureaucratic, and hierarchical. My experience as an officer in the U. S. Navy was a good preparation, and I was well indoctrinated to work through a given chain of command. In the course of the relationship, we had developed warm and cooperative working conditions with many fine, hard-pressed professionals and had established numerous concepts, standards, and criteria of design and detailing. One of these stands out in my memory. It was the dictum, nay the absolute taboo, "Never use the color green in any store's interior design." I accepted this direction, perhaps not without question, but as a given inarguable rule: "The Chairman hates green!"

One day, early on in my relationship with this client, I was summoned by the executive secretary to meet with the chairman. I had no idea what the subject of the meeting would be. Mister Jack was ordinarily as inaccessible to hirelings as the Pope himself. Needless to say, I had a few sleepless nights before the meeting. I entered the hallowed executive office, spacious, vaulted, literally unpopulated except for the receptionist-security guard. Finally, I was shown into the chairman's office. It was awesome: large, all paneled, overlooking a landscaped terrace and the entire city of New York. What stopped me cold, however, was the inescapable: the entire chairman's office—his private, personal abode and workplace, reflecting his taste and quality—was decorated entirely in GREEN!

LESSON: Try not to accept directives or opinions at second hand (or determine whether or not the client's spouse had a hand in decorating the office).

MISTER JACK, II

As background to the meeting with the chairman, I should sketch here the personality of Mister Jack as seen in action when he was presented with design proposals. He was absolutely, keenly interested in the style and quality of designs for his stores. I had sat in during several presentations and had watched famous, world-renowned architects and store designers—heroes in the field whom I idolized—bow and succumb to the chairman's reactions and his scathing, pitiless, rabelaisian criticism. As I waited in the anteroom in preparation for our firm's design presentation, I often saw these heroes leave the conference room bowed, bloody, seared, shocked, and beaten.

When I entered Mister Jack's office, I still had not a clue as to the purpose of the meeting. He was benign, fatherly, and gentle. He offered me a chair near his desk, magesterial and yet warm. "Did you fellows design the recently altered Au Printemps in Paris," he asked out of the blue. Not being guilty of this act, I answered honestly, "No, sir." "Good, " he said. "It is terrible. I understand you have been commissioned to do the designs for their rivals in Paris. You should know that they are my good friends and that I recommended your firm for the job." I thanked him in my best, still youthful, professional manner and tried to assure him that we would do a great design job. He answered, "I'm sure you will. Let me tell you one thing only: Stick to your beliefs; do what your training and instincts tell you; do not change your opinion because of a client's pressure."

And this unforgettable, fatherly encouragement came from a chief executive officer who was notorious for destroying architects and designers!

CHARLIE

Another major New York retail empire had just assigned an executive to direct its store's expansion program. It had ambitious plans for building new suburban stores throughout the eastern and central part of the United States. Charlie, the former president of its Midwest operation, as the new head of store design and construction, would be solely responsible for the direction and management of a multimillion dollar venture. He, too, had a notorious reputation. He was an Old-World autocratic type, powerful and ruthless. He was big, craggy, and austere in manner. He was volatile, imperious, or loudly jovial in turns—and unpredictable. He awarded contracts that were in the millions of dollars, and he took childish delight in slashing proposals indiscriminately. A hard-headed retailer and businessman, he was enormously wealthy, and had collected an enviable treasure of many world-famous modern artists.

It was our first interview with Charlie. We had won a commission to design the first major new store to be built under his command. We knew that he wanted the store to be outstanding. Behind his back, his associates taunted us to produce a new Parthenon. We wanted to clarify the process and responsibilities. Since it was our first project with him, we wanted to understand his objectives and methodology, in order to assure both parties that the work would be professional and inspired. We tried to establish esthetics, budgets, operating procedures, time schedules, and responsibilities.

The kick-off meeting was held at our offices. We all trudged into the conference room—an entire team of project planners and designers—together with Charlie's staff. All together there were at least 30 people present. At that time in the development of branch stores, during the planning process, one of the chief stumbling blocks in trying to determine merchandise classification requirements and appropriate selling fixtures was the opinion of each department's store buyer. This process became inordinately long-winded and political. In addition, a buyer was frequently replaced before the store was built. We were just at the point at which most stores were beginning to eliminate the buyer's role and to place the merchandising responsibilities in the hands of senior merchandise executives. With this is mind, I piped up with the following question to Charlie: "What is the role of the buyer?"

Charlie looked at me and then at everyone. He was seated at the head of the table, with his hands clasped upon his middle-age paunch, looking like Buddha. He gradually closed his eyes and went into a meditative trance. He sat that way for at least ten minutes. Everyone thought he had fallen asleep. Finally, he opened his eyes, looked around again, this time with a mischievous and childish glint in his eyes, and said, "Well, you see, fuck the buyers!"

LESSON: Don't ask silly questions.

A PHILADELPHIA STORY, I

Marty and I met in the early 1950s. It was after World War II, and we had both finally found a home in the expanding suburbs of New York. Marty worked at Macy's in the executive training squad and was totally absorbed in, and dedicated to, the challenges of retailing, which then was also expanding into the suburbs. We became friendly neighbors. We commuted together to New York City for several years, zealously sharing the new ideas in retailing and store design. Eventually, he moved up the corporate ladder and took an executive job out of town. We lost touch for a while, although I would hear from time to time about his upwardly mobile wanderings. Then he disappeared.

After many years, I met Marty again. Now he was chairman of the same store empire as Charlie—a plum assignment. We renewed our friendship, although now he was a little remote because of his exalted position. My firm was still actively involved in designing stores for his group. One day, a few weeks before Christmas, he invited me to ride with him in his company's limousine to a branch store in Philadelphia. He had sheaves of plans, which we pored over in the car. The visit was a kind of "Captain's inspection" of the store on Christmas Eve to determine an ultimate program of replanning and rebuilding. (While Charlie's philosophy was, first of all, to control costs, Marty's philosophy was to spend money to make money.)

When we arrived at the Philadelphia branch store, we were met by a large contingent of staff from both corporate and Philadelphia headquarters. An entourage of 25 people followed us as we solemnly inspected all aspects of the store. Finally, we marched up to the store manager's office and seated ourselves around the large conference table. Marty, having closely observed Charlie's psychological treatment of staff and consultants, sat very still, with his eyes closed, in a deep, meditative trance. For ten minutes, there was total silence. Everyone waited for the chairman's views and comments. The tension built and became palpable. Finally, Marty opened his eyes, looked up at the manager, and made his magesterial pronouncement: "This store is a shit house."

To the manager: No comment.

SOUTH AFRICA

It was the first overseas department store project for Copeland, Novak, and Israel (CNI). Peter Copeland, my partner, not only made this a marketing coup but also developed a warm and deep friendship with Norman, the chairman of a dominant chain of stores with headquarters in Johannesburg, South Africa. Norman was young, bright, warm, impulsive, with a cynical but realistic sense of humor. What a wonderful opportunity, we thought. Here was a first foreign job, to be developed in partnership with a client with whom we could comfortably relate and, in addition, enjoy the process.

Our design team, who were all excited but naive and inherently provincial, began dreaming about a new look, a theme based on Picasso's cubism and on native, tribal, cultural icons: wood-carved masks, weaponry, local materials.

During the preliminary design review that was held with the chairman, this concept was sketched out and presented to him. Without hestitation, he vetoed it. "Absolutely not," he said. "We are surrounded every day by these motifs. We are sick and tired of them." What they desperately needed and wanted, and what they had traveled halfway around the world to find was a new, cosmopolitan, urban expression of fashion and service—*new* design directions.

It was our first exposure to the challenges of "the global village." It drove home to us the realization that we had to understand the diversity of regional cultures. More importantly, however, it accentuated the absolute requirement that we steep ourselves in and master all of the elements of that culture—the taboos and the needs of a foreign and very different client. To undertake a major design project without that mastery and understanding could be suicidal.

VIVE LA FRANCE

This was to be our first major store project in Western Europe. A leading department store had made an exhaustive tour of new department stores in America. It was planning its first postwar suburban store. It was convinced that America was the mecca, the scene of the contemporary store, which in technology, esthetics, marketing, and presentation techniques would be the paradigm of all future retailing. In the French manner—intellectual, searching for perfection, struggling with a postwar malaise that contrasted the old grandeur of France as the cultural world ruler with modern France as a second-rate power—we were short listed and ultimately selected, based on several new stores that we had designed for a prominent American retailer.

The directive was simple: "We want our store to look like those." We developed an excellent working relationship with the store's planning and design committee, consisting of a merchant, an architect, and operations officers. We got along well. There were few language barriers, After several months of working together, we became warm friends and had developed a mutual respect. We discussed and debated every issue: building code compliance, adjacencies, plan flow, design, fixturization, lighting, and, especially, color. The issue of color was a special problem. We had many sessions in which we sought to define a color theme and to equate the lighter colors used in American stores in subservience to their merchandise presentation, to the bolder color style of French stores at that time dominated by vigorous purples and oranges.

Finally, we were prepared to present our design to the board of directors. I made a sincere, enthusiastic and (I thought) professional presentation. We had done our homework, and the plans, perspective drawings, and color and materials boards were great. The board room was huge, quite contemporary, overlooking a garden cloister and the massive stage facade of Tony Garnier's opera in Paris. The board was regal, aged, attentive and . . . silent. Finally, a spokesman rose and spoke. He said, "This is all very well, but the design and colors are not for us, the French!"

The preference for a color, of course, is subjective, based on strong personal and national preferences. But how does one satisfy a client that selected you specifically because it wanted you to replicate projects that you had already completed and then chooses to override its own directive? I don't know whether there is any answer to such a dilemma. All of the exposure to, and application of, ancient and modern French art, style, and culture cannot resolve the problem of strong egos still imagining the former glories of France.

Much has been written about a Canadian developer and entrepreneur who acquired several divisions of a dominant American store group. We had been awarded a contract for the planning and design of several stores in their Northwest division. There was national publicity attending the acquisition. I was invited to be present at a meeting of the press in which the magnitude of the proposed store's expansion and upgrading program was to be presented to the local politicians and the public. Later I accompanied the chairman on an inspection tour of the various branch stores involved.

At that time, we were briefed on the chairman's philosophy about store planning. He loved the idea of a large central atrium, the most recent installation of which was to be found in London and which he referred to at every opportunity.

The particular branch store that we visited had just gone through a major renovation. At a cost of several million dollars, two of its three floors had been rebuilt and updated. It was the pride of Bill, the branch store's president, who had directed and supervised the project. One of the major stores originally built as part of an outstanding regional shopping center during the 1950s, it was a classic installation representing the viewpoint of the original corporate owner. Monumental in scale, it was built around a budget-conscious, engineer-oriented plan. It had central escalators, surrounded by a large system of electrical and air conditioning risers, leading up to a central mechanical equipment penthouse located directly overhead. From an engineering aspect, it was an extremely compact system, with an efficient network of risers, ducts, heavy electrical buses, and switch panels, ramifying from the geometric center of the structure. Efficient but totally inflexible, central nervous system of the store surrounded the escalators on both sides as well as overhead.

One of the operative truisms in store alteration work is that the cost of investment for the improvements must be justified by a corresponding increase in dollar sales volume and profit: the awesome ROI, or return on investment, that haunts the life of every executive in the business. Surely Bill at this precise time was trying heroically to increase store sales in an effort to prove the cleverness of his just completed, upgraded project.

So here we were now, parading through the store: the new chairman, Bill, all of the local executive staff, the senior staff from corporate headquarters, consultants, the press, and my project team. The chairman was all smiles, impeccably groomed, charming, nodding his appreciation of the style of the new installation. Quickly he came to the center of the store, the escalators, quite hidden by walls which contain all the massive, mechanical, and electrical systems. He scowled, called Bill to his side, and issued his peremptory command: "This bloody thing must go!"

Bill turned green, then white, sweat glistening on his face. To rip out the very heart of the store, which had just been rebuilt, meant destroying the new work and starting all over again, compounding the costs astronomically. How in the world would he be able to justify the expenses, on top of those just completed?

Ultimately, the alterations were completed, after many studies, modifications, and struggles with cost. The store was, in fact, brilliantly transformed by the new central atrium and became a regional showcase. I cannot, however, provide a report on the ROI!

INEVITABLE CONFLICT

We had developed a special warm relationship with Harry, owner and chairman of an independent group of department stores in the Tennessee Valley. We had enjoyed designing and building several new stores that were highly sophisticated and advanced in their design. This was a client whom everyone in the office responded to. As a result, the work was good, and both parties—client and designer—profited.

That year Harry offered us the commission to design a new unit in a proposed major regional, enclosed mall shopping center. We had completed our contract proposal, and it was now in his hands for signing.

Unexpectedly, we were called into conference by another long-term client. This client, however, operated a major department store group that had numerous divisions, each one of which was prominent in its own region. We had been working with them for many years. They gave us a steady flow of commissions, which represented a large percentage of our fees. In addition, most of their stores were prestigious and offered stimulating challenges to us to produce outstanding designs with international visibility. Inevitably, one of the divisions had committed to building a new unit in the same shopping center as Harry's. The impending conflict was impacted by this client: their offer to us was not only to build on the location in question but also to design and build a cluster of several units immediately, on an accelerated schedule. Furthermore, recognizing the anticipated competition in this new market and recognizing the highly unusual, if not irregular, or even unconstitutional, nature of their next condition, they sprang this qualification on us: You cannot work for Harry if you accept our projects.

What a dilemma! We had frequently designed for competing stores in a given location. While neither client was happy about it, they tolerated it. We were able to convince each that we would keep their data, projections, and plans absolutely confidential; that the requirements, personalities, and objectives of each were different; and that we would set up completely separate, discrete project teams to handle each, thus assuring that the concepts and details would be absolutely different. Now, however, the situation was different. The condition was clear and immutable.

My partners and I debated the problem long and deeply. Finally, we made the extremely unpleasant decision to stay with our long-term client and cancel our agreement with Harry. It was a business judgment—an objective weighting of the proposed income that each might generate that year and in the future.

I flew down to meet Harry and to explain personally what had happened. It was the most difficult meeting of my professional life. Not only was it the end of a wonderful friendship, but also there existed the possibility of being sued for breach of contract and damages due to valuable time lost.

The end of this story is still more ironic and sad. Not more than two months after we had started planing the other projects, that client was acquired by another major department store. We were ordered to stop all work: The acquiring store had its own in-house planning and design department, which would work on the projects.

This was our first exposure to the tumultuous 1980s, during which the liquidations, sales, acquisitions and bankruptcy proceedings changed the face of retailing forever. The number of casualties resulting from this explosive revolution remains hopelessly uncounted.

A PHILADELPHIA STORY, II

One of the great stores of America, active in Philadelphia and its vast regional hinterland, had remained an inaccessible but frequently targeted client. Eventually, partly as the result of a changing executive leadership and partly because of Copeland, Novak and Israel's (CNI's) growing prestige and reknown, we were called in for a consultation. The project was the total renovation of a major branch store, located in a key shopping center that was in the process of undergoing a huge expansion program. It was known that a New York store division was planning to put a new unit in this expansion, its first in the Philadelphia region. It was a powerful operation. Its store designs were outstanding, at the cutting edge of the field. It represented formidable competition.

I spent several days walking through the existing store. It was entirely out of date and required a comprehensive total overhaul in order to compete with the New York unit. I consulted many senior staff people in an attempt to develop a coherent and exciting program for the alterations. I drooled for this account.

Finally, a meeting was set for the presentation of our proposal. The new chairman was gracious and businesslike. We discussed the scope of the alterations—the esthetics, style, the expression of a great, traditional store evolving in the face of vicious, brash competition—and, ultimately, the budget, or estimated cost of the job.

Sitting in one of America's most famous mercantile buildings, which exuded from its every surface tradition, dignity, refinement, upper-class superiority, we now began to discuss a budget. The chairman put his dollar amount on the table: a dollar per square foot cost guideline. I was shocked. It was incredibly low, not half enough to do a decent job. At first I was speechless. Then I tried to indicate how unrealistic that amount was, how vital it was to meet the new competition with a strong and excellent statement, and how complex and massive the alteration would be, effecting structure, lighting, the relocation of literally every selling department—everything.

The chairman looked at me. "Are you trying to tell me you don't want this job?" he asked. I answered firmly, remembering somewhere in the back of my mind Mister Jack's fatherly advice not to retreat. "No, I want this account desperately. But I will not lie to you or lead you on in expectations that are doomed to fail. That would be disastrous for both of us." Silence. A long, keen regard. A handshake. And, farewell.

As far as I know, the renovation was never done.

A THOUSAND OAKS

This prestigious community in the outer suburbs of Los Angeles, named for a hallowed grove of live oak trees, was the site for the new addition of a major department store in a fine regional enclosed mall. My firm had been selected as store planner/designer, and we were consulting with the local architect who had been commissioned to design the building.

The project was developing well. Our interior plans and designs had been approved on schedule by the store's top management, and the building footprint and working drawings had reached the stage of filing for local building department and zoning approvals. Then disaster struck. Architectural plans were rejected. It seemed that the location and the footprint of the proposed building overshadowed and threatened the root structure of one single dedicated oak tree.

The building had to be relocated and reduced in bulk. Back to the drawing board. We literally had to start the planning and design process all over again. We had to take a loss on all of the additional man hours of effort through the planning, design, and construction document phases of services, without any additional fee compensation. Never in our firm's history did we have to totally rework a plan because of a building department refusal, and our designer-owner agreement did not protect us if this contingency occurred. It was a costly oversight. And it was primarily not even under our own responsibility for services rendered. It was a costly lesson. It made us immediately aware, however, of the new ecological responsibilities: Everyone must contribute to the preservation of every minute part of the environment on our cherished earth.

TRIVIAL PURSUITS

It was the final design presentation of a new branch store for an outstanding department store that had been our client for many years—a client that represented an extremely important percentage of our annual fees. Copeland, Novak and Israel (CNI) was, at that time, evolving its own internal organization and had promoted several of its key project managers to vice presidents. So it was that Andy was to make the presentation to the store chairman, Ed, a world-renowned merchant who had won numerous awards as retailer of the 1990s. In the past, he had shown extraordinary interest in store planning and design and had put his personal stamp on many successful projects.

For some reason, Andy and Ed got into a rather heated confrontation. To this day, I cannot remember the initial cause of the dispute. At any rate, taunted by the chairman, Andy responded, "Well, anyhow, I buy my clothes at B_____'s," referring, of course, to Ed's archrival. There was total shocked silence in the conference room. Andy was banished, excommunicated. He was never again to meet with this client in any capacity whatsoever!

LESSON: Never lose your temper.

TOO MANY CEOS

Once our firm worked for four separate clients on a single project. It was a vital new downtown store. The client, for whom we had been working exclusively for many years, had agreed to relocate literally across the street in the inner core of a large metropolitan area. He would vacate his old, obsolete building and build an anchor to a downtown regional enclosed mall that was being planned by a leading national developer. It was to be an advanced, monumental project, an outstanding example of the trend at that time to revitalize the inner cities.

We started with chairman Bernie. He saw the project as a major work, but his experience was conditioned by a primary concern for economic solutions that he felt reflected the value traditions of his stores. He retired within a year after we had started the project. Manny came next. We knew that he was dedicated to esthetics and refinement of design. In fact, he completely overturned Bernie's program. The adjacencies of departments, the layerage, the dynamics of the plan, the striving for outstanding design—it was a new project. Manny brought onto his team wonderful consultants in color, design, and visual merchandising. His enthusiasm and pursuit of perfection in every detail was contagious to us all. We were producing a new downtown department store that, by its sheer magnitude and advanced concepts, would revolutionize store design.

Alas, Manny was replaced by Marty. In one day, Marty studied the plans and the scope of the entire project. He decided to cut the gross store area by one-half. To him, downtown represented merely another branch in the store chain. The projected dollar volume of business downtown could no longer justify a traditional metropolitan headquarters store of over 800,000 square feet. So the lawyers renegotiated with the developer, and we started replanning. Fortunately, many of the design ideas developed under Manny's direction could be reasonably applied to the revised version. Plans and details were virtually complete by the third year.

However, Marty was promoted to corporate chairman. The local chief executive, Kai, was appointed division chairman. Fortunately, Kai was familiar with the Byzantine history of the project and chose to exercise only superficial changes to the plan and design. The project was finally completed and opened in a blaze of glory.

It was truly a miraculous achievement. Each chairman had his own strong personality, ultimately reflected in plan and design solutions; each had a different program, different objectives, budgets, and merchandise philosophy. The constant modifications made us dizzy. But we persevered by sheer will, a sense of humor, and the equally strong desire to produce an outstanding and successful store.

LORD JIM

Jim was a maverick. He was, however, a brilliant planner and designer. He was bright, highly presentable, articulate, and dedicated. He did things, however, on his own terms. He was hopelessly unpunctual. He could never justify his expense account submissions. The office hated him for his excesses and disregard of the rules. My partner, Adolph, could not tolerate his rebellious spirit of independence. Adolph constantly pressed me to cashier Jim. I was reluctant. With all of his faults, he was an extremely gifted, highly creative architect and designer. He could draw like an angel.

Ultimately, under Adolph's constant nudging, I suggested that we take the case to a client with whom Jim was working. Bob was the chairman of a prestigious, high-fashion, national store group. I knew Bob well for many years and felt that he might help us make an intelligent decision.

I discussed the matter as objectively as possible. Bob's answer was quick and decisive: "Keep him. Accommodate him. He is one in a million!" Here was a chief executive, in contact literally every day with thousands of talented people in every creative field—architecture, interior design, store design, fashion, advertising—instructing us in the incredible value of one unique, special, irreplaceable talent.

Alas, Jim died of AIDS many years later, after having left a brilliant legacy to the store design profession.

Epilogue

Not casually have I concluded the anecdotes with a story celebrating the value of one talented human being. While I have never in the least subscribed to the Carlylean theory of the "Hero" as a prime mover of history—a theory that led to Nietzche's concept of the "Superman" and, penultimately, to the cataclysmic and catastrophic actions of Hitler—there is nothing more beautiful and noble to me than an outstanding person. A talented designer, like geniuses in every field of human endeavor, can easily disregard analysis and theory. In many ways, he or she is indeed above the law. To the rest of us, however, I have tried in this book to demonstrate and illustrate those logical laws and ideas that we must strive to master if we wish to be successful in our chosen discipline and if we are to succeed and contribute to the metamorphosis of store design.

Especially now, in this crucial stage in the evolution of retailing, I have refered, particularly in my review of the 1980s and the 1990s to the revolution that has occurred, to the unparalleled competition between department store peers and between different sectors of the market, and to the demise and liquidations of innumerable ownerships. In searching for the current owners of many of the historic stores cited, I felt more like a detective than a store design historian; nay, more like one mourning at a cemetery strewn with countless tombstones of failed operations.

But I do not mean this book to be an epitaph to a lost art. Rather, I wish to suggest positively and sanguinely that this critical time is, in fact, a chance for the imaginative and smart store planner/designer to seize the opportunity to contribute ideas, forms, and structures, and to help lead the department store creatively back to its former glory and dominance in our civilization. I hope it will instruct and inspire.

Bibliography

Artley, Alexander, ed. *The Golden Age of Shop Design: European Shop Interiors, 1880-39*. New York: Whitney Library of Design, 1976.

Barber, Bruce, *Designer's Dictionary*. Lockport, NY: Upson Co., 1974.
Barmash, Isadore. *For the Good of the Company*. New York: Grosset & Dunlap, 1976
—*Macy's for Sale*. New York: Weidenfeld & Nicholson, 1989.
Barr, Vilma, and Charles E. Broudy. *Designing to Sell*, 2d ed. New York: McGraw-Hill, 1991.
Birran, Faber. *Color and Human Responses*. New York: Van Nostrand Reinhold, 1978.
Brady, Maxine. *Bloomingdale's*. New York: Fairchild, 1970.

Campbell, Joseph, with Bill Moyers. *The Power of Myth*. New York: Doubleday, 1988.
Chidilwa, Hideaki. *Color Harmony*. Rockport, MA: Rockport Publishers, 1987.
Colborne, Robert. *Fundamentals of Merchandise Presentation*. Cincinnati, OH: The Signs of Times Publishing Co., 1982.
Conrad, Joseph. *The Nigger of the Narcissus*. New York: Doubleday and Company, 1914; Bacheller Syndicate, 1987.

de Chiara, Joseph, Julius Panero, and Martin Zelnik. *Time-Saver Standards for Interior Design and Space Planning*. New York: McGraw-Hill, 1991.
Drew-Bear, Robert. *Mass Merchandising*. New York: Fairchild, 1970.

Ferry, John William. *A History of the Department Store*. New York: Macmillan, 1960.
Fickes, Michael. "Nordy's Forte." *Retail Store Image*, Communications Channels, Inc. Nov.-Dec. 1992, pp. 31–37.
Fitche, Rodney, and Lance Knobel. *Retail Design*. New York: Whitney Library of Design, 1990.
Follis, John, and Dame Hammer. *Architectural Signing and Graphics*. New York: Whitney Library of Design, 1979.

Gill, Penney. *"What's a Department Store?'* New York: NRMA Enterprises, 1990, pp. 8–17.
Giovannini, Joseph. "Revolution by Design." Lakewood, CA: *Modern Maturity*, Published by the AARP, Oct.-Nov. 1992, pp. 41–81.
Gosling, David, and Barry Maitland. *Design and Planning of Retail Systems*. New York: Whitney Library of Design.
Green, William R. *The Retail Store: Design and Construction*. New York: Van Nostrand Reinhold, 1991.

Harris, Leon. *Merchant Princes*. New York: Harper & Row, 1979.
Hartley, Robert. *Retailing*, 3d ed. Boston: Houghton Mifflin, 1984.
Hendrickson, Robert. *The Grand Emporiums*. New York: Stein & Day, 1979.

Katz, Donald, R. *The Big Store: Inside the Crises and Revolution at Sears*. New York: Viking, 1987.
Ketchum, Morris Jr. *Shops and Stores*. New York: Reinhold Publishing Corp., 1948.
Klein, Jerome E., and Norman Reader. *Great Shops of Europe*. New York: National Retail Merchants Association, 1969.
Kowinski, William. *The Malling of America*. New York: William Morrow, 1985.
Kreft, Wilhelm. "Laden Planning." Verlagsanstalt Alexander Koch CombH. 1993.

Lapidus, Morris. *Architecture: A Profession and a Business*. New York: Reinhold Publishing Corp, 1967.

Le Corbusier. *Towards a New Architecture.* New York: Dover Publications, 1986 (John Rodker, London, 1931).

McAusland, Randolph. *Supermarkets: 50 Years of Progress.* Washington, D.C.: Food Distribution Institute, 1980.

Mahoney, Tom, and Leonard Sloane. *The Great Merchants* enlgd. ed. New York: Harper & Row, 1966.

Maitland, Barry. *Shopping Malls: Planning and Design.* London: Construction Press, 1985.

Marcus, Stanley. *Minding the Store.* New York: New American Library, 1975.

McLuhan, Marshall. *Understanding Media: The Extensions of Man.* New York: McGraw-Hill, 1964.

Munn, David. *Shops - A Manual of Planning and Design.* New York: Architectural Press, 1986.

Novak, Adolph. *Store Planning and Design.* New York: Lebhar-Friedman, 1977.

Olins, Wally. *Corporate Identity.* London: Thames and Hudson, 1989.

Parnes, Louis. *Planning Stores That Pay.* New York: F.W. Dodge Corp., 1948.

Pegler, Martin M. *The Language of Store Planning and Display.* New York: Fairchild, 1982.

—*Stores of the Year*, 7th ed. New York: Retail Reporting Bureau, 1993.

—*Visual Merchandising and Display*, 2d ed. New York: Fairchild Fashion & Merchandising Group, 1991.

Proust, Marcel. *Remembrances of Things Past*, Vol. II. New York: Random House, 1932.

Rothchild, John. *Going for Broke.* New York: Simon & Schuster, 1991.

Stevens, Mark. *Like No Other Store in the World: The Inside Story of Bloomingdale's.* New York: Thomas Y. Crowell, 1979.

Stuart, Albert. *Retail Merchandising and Control.* New York: Lebhar-Friedman, 1982.

Telchin, Charles, and Seymour Helfant. *Planning Your Store for Maximum Sales and Profits.* New York: National Retail Merchants Association, 1969.

Van de Bogart, Willard. *Computerized Fashion and a 21st Century Retail Store.* New York: The FIT Review, Fall 1989.

Venturi, Robert. *Complexity and Contradiction in Architecture.* New York: Museum of Modern Art, 1966.

Wayne, Leslie. "Rewriting the Rules of Retailing," *The New York Times*, October 15, 1989.

Weishar, Joseph. *Design For Effective Selling Space.* New York: McGraw-Hill, 1992.

Wood, Barry J. *Show Windows: 75 Years of the Art of Display.* New York: Congdon & Weed, 1982.

Woutat, Donald. "Ultimate Challenge Awaits Shop-Till-You-Drop Crowd," *Los Angeles Times*, July 27, 1992.

Zimmerman, M. M. *The Supermarket: A Revolution in Distribution.* New York: McGraw-Hill, 1955.

Market Supermarket and Hypermarket Design/2. New York: Retail Reporting Corp.

Retailing Store Planning and Design Manual. New York: National Retail Merchants Association.

Storefronts and Facades/4. New York: Retail Reporting Corp.

Store Windows That Sell/6. New York: Retail Reporting Corp.

Successful Sign Design/2. New York: Retail Reporting Corp.

Time Saver Standards, F. W. Dodge Corp. New York, 1946.

Visual Merchandising. New York: National Retail Merchants Association, 1976.

Visual Merchandising: Best Designs from Leading Designers. New York: National Retail Merchants Association, 1986.

Visual Merchandising and Store Design, published monthly by IST Publication, Inc. Cincinnati, OH.

Index